L'Institut Roeher Institute

Canada's National Institute for the Study of Public Policy Affecting Persons with an Intellectual Impairment and Other Disabilities

Institut Roeher Institute is Canada's leading organization to promote the equality, participation and self-determination of people with intellectual and other disabilities, by examining the causes of marginalization and by providing research, information and social development opportunities.

To fulfill this mandate, l'Institut Roeher Institute is engaged in many activities: research and public policy analysis; publishing; information dissemination; and training, education and leadership development.

L'Institut Roeher Institute acts as a centre for the development and exchange of ideas, all of which are founded on a new way of looking at disability and society. It critically examines issues related to the well-being and human rights of persons with an intellectual impairment and other disabilities. Based on its examination of these issues, The Institute raises awareness about the barriers that affect people's full participation and prevent them from exercising their rights. The Institute also presents policy and program alternatives.

For more information about l'Institut Roeher Institute please contact us at:

Kinsmen Building
York University, 4700 Keele St.
North York, Ont. M3J 1P3
Tel: (416) 661-9611
Fax: (416) 661-5701
TDD: (416) 661-2023

Contents

Foreword

Two discordant sets of research findings have made some researchers in the field of disability uncomfortable. On one hand, research and development has moved rapidly in the biomedical field and in designing sophisticated technology for use by people with disabilities. On the other hand, research in the social sciences and in law show that, despite biomedical and technical developments, the barriers to equality and full inclusion have changed very little for people with disabilities. This discordance suggests that we are at a juncture. It suggests the need to step back and reflect upon the research enterprise itself. Theoretical frameworks and research paradigms in the field of disability illuminate some possibilities for people and foreclose others. The nature and influence of these frameworks have mostly been ignored in terms of defining the direction of research, the way in which research questions are structured and the significance of the findings. Although a process of reflection has begun, enough barriers remain to the equality and full inclusion of people with disabilities to suggest that we may not be stepping back far enough in our reflection. In other words, we sometimes forget to question how the questions are being asked.

This is the task the contributors to this book have set for themselves. In exploring issues that have gone unaddressed in the predominant framework for thinking about disability, they look outside the field of disability for research paradigms and methodologies that can be used fruitfully in this field. Together these explorations expand the boundaries of what can be considered serious research in the field of disability.

By not limiting themselves to the parameters of the prevailing framework, these researchers act as a catalyst for critical disability research. The directions they chart not only satisfy the requirements of rigorous research, they also provide theoretical justification and practical tools for bridging the gap that creates silences between the research community and people with disabilities.

All the chapters in this collection point towards, and work within, a critical paradigm for disability research. A central element of this paradigm is a critique of the reification of disability that has been entrenched through a positivist theory of knowledge. In doing so it unsettles this "fallacy of misplaced concreteness" that has dominated disability research and acted to narrow the scope of questions that have been considered legitimate. By focusing on the social, economic, political and legal construction of disability, a critical paradigm unmasks the process of reification.

In this vein, Rioux argues in the introduction to this book that disability remains a poorly theorized concept in sociology, law and politics because the political implications of the category have not been taken into account. Consequently, the political context for the construction of disability must receive explicit focus in a new research paradigm. Radford locates one of the sources of the construction of disability as a scientific category in the social relations that tied the university and the asylum together. He suggests that the hold science has had on the definition of, and the response to, disability can only be challenged within a critique of the broader context of modernity.

A second element of the emerging paradigm for critical disability research builds on the recognition that disability is socially constructed. If disability is not an inherent and fixed feature of a person but the product of a social, legal, political and economic context, then this context must be brought into question. Critical disability research questions this context through the lens of human rights and ethics.

Ward and Flynn argue that because disability is socially produced, we have to change the social relations of research production, which has not to date happened within the positivist and even the qualitative research traditions. They point to an emancipatory research paradigm that challenges how research is funded, how it is used and the relationship struck between the researchers and research subjects. The ongoing web of social, economic and political forces, Zola argues, shapes the relationship of disability to research and to public policy. He examines the historical context of this relationship in the United States and suggests that through the voice given by social movements to people with disabilities the exclusionary effects of research and of public policy are being effectively challenged. He cautions, however, that because "prejudices and paradigms run deep" it will take tools and time to develop the voice of people with disabilities.

Rioux argues that the fundamental basis for a critical perspective is the principle of equality and the aim of well-being. However, these concepts are not self-explanatory, they are subject to multiple interpretations and, as she suggests, these interpretations are political in nature; different interpretations lead to very different obligations. She argues for a concept and standard of equality that can take into account the discrimination faced by persons with disabilities and the different needs they have. Bickenbach argues as well that we need a framework for thinking about disability that is rooted in a moral and political commitment to equality. Without such a commitment, he suggests, people with disabilities will continue to be the subjects of a culture and policy of paternalism and pity. Bach contends that because disability has not been viewed within a framework of rights and ethics, disability research has tended to reinforce the marginal status of persons with disabilities rather than challenge it. In his critical examination of different models of quality of life research, he points towards the need for a methodological framework that makes explicit its moral and ethical commitments.

Critical disability research also takes a self-critical stance on the "discourse of disability" and is founded on a recognition that language and power cannot be separated. By bringing the discourse of disability into view, researchers can begin to illuminate those practices and forces that reinforce certain social, legal and cultural constructions of disability. Research can also point to the sources of more enabling social constructions and the ways in which the voices of persons with disabilities can begin to be heard in discursive spaces that have excluded them. Some of the contributors to this volume explore how the discourse of disability has evolved and how it operates.

In Stockholder's analysis of how the naming of people with intellectual disabilities has evolved, he argues that language is an instrument for the shaping of consciousness. As names are challenged and changed, consciousness of the social, economic and political possibilities for groups also changes. He provides a historical overview of this development in relation to children, women and other marginalized groups and shows how language is rooted in the trajectory of each group's particular history. Wight Felske explores the different ways in which language can be constructed to name the experiences and the needs of persons with disabilities and the implications for individuals' treatment and status in society. She argues that these different constructions are rooted in differing epistemological paradigms — the positivist, the interpretive and the critical social science paradigm. Rather than being critical simply of our research methods, we need to be critical also of the epistemologies that have given rise to particular ways of viewing and naming the experience of people with disabilities.

Woodill provides a framework for a "social semiotics of disability" and examines how the meaning of disability is constructed through popular culture, professional discourse and the language of people with disabilities. He suggests that the task is to uncover the representations of disability to show that they perpetuate oppression and to point toward the deployment of new signs of disability in cultural practice.

A paradigm of critical disability research must also question the relationship between researchers and the subjects of research. The predominant research methodologies and processes have vested enormous power in the researcher to define the questions and to shape what is to be known about persons with disabilities. The consequence has often been that research has reinforced the objectification and, thereby, the marginalization of its subjects. All of the articles in this volume address this issue and point to research methods to counter the predominant approach, some more implicitly than explicitly. Ramcharan and Grant make this the focus of their contribution. They critique the prevailing "tokenistic" model of the research process in which persons with disabilities are excluded from all the decision making. They carry out their critique from the vantage point provided by an ideal type — a "devolved" research model in which the subjects of the research establish the agenda and manage the process.

Working from an empirical level, Gleason documents a five-year ethnographic study he undertook on persons labelled with intellectual impairment and severe and profound disabilities. He explores the process of making sense of what persons with disabilities actually do, the interpretive challenges such an exploration raises and the implications for reframing relationships with people and responses to them. In Munford's analysis of care-giving, she argues that we must focus attention on the power relations that underlie care-giving. She argues that researchers must look at why the daily experiences of persons with disabilities have been excluded from our culture. They must also make people's realities visible in research. In doing so they must connect these realities to a structure of discourses on disability and to the social policies that shape people's lives.

Putting a critical disability research paradigm into practice presents enormous challenges. It is difficult for any research study to meet such rigorous standards at this point in the history of disability research. Although no single study may be able to meet all the demands of the paradigm, some researchers are moving resolutely in this direction. This volume includes contributions that provide theoretical reflections on shifting to a new paradigm. At the same time they apply these insights to particular research projects. The paradigm suggests that we need to think about disability within a social, economic, legal and political context that has often been outside the parameters of disability research. It points to the need for an ethical and moral framework to view this context and the social construction of disability, a framework that has been at odds with the positivist research tradition. It means that researchers must always be critical about the language they deploy, given the recognition that language has such power to shape the place of people with disabilities in our society. Finally, it means that we must challenge the divisions between researchers and the researched that have kept the perspectives of people with disabilities outside the research process and the production of knowledge.

Disability Is Not Measles was sparked by our decision to organize a forum on New Research Directions and Paradigms at the IXth Congress of the International Association for the Scientific Study of Mental Deficiency (IASSMD) in Australia in August 1992. Having worked from a rights and equality paradigm in Canada in carrying out research on public policy and disability, we were curious to make connections with other researchers who were also re-examining the premises of the study of disability. The IASSMD provided us with a place to begin those discussions on an international level and to begin thinking about the implications and challenges for traditional researchers.

This collection reflects the work of only a few of the contacts we made in Australia and have made since that time, and only the tip of the iceberg of research that is heading in this direction. We anticipate with excitement the further development of a critical framework for research in the disability field.

Marcia H. Rioux and Michael Bach

Introduction

New Research Directions and Paradigms: Disability Is Not Measles

by Marcia H. Rioux

Research in the field of disability is at a turning point. For the first 80 years of this century, the policy and research agenda in disability was driven first by biomedical concerns and second by service delivery models. The wider political implications of disability were all but ignored, leaving disability as a poorly theorized subject in sociology, law and politics. Within traditional research, a professionally dominated functionalist theory was applied. Disability was explained as an individual problem rather than as a social relationship. Methodological individualism and positivism dominated the research. Substantial research funding continues to be directed to this stream.

It is important to recognize that research was not apolitical despite the claims of positivist researchers and scientists. It fit (and continues to fit) a political agenda that can be traced historically in the Western democracies. The example of the treatment of people with intellectual impairments in Canada helps illuminate this agenda. In the 1800s in Canada people with intellectual impairments (then called "lunatics", "idiots" and "imbeciles") were put on poor farms and in asylums that housed, along with them, all the other poor and deviant people of society who could not look after themselves.

By the 1920s large institutions were built, especially for the people who were by then labelled "idiots", "imbeciles" or "morons". The initial rationale, a contribution of scientific study, for putting people in these large institutions housing up to 2000 people was that society had to be protected from the effects of such people. There were fears that they might reproduce and that society would be overridden by people who would be unable to work, contribute or take care of themselves. The immigration laws precluded people with intellectual impairments or their families from being admitted into Canada on the basis that people who were "retarded" would be a "drain on society". Laws enabling them to be sterilized without consent were put into effect. Eugenic theory was very much in scientific vogue at that time and a great deal of the scientific community's research efforts went into the development and use of IQ tests. Research was important to support policy based on the presumption that the country needed to be rid of this so-called "blight".

Human biology research was important to the political enterprise of the time. This research included all aspects of biological and medical health within the human body as a consequence of the basic biology of human beings and of individual organic make-up, including genetic heritage. The concentration of research in disability continues to be in this area. This includes research into the genetic structure of the human being and ways of preventing the malfunctioning of biological systems.

By the 1950s theory and practice had changed and the genetic theories of the earlier period had been significantly discredited. Although medical and biological research continued to seek ways to prevent disability, as it was by then termed, the field of rehabilitation had opened up. People were beginning to look for ways to enable people with disabilities to develop the potential they had. Programs were developed to enable people to learn skills and take care of themselves. Special segregated classes with specially trained teachers were developed and research into new pedagogical methods designed for those with disabilities was undertaken. In the 1970s large group homes in communities were constructed for people to live in and sheltered workshops were built for them. A whole new group of professionals and researchers put their energy into rehabilitation theory, into designing a service system to meet their needs and into seeking political recognition for these mandates. Research in therapies for treating disability was widespread, with an emphasis on ameliorating the problem that continued to be defined as residing in the individual. The pathology approach of the earlier period remained. A theory of services developed.

The earliest assumptions of medical and biological research, that an individual pathology was the basis of the research question, have not changed a great deal over the past century. Although the placement of disability under the auspices of medicine has been heavily criticized and has partially shifted to come under the auspices of a rehabilitation or habilitation paradigm, the domination of the field by experts, the positivist perspective of the research agenda and the location of the research question in the individual have not changed significantly.

What does the preponderance of research in the field look like now? It looks a great deal like the research into measles. The goal is prevention. Consequently, identifying the condition and its biological origins is still a preoccupation of much of the work. Cures are sought — now euphemistically called prevention — and divided between biological prevention and environmental prevention. Although the latter has traditionally been of much less interest to the research community than the former, it has come into vogue in the past 20 years with new research showing the relationship between such elements as workplace toxins, alcohol use, age of women at conception and rates of disability.

This positivist paradigm has, built into it, a number of assumptions about the nature of the social world and appropriate methods for investigating it. These assumptions consist of the following: a belief that the social world can be studied in the same way as the natural world — that there is a unity of method between the natural and social sciences; that the study of the social world can be value-free; that, ultimately, explanations of a causal nature can be provided; and that the knowledge obtained from such research is independent of the assumptions underpinning it and the methods used to obtain it.[1]

Quality-of-care studies, again concentrated on issues of importance to professionals and a professional service paradigm, have dominated service research. Success in designing and evaluating services and service delivery is measured by how closely people with disabilities who use the service can approximate "normal" people. These studies, predominantly functionalist in nature, assume a congruence of interest between the service provider and service user and fail, consequently, to analyze opposing interests, inequality and the distribution of power.[2]

The example of research in behavioural therapy as a procedure to reduce self-injurious behaviour is instructive in this regard. Traditional research frames the question as discovering the means of reducing the undesired behaviour through technical and professional expertise. Similar to biological research it asks: Does a particular intervention decrease the behaviour identified? The positivist then approaches the research with an experimental design that is formulated outside the political and social context of the behaviour. He or she proves that the intervention is effective in a laboratory setting. The distorted claims as to the benefits of the procedure fail to take into account the malevolent side-effects of the treatment, the underlying cause of the behaviour (assuming as it does that the cause is the disability itself) or the experiences of the research subjects themselves. The powerful ideological role of scientific objectivity is clear.

What is evolving in certain recent research, in the critique of positivism and in the critical evaluation of traditional research methodology and practice, is a theory of disability that takes into account the material constraints in the lives of people with disabilities. To understand how new research questions are being structured it is important to understand the shift from an eclectic set of positivist scientific studies to a critical theory of disability.

4

The real nature of the issue of disability has only recently begun to be addressed. New research directions are challenging the "measles approach" to disability.

The redefinition of the problem of disability puts in question the whole body of research that concentrates on the biological classification of disability and the elimination of the biological condition. It also questions quality-of-life and service research premised on assumptions that bettering service systems will result in ameliorating the condition and the individual effects of disability.

In this new framework, eliminating social and physical barriers that create handicaps and promoting social well-being are priorities. Conceptualizing prevention within a social and political context, the research is premised on the presence of disability and seeks to prevent the conditions that make the disability a liability in social and economic participation. It identifies ways to increase individual control over social well-being, rather than defining social well-being as the absence of disability.

Disability in these new research agendas is located within a political context. This new theoretical framework of disability, which is beginning to surface in research literature, identifies the causal role of objective economic conditions in the explanation of oppression. This body of research challenges the position of the dominant positivist research as the only valid and legitimate source of knowledge about disadvantage resulting from disability. It also debunks the illusion that ideas and attitudes alone cause disadvantage and discrimination.

A combination of factors including biological condition, service delivery and systemic elements all have an impact on the ability of persons with disabilities to exercise citizenship rights and autonomy. The exclusion of an analysis of the systemic factors that affect disability in biological and genetic research and service delivery research limits the potential of that work and in some cases negates its usefulness.

In a materialist analysis, disability comes from the social and economic restrictions imposed on the individual that disable him or her. This analysis recognizes the implications of power relations in enabling well-being. Recent research recognizes the role of poverty as a major cause of disempowerment and marginalization. It includes the analysis of power relations and barriers to integration that persist within government policies and programs. It also recognizes the conflict within the existing structure of research production and the importance of engaging in debate with funding institutions over these issues.

The connection between the research methodology and the research agenda is being debated by those researchers who accept the political nature of disability. An argument is being made for a paradigm that takes into account both the phenomenon of disability and the experiences of those with disabilities — elements missing from the objective, technical agenda that has dominated the field.[3] Empowerment and reciprocity are central to this notion of research that encourages qualitative methodology.

There is, however, another important policy agenda that must be addressed in the research of the 1990s on disability. The philosophical foundations of notions of citizenship and equality are important to the critique of traditional research in the field. The underlying assumption of the lack of status of persons with disabilities has promoted, or at a minimum left unquestioned, the funding and undertaking of research that would be ethically and legally unacceptable if it involved other groups. Studying the genetic make-up of people from non-white racial groups is sceptically viewed. Research into genetic engineering that could be used to prevent female children is sceptically viewed. The development of technology that involves pain as a mechanism of control for criminal behaviour is sceptically viewed. All of these are unacceptable from ethical, social and rights perspectives. Disability ought not to provide a rationale for research that is unacceptable for other groups in society.

Equality and citizenship can no longer be ignored in the

research agenda. Disability is not measles. It is not a medical condition that needs to be eliminated from the population. It is a social status and the research agenda must take into account the political implications attached to that status. The developing theory of disability is an exciting advance in this field and promises much more fruitful results than the limited and singular positivist, scientific research of the past.

Notes

1. M. Oliver, "Changing the Social Relations of Research Production", *Disability, Handicap and Society*, 7(1), 1992, pp. 101-114.

2. A.L. Chappell, "Towards a Sociological Critique of the Normalization Principle", *Disability, Handicap and Society*, 7(1), 1992, pp. 35-51.

3. Oliver, "Changing the Social Relations", 1992, (see n. 1); C. Barnes, "Qualitative Research: Valuable or Irrelevant?", *Disability, Handicap and Society*, 7(2), 1992, pp. 115-124; G. Zarb, "On the Road to Damascus: First Steps towards Changing the Relations of Disability Research Production", *Disability, Handicap and Society*, 7(2), 1992, pp. 125-138. L'Institut Roeher Institute, *Research by/for/with Women with Disabilities*, North York, Ont.: L'Institut Roeher Institute, 1991.

Chapter 1

Intellectual Disability and the Heritage of Modernity

by John P. Radford

The prevailing twentieth-century construction of intellectual disability has been characterized by an insistence on the authority of measurement and classification and an obsession with terminology. It has been associated with discrimination, institutionalization, segregation and sterilization. Over a period of many decades countless well-meaning, responsible, moral people, including some of the most "progressive" of their day, became convinced that such measures would not only protect society, but were enacted on behalf of disabled people "for their own good". The dominant construct cut across boundaries of national identity, political persuasion, ethnicity and gender, though not, it is true, indiscriminately across lines of social class and religious affiliation. Its local expressions varied, but the main tenets spread a certain underlying uniformity of principle across much of Western Europe and North America.

How did such notions become so widespread and endure for so long? How were they able to withstand challenges to their dominance? Individually many of the diagnoses, protocols, remedies and assumptions would have seemed indefensible. Collectively, however, they constituted what might be termed a "problematic of mental deficiency". This problematic defined which questions were relevant and which were trivial. It was not static but its dynamism was circumscribed. It was dominated, as Wolfensberger clearly demonstrated, by the notion of the person with an intellectual disability as a social deviant. But the problematic of "mental deficiency" could not have endured and remained so pervasive had it been out of balance with the times. Clearly such was not the case. The genealogy of "mental deficiency" is a shared one, part of a broader inheritance.

In the first part of this chapter, I argue that the problematic of "mental deficiency" was legitimated by the institution of the university through the authority of "science" and the rise of professionalism. In essence, the university sanctioned the asylum, both as a concrete custodial institution and as an enduring asylum *mentalité*. As a result, with a few notable exceptions, the role of the university in engendering a critique of this problematic has been indifferent at best. Sometimes its stance has been obstructionist. This reflects a residue of the hostility with which, for most of this century, forces within the university pursued the creation and legitimation of a dogma of "mental deficiency".

I then attempt to place this production of dogma in context. I argue that the asylum *mentalité*, sustained in the immediate largely from within the university, is best understood in broader terms as a product of modernity. Some recent work on modernity is presented as worthy of further exploration as a means of contextualizing the problematic of "mental deficiency". I conclude by suggesting some implications of the critique of modernity in challenging the dominant paradigm of research and practice and the problematic of "mental deficiency" it has established.

The University and the Asylum

The contrasting physical locations of university and asylum reflect their differing social positions, one at the crux of modern society, the other at its margin. Whether situated in the metropolis or in their own exclusive college towns, universities have characteristically occupied privileged and highly visible locations. Many of the early asylums aspired to a similar status, and their buildings were designed to act as symbols of progress and therapy. Sooner or later, however, concessions were made in all jurisdictions to societal demands for custodial protection. Asylums became hidden places, located in the hinterlands of major population centres. They were also pushed to the margins of our social consciousness. Yet, as the writings of Foucault, Goffman and others have shown, they maintain a central position in power-knowledge relations, epitomizing the very society that enforces their peripheralization.

Although apparently occupying separate physical and social worlds, the modern university and the custodial mental handicap asylum emerged from a common origin in the Enlightenment. In a sense, they represent its positive and negative personae. At its best the modern university has been a champion of truth, learning and scholarship. It has been increasingly outward-looking and cosmopolitan, its self-image identified with a secular search for knowledge and truth in the interests of human progress. The asylum represents its antithesis: a closed world of ignorance and failure. This, I shall argue, is especially true of those asylums established to confine people diagnosed as "mentally deficient".

The diverging paths of university and asylum in the modern era conform to the fundamental dialectic which Horkheimer and Adorno claim to find at the heart of the forces of enlightenment.[1] The asylum can be seen as part of what they call the Enlightenment's "recidivist element". Ironically, as the ideals of university and asylum became more incompatible in the nineteenth century, authority over the asylum was increasingly vested in certain of the newly emerging academic disciplines and related professions, especially law, education, medicine and psychology.

A key development was the modern separation of mental illness from intellectual disability, representing the formal professionalization of a legal distinction between lunacy and idiocy dating from the medieval period. Intellectual disability has received much less scholarly attention than mental illness and the significance of its social history is only now beginning to become widely understood. Whereas universities have expressed few reservations about incorporating the study of mental illness into their curricula, they have often distanced themselves from intellectual disability. Professional confidence in the potential curability of mental illness tended to produce strategies and agendas attractive to Enlightenment perspectives. Those diagnosed as mentally ill might offend rationality but they were not uniformly regarded as totally beyond redemption. However misguided or bizarre the various treatments may have been, they were at least founded in the possibility of a cure. The apparent incurability of "mental deficiency", by contrast, challenged the very foundation of the Enlightenment ethos. Even rudimentary optimism was quickly abandoned in such cases. In more recent times academics have produced significant studies on the definitions, causes, prevention and measurement of mental deficiency. It is instructive, however, that these topics have tended to be pursued on the margins of established disciplines. Traditional reliance by "scientific" studies on data from incarcerated populations has intensified the aura of deviance and the dominant philosophy within the professional-academic mainstream has tended to pronounce "mental deficiency" a lost cause. We deal today with the residue of a mind-set that readily dismissed the supposed "victims" of "mental deficiency" as "hopeless cases".

It is this hopelessness that the closed, custodial mental handicap asylum came to represent. From the beginning the plight of the "idiot" perplexed the Enlightenment mind. Whereas the "lunatic" was also a deviant, as were the criminal, the inebriate and the pauper, the "idiot" was condemned several times over. In an age that celebrated intelligence as much as beauty, perfection and rationality, the "idiot" was dull, flawed, defaced with stigmata and above all incurable. In the blunt terms of the philosopher John Locke: whereas the "lunatic" had lost his mind, the "idiot" never had one. A lost mind might be restored to normality in some way by coaxing or shocking it out of its disorder but what had never existed could not, so Locke maintained, be artificially created. And whereas the criminal might potentially be reformed and the poor rescued, the "idiot" was irredeemable.

Although the roots of this pessimism lie in Enlightenment thought, it did not attain its virtual monopoly over the modern view of "mental deficiency" until the last quarter of the nineteenth century. During most of the Victorian era opinion was much more varied and tended to swing from one pole to another. The earliest mental handicap asylums were founded in a period of intense optimism that flourished in the 1850s and 1860s around new ideas about the educability of "idiots". In North America the major actor was Eduard Seguin, a pupil of Itard, the physician known for his investigation into the "wild boy of Averyon". Seguin was an enthusiastic supporter of Saint-Simon's views on the modern scientific industrial state. He believed in the educability of all children and advocated the intensive use of sensory-motor activities as an aid to learning. In 1844 the Paris Academy of Science proclaimed that Seguin had solved the problem of "idiot education".[2] Four years later he left France for North America and became influential in the establishment of numerous institutions in the northeastern states. He was the principal organizer of the American Association on Mental Deficiency, founded in 1866, and the English version of his text *Idiocy and Its Treatment by the Physiological Method* became the standard work in the field. The other founders of the early institutions also considered them to be educational establishments and shared Seguin's belief that most of the children accepted into their programs would respond to the training provided and graduate to relative self-sufficiency in the outside world.

The career of Langdon Down provides one illustration of the curious mixture of optimism and hopelessness that characterized mid-nineteenth-century professional attitudes towards intellectual disability. As medical officer of the Earlswood Asylum, Down seemed to support without reservation the asylum's role as an educational institution. According to Edwin Sidney, who toured Earlswood in 1859 and again in 1861, Down used his collection of natural history specimens to develop the pupils' powers of observation. He also encouraged the classroom use of coloured wooden shapes for counting and fitting together and gave full approval to programs in carpentry, gardening, farming and other activities.

Within five years of conducting Edwin Sidney on his tours of Earlswood, however, Down published the paper for which he is best known, a paper imbued with highly deterministic notions of class, race and intelligence.[3] Seeking a framework within which to interpret the meticulous observations he had made of the physical and behavioural characteristics of the children in his care, Down noticed a set of recurrent patterns of stigmata in several individuals, notably the shape of the head and ears and the epicanthic fold. These children, he suggested, represented the birth in a Caucasian family of a biological throwback to an earlier stage in the evolution of the "race". Such an atavism appeared to be an emanation of a race just one step down in a supposed racial hierarchy, that is, from Caucasian to Mongolian. These associations became fixed in the genealogy of "mental deficiency", and the label "mongolian idiot" remained part of its lexicon for more than a century. It is important to realize, as Gould has made clear, that the connections postulated in this work between human evolution, race and intelligence were not the work of an isolated eccentric. Rather they represented an "earnest attempt to construct a general, causal classification of mental deficiency based upon the best biological theory (and the pervasive racism) of the age."[4]

The implications of this kind of research finding were enormous. The "fool", whom the medieval church had tended to see as an object of pity or a holy innocent, was now exposed by science as a biological freak. At the same time, first-hand experience in asylum praxis was suggesting that the early optimism on the question of educability had been ill-founded. Asylum staffs were frustrated by what they perceived as a lack of success, the "idiot" having failed to respond to perfectly reasonable methods of training and education. The blame was placed firmly on the shoulders of the victim. As had happened in the mental illness asylum a decade or two earlier, the ideal of the "idiot asylum" began to evaporate almost as soon as it was born.

By the last quarter of the nineteenth century, the rationale of the asylum had begun to shift from education to control. Simmons has articulated a sequence of four models that can be traced in Britain and North America in which a new policy thrust largely supesedes its predecessor without entirely obliterating it.[5] On top of the original educational model of the so-called asylum was grafted a true asylum model — institutionalization for the protection of the disabled themselves. This gave way to an overlay of social welfare which in turn spawned a custodial model — incarceration for the supposed benefit of the rest of society. The result was a policy palimpsest, the earlier layers of which are barely visible beneath the later ones. During the last quarter of the nineteenth century the custodial model took preference and custodialism was writ large on the policy landscape.

By the turn of the century the stigma of "mental deficiency" had become firmly embedded in the culture. At that point it could be used to ensnare supposed deviants of any kind. The diagnosis "mentally deficient", especially when supported by the whole armory of statistical procedures, became convincing evidence for the necessity of removal of the "afflicted" from free society. The role of the state in this process varied over time and place. By the early years of this century, people in countless jurisdictions were being routinely incarcerated in custodial mental handicap asylums for reasons that had nothing to do with intelligence and everything to do with their social undesirability.

Science (including the medical and social sciences) in general and the university in particular provided legitimation for this sequence of events. There were, of course, opponents, most notably Lester Ward and Franz Boas. But the indifference of the majority of the general population gave credibility to the hostility of a few. The most powerful academic support was given during the lamentable denouement in the first half of this century: the custodial incarceration, sterilization and even extermination of many people diagnosed as "feebleminded" on the basis of a perceived eugenic threat. Here the doctrine of degeneration was fully developed; more rapid breeding by the least intelligent was supposedly dragging down the race or, more immediately, the nation in its competition with rival states. The success of medical science in Western nations had, so it was frequently claimed, artificially prolonged the average life span of "mental deficients" so that they were now being kept alive well into their reproductive years.

During the early years of this century, it was not the "idiot" who was deemed the most potent threat, but the "mildly disabled" who might "pass for normal". The role of Robert Goddard has been much discussed as the inventor of the term "moron" to describe people regarded as "mildly mentally deficient" and as the importer of the Binet-Simon tests into the United States to provide a way of weeding them out. Yet, as Gelb has pointed out, Goddard's role has often been exaggerated to the detriment of a full appreciation of the generality of the notions which he presented.[6] The intelligence tests merely operationalized a long-felt need in psychology and education, and Goddard's claims for their results were in fact more modest than those of many others.

Postulated causal links between the distribution of intelligence and a supposed hierarchy of racial groups, articulated by physicians such as Langdon Down in the mid-nineteenth century, were elaborated by eugenicists in the early years of the twentieth. To the old arguments were added a new faith in the explanatory powers of measurement and unprecedented levels of funding from major corporate benefactors for eugenic research. Credited academic protocols unearthed frightening and largely groundless statistics on the prevalence of "mental deficiency", developed and refined questionable intelligence tests and conducted largely fanciful pedigree studies. In the United States, segments of the academic world thereby supported the eugenic imperative, with its emphasis on segregation and sterilization, and provided, on cue, the new procedures of vasectomy and salpingectomy. In interwar Britain, the state readily accepted alarming incidence statistics avowed by credited experts and, while managing to avoid calls for involuntary sterilization, embarked on an unprecedented program of asylum construction. It is no exaggeration to say that some of the major research universities in the United States, and an academic-medical establishment in Britain, provided a base for the production of dogma. They were catalysts in the development of an enduring asylum *mentalité*.

The Critique of Modernity

One of the most notable trends in recent intellectual history is a growing recognition that, since the 1970s, Western nations have been moving beyond the age that (since early Victorian times) has described itself as "modern". This view is not confined to those who characterize our present society as "postmodern". It is also shared by some who regard postmodernity as a chimera and argue that we have graduated into an intensified version of modernity, or "hypermodernity". This sense that society has moved beyond the modern epoch has led to a greater interest in the chronology of the era and a heightened awareness of the singularity of modernity as a phenomenon. As part of these new directions in research, the writings of many of the theorists of the last 200 years are being subjected to re-evaluation as contributions to the search for a coherent theory of modernity.

This rapidly expanding literature exploring the essence of modernity pays little attention to any implications for the construct of intellectual disability. Yet the links which connect the "problematic of mental deficiency" to the broader concept of modernity are numerous and varied. One striking parallel is in the chronology of events. Just as the asylum era emerged in parallel with the intensification of modern thought, the inception of "normalization" coincided with the period generally acknowledged to have seen the demise of modernity in several arenas. Charles Jenks,[7] for example, claims to be able to date with precision the symbolic death of modernism in architecture. On July 15, 1972, the huge, award-winning modernist Pruitt-Igoe housing development in St. Louis was systematically destroyed with dynamite, having earlier been officially declared uninhabitable. There were many reformers in this era who, in the light of a series of scandals in mental handicap "hospitals" in Britain and "training schools" in the United States, would have seized the opportunity to consign such asylums to a similar fate. The reality was less dramatic: closures (and a few demolitions) took place within jurisdictions all over Britain and North America at a relatively modest rate throughout the next 20 years. There can be little doubt, however, that by the early 1970s the asylum was widely regarded as the icon of a bankrupt system.

What were the main characteristics of this modernity that apparently began to unravel in the early 1970s, and how can it help to explain the problematic and the public policy for which it provided a foundation? I can attempt no more here than an outline of an answer to these questions. I do so by listing five recurrent themes in the recent literature on modernity and by offering in each case a suggestion as to how each contributed to the *mentalité* of deviance (see Figure 1).

1. A dominant theme in the discussion of modernity is the penetration of market forces into every aspect of life. Whether or not one takes the Marxist view that this provided the material context for individualism, fragmentation, alienation and crisis, it clearly engendered a re-evaluation of the individual's role in society. Performance, evaluated according to market criteria, became a key measure of social status, and poverty was closely associated with failure and suspected criminality. Even when mitigated by charity directed towards the "deserving poor" it was the lot of the vast majority of people

with disabilities to share the stigma of poverty. It is worth noting in passing that Marx himself was sufficiently a child of the Enlightenment to be impressed by the power of human intellect. He retained some respect not only for the secularism of the bourgeoisie but also for its cunning urbanity when contrasted with what he referred to as "the idiocy of rural life".

2. No theme more clearly characterizes recent discussions of modernity than "creative destruction". In a frequently quoted essay written in 1863, Baudelaire characterized modernity as "the transient, the fleeting, the contingent". Another ringing phrase sounding through much recent writing is "All that is solid melts into air...", a quotation from Marx and Engels' characterization of the bourgeois epoch as one of uninterrupted crisis. Berman takes the phrase as the title for his lengthy and influential explication of the impact of modernity on urban life.[8] Schumpeter's view of the same phenomenon is expressed in terms that are ideologically opposed to Marx, casting the entrepreneur in the role of a heroic agent of positive change.[9] Yet the outcome is remarkably similar. In both versions the forces of capitalism are seen as inducing a state of constant economic and social change. The pace of change is set by aggressive accumulators of wealth and it is up to others in society to adapt as best they can. In such an environment of apparent chaos and unpredictability, people with disabilities are likely to be especially vulnerable to dislocation and a lack of control over their own lives.

3. Surrender of control is at the heart of a theme that characterizes another section of the modernity literature, one dominated by the writings of Foucault. This discussion focuses on the exercise of power at different scales, postulating hierarchies of control ranging from localities to

global systems. Many of Foucault's local sites are closed institutions, including prisons, hospitals and asylums. Although he had little to say about the mental *disability* asylum per se, the clear implication is that this institution too is to be regarded as a site of control. Indeed, the site to which all such localities reduce for Foucault is the human body. Control is achieved through surveillance — as expressed in Foucault's use of the image of the panopticon. Perhaps the major significance of this thrust in the literature on modernity for our purposes lies in the implication that the local sites of control, although seemingly at the margins, are actually central to power-knowledge relations within society as a whole.

4. Another important theme in discussions of modernity is its use of language. Bourdieu, for example, has described the social consequences of the imposition of a national language and the discrediting of local dialects.[10] Pred has discerned elements of modernity in the bureaucratic renaming of districts in Stockholm.[11] There is much scope for the exploration of labelling theory in the area of intellectual disability. The peculiar lexicon of "mental deficiency" is clearly an integral part of its construction.

5. Perhaps most illuminating of all is the theme of modernity's obsession with instrumental rationality. This is nowhere more vividly illustrated than in Max Weber's image of modern bureaucracy as an "iron cage" from which there can be no escape.[12] Means and ends become endlessly confused. In similar vein, Ellul argued that modern society is dominated by a "rule of technique" which defies any kind of regulation. Technique, he wrote, is "nothing more than means and the ensemble of means".[13]

More recently, Zygmunt Bauman has argued that the mind-set of modernity was a necessary precondition to the Holocaust.[14] Several authors have argued over the years that Nazi Germany represented the most horrific conflation of modernity and disability. It is now even clearer that developments in Germany in the interwar period, though more extreme than elsewhere, were by no means unique to that nation. One of the first enactments of the Third Reich, the Hereditary Health Law of 1933, was based to a large extent on an American model.[15] In the hands of the Nazi regime the law proved to be just one step on the road to a systematic extermination program of "persons worthless to live", a significant proportion of whom had been diagnosed as "mentally deficient".[16] As Wolfensberger has stated, the philosophy, personnel and equipment used to kill persons with disabilities evolved into those employed in the devastation of Europe's Jews.

Bauman's writings remove the Holocaust from its specific context and locate it firmly within the broader scope of modernity. Bauman treats the Holocaust as a "significant and reliable test of the hidden possibilities of modern society",[17] arguing it demonstrates that "the rules of instrumental rationality are singularly incapable of preventing such phenomena". He suggests that modern bureaucracy rendered "Holocaust-style solutions not only possible, but eminently 'reasonable'". He argues further that an obsession with the technical order — the classification and labelling of victims, the efficiency of equipment and so on — blinded the operatives to the horror of their deeds, "by emancipating the desiderata of rationality from interference of ethical norms or moral inhibitions".[18] Such ideas are extensions of those already explicit in the writings of Wolfensberger[19] and of Nirje,[20] the two acknowledged founders of the principle of "normalization" within the intellectual disability movement. Bank-Mikkelsen's statement that "normalization is basically an attack on the various dogmas"[21] retains its plausibility today in an era with an expanding post-Holocaust awareness of the potential consequences of the abuse of power.

This attempt to integrate five traditions in the writing of modernity with some of the dynamics of intellectual disability is intended merely to be suggestive of an approach. Further research along these lines can be expected to enhance our understanding of the dominance of the "problematic of mental deficiency" and articulate the ways in which it has affected our attitudes towards intellectual disability. It is possible at this point to offer only a preliminary assessment of this research direction and this I attempt in a brief concluding section.

Conclusion

A number of recent studies, such as *On Target?* and *Poor Places*, published by l'Institut Roeher Institute,[22] have demonstrated the marginal status in contemporary society of people with an intellectual disability. Such studies, and our experience over more than two decades, show clearly that successful community living does not flow automatically from deinstitutionalization. Given the extent that notions of deviancy remain embedded in the culture and the extent that they continue to be authorized even passively by the academy and the professions, mere policy changes are powerless to effect a major transformation.

The concept of modernity allows us to appreciate how firmly sedimented were the notions of deviance in the recent past and how lukewarm are the current institutional endorsements of reform in comparison with past justifications of repression. Modernity is a lens through which we can see that our culture has not only marginalized people with an intellectual disability, *it has also marginalized the study of intellectual disability as a phenomenon.* Traditionally, "mental deficiency" was given a place on centre stage only when this served to further some cause. Eugenicists, proponents of restrictive immigration and opponents of social, environmental and housing reform have all used the issue instrumentally to further their own agendas.

In so doing, they have frequently called on the authority of science and were always able to find both natural and social scientists willing to oblige. Supportive research was all too often based on inferences imbued with unacknowledged social values, usually grafted onto an unreflective empiricism and reinforced by the added authority of "statistics". The repeated "demonstrations" by eugenic researchers of an exclusively genetic basis for intelligence provides the best example of this pattern. Yet before we dismiss such methods entirely let us remember that, when governed by alternative values, the methods have been capable of reaching quite different conclusions. In the 1930s R.A. Fisher, though he never ceased to be a eugenicist, nevertheless undertook statistical research that convinced him of the importance of environmental influences on measured intelligence. Lancelot Hogben and J.B.S. Haldane went further, using quantitative methods to undermine much of the eugenic argument.[23] In addition, the work of Lionel Penrose contributed enormously to the destruction of the supposed single-cause etiology of intellectual disability. Subsequent developments in medical science have increased the potential for accurate diagnosis and effective treatment of some of the conditions previously thought to be endemic in "retardation". Our goal, then, should not be to devalue the contributions of formal science, but to open them up to critique and to use scientific methods within a pluralistic framework rather than in the rigid pursuit of a supposed "one best way".

Whatever may be the trends within the university, the fact remains that the impetus towards normalization in the 1970s and subsequent reconceptualizations of intellectual disability were neither mainly derived in, nor mainly implemented from, the universities or any of the established professions. The advances were, and continue to be, grounded in the voluntary sector and are sustained by the enthusiasm and convictions of parents, colleagues, self-advocates and friends. Professionals have contributed richly to its progress but it is instructive that in doing so they have often been forced to rethink a largely inadequate professional training. And they, like the rest of us, are thankful that within a sea of indifference and (even now) occasional hostility, there have existed in academia a few vital islands of hope and inspiration.

There lies in the critique of modernity a rich potential for establishing conditions that can lead to the liberation of people with an intellectual disability. The modernity perspective can illuminate the former dominance of an ethos of a "one best way", codified, professionalized and bureaucratized, which viewed the subject less as an individual with unique strengths and weaknesses than as the representative of a particular problem category. Equally as important in the long term, the critique of modernity also provides a method for undermining the spurious but persistent academic authority of the "mental deficiency problematic" and its lingering asylum *mentalité*. Above all, the critique of modernity provides a means of dissolving that resistant mass of dogma which represents not only, as Bank-Mikkelsen pointed out, the antithesis of normalization[24] but also the total negation of human rights.

CHARACTERISTIC	REPRESENTATIVE AUTHORS	IMPACT ON INTELLECTUAL DISABILITY
PENETRATION OF INDUSTRIAL CAPITAL	MARX, HARVEY, SAYER	UNEMPLOYABILITY
CREATIVE DESTRUCTION	MARX, SCHUMPETER, BERMAN	DISLOCATION AND DISEMPOWERMENT
SURVEILLANCE	FOUCAULT, DANDEKER	CONTROL
RENAMING	BOURDIEU, PRED	CLASSIFICATION AND RELABELLING
RATIONAL BUREAUCRACY AND TECHNIQUE	WEBER, ELLUL, BAUMAN	CLASSED AS "INEFFICIENTS"

FIGURE 1. MODERNITY AND INTELLECTUAL DISABILITY

Notes

1. Max Horkheimer and Theodor W. Adorno, *Dialectics of Enlightenment*, New York: The Seabury Press, 1969.

2. Alfred A. Baumeister, "The American Residential Institution: Its History and Character", in Alfred A. Baumeister and Earl Butterfield (eds.), *Residential Facilities for the Mentally Retarded*, Chicago: Aldine, 1970, pp. 1-28.

3. Langdon J. Down, "Observations on an Ethnic Classification of Idiots", *Journal of Mental Science*, 13, 1867, pp. 121-123.

4. Stephen J. Gould, *The Panda's Thumb*, London: Penguin Books, 1980.

5. Harvey G. Simmons, *From Asylum to Welfare*, Toronto: National Institute on Mental Retardation, 1982.

6. Steven A. Gelb, "Henry H. Goddard and the Immigrants, 1910-1917: The Studies and Their Social Context", *Journal of the History of the Behavioral Sciences*, 22, 1986, pp. 324-332; Steven A. Gelb, "Social Deviance and the 'Discovery' of the Moron", *Disability, Handicap and Society*, 2, 1987, pp. 247-258.

7. Quoted in David Harvey, *The Condition of Postmodernity*, Oxford: Blackwell, 1990, p. 39.

8. Marshall Berman, *All That Is Solid Melts into Air: The Experience of Modernity*, New York: Penguin, 1982.

9. Joseph A. Schumpeter, *Capitalism, Socialism and Democracy*, New York: Harper, 1950.

10. J.B. Thompson (ed.), *Language and Symbolic Power*, writings of Pierre Bourdieu, Oxford: Polity Press, 1991.

11. Allan Pred and Michael John Watts, *Reworking Modernity*, New Brunswick, N.J.: Rutgers University Press, 1992.

12. Max Weber, *From Max Weber: Methodology of the Social Sciences*, Edward Shils and Henry Finch (eds.), Glencoe, Ill.: The Free Press, 1949.

13. Jacques Ellul, *The Technological Society*, New York: Vintage, 1964.

14. Zygmunt Bauman, *Modernity and the Holocaust*, Cambridge: Polity Press, 1989.

15. J. David Smith, *Minds Made Feeble: The Myth and Legacy of the Kallikaks*, Rockville, Md.: Aspen, 1985; Philip R. Reilly, *The Surgical Solution: A History of Involuntary Sterilization in the United States*, Baltimore, Md.: Johns Hopkins University Press, 1991.

16. John F. Kane and Johannes Rojahn, "Development of Services for the Mentally Retarded in Germany: A Survey of History, Empirical Research, and Current Trends", *Applied Research in Mental Retardation*, 2, 1981, pp. 195-210.

17. Bauman, *Modernity*, 1989, p. 12 (see n. 14).

18. Ibid., p. 28.

19. Especially Wolf Wolfensberger, *The Principle of Normalization in Human Services*, Downsview, Ont.: National Institute on Mental Retardation, 1972; Wolf Wolfensberger, *The Origin and Nature of Our Institutional Models*, Syracuse, N.Y.: Human Policy Press, 1975; and Wolf Wolfensberger, "A Brief Overview of the Principle of Normalization", in Robert J. Flynn and Kathleen E. Nitsch (eds.), *Normalization, Social Integration and Community Services*, Baltimore, Md.: University Park Press, 1980, pp. 7-30.

20. Bengt Nirje, "The Normalization Principle and Its Human Management Implications", in R. Kugel and Wolf Wolfensberger (eds.), *Changing Patterns in Residential Services for the Mentally Retarded*, Washington, D.C.: President's Committee on Mental Retardation, 1969, pp. 179-195.

21. Neils E. Bank-Mikkelsen, "Denmark", in Robert J. Flynn and Kathleen E. Nitsch (eds.), *Normalization, Social Integration and Community Services*, Baltimore, Md.: University Park Press, 1980, pp. 51-70.

22. L'Institut Roeher Institute, *On Target?: Canada's Employment-Related Programs for Persons with Disabilities*, North York, Ont.: Author, 1992; L'Institut Roeher Institute, *Poor Places: Disability-Related Housing and Support Services*, North York, Ont.: Author, 1990.

23. Pauline M.H. Mazumdar, *Eugenics, Human Genetics and Human Failings*, London and New York: Routledge, 1992.

24. Bank-Mikkelsen, "Denmark", 1980 (see n. 21).

Chapter 2

What Matters Most: Disability, Research and Empowerment

by Linda Ward and Margaret Flynn

It is a hot summer day in London in the late 1980s. Gathered together in one of the capital's most venerable colleges is a large number of academics, researchers and representatives of research funding bodies. Their purpose? A symposium on researching disability comprising presentations on a variety of different methodological and other themes, given and chaired by a panel of experienced disability researchers.

Those convening the event are proud that it will shine a spotlight on a usually neglected area of social science research. But some in the audience (and one or two others who have chosen not to attend) hold a different view. What credibility can such a seminar muster, they ask, when none of those chairing or presenting papers are themselves disabled? What does it say about current understanding of disability research issues that such an event has been allowed to go ahead in this form, when a symposium on researching gender issues given entirely by men, or on race relations research given entirely by white people, would have been laughed out of court?

During the discussions, there is a fierce, short-lived debate on the nature, purpose and future of disability research, spearheaded by an articulate wheelchair user (one of the two or three people present who have a disability). The session ends inconclusively, but the debate and struggle for a research process that contributes to the empowerment of people with disabilities, rather than disempowers them, will continue.

Introduction

Disability is *not* the measles. Disability is socially produced. The wheelchair user with an adapted car, the personal assistance she wants (at the times that she wants it), an allocated parking place and an accessible and adapted home and workplace is not disabled at home or at work in the same way as the wheelchair user who is contending with inaccessible home and work environments, without personal assistance or transport. The disability experienced by the latter is created by the disabling society in which we live.

Over the last 20 years our models for understanding disability have shifted from the traditional medical model, focusing on individual impairments, conditions and medical interventions, to a socio-political model, emphasizing our disabling society. Gradually, disability research paradigms have shifted also. First, there was the traditional positivist research paradigm, with its unquestioning assumptions — that the social world could be studied in the same way as the natural; that research could be "value-free"; that the knowledge and causal explanations obtained would be independent of the methods used or the beliefs of the researchers involved.

Then came the interpretive or qualitative paradigm that challenged these assumptions. All knowledge is socially constructed; the social world differs from the natural in that those studied are active participants not passive objects; research should try to understand the meaning of events, not just their causes; knowledge and understanding obtained from research will be influenced by the researchers' values and are not independent of them.

The two paradigms differed — but in one respect they were similar. Both entailed research which was — and is — carried out by relatively powerful *experts* on relatively powerless "subjects". Despite the liberal trappings of the qualitative paradigm, the "social relations of research production" had not changed. Hence, there was a need for an "emancipatory" research paradigm: one which places people with disabilities and their concerns centre stage at every point in a research process aimed at facilitating their empowerment.[1]

What would such a fundamental shift in the way disability research is conceptualized, organized, produced and used look like in practice? If we think of the research process as a continuum, this new paradigm will involve changes at every stage. That means changing:

- the processes followed by funding bodies in deciding what disability research should be supported;

- the relationship between disability researchers and those they research;

- the ways in which the products or findings of research are written up, disseminated and utilized.

In this chapter we look at each of these three areas in turn.

Changing Attitudes and Practice in Funding Bodies

Research costs money. People with disabilities, because of their disadvantaged position in a disabling society, are usually poor. They are also under-represented as researchers, academics and, significantly, as directors, trustees, employees or advisers to those organizations that fund disability research. Many funding bodies still subscribe (albeit unthinkingly) to a positivist research paradigm, sometimes leavened by a dash of the liberal or interpretive. Shifting to a more emancipatory research paradigm means educating funders so that the work supported by them will contribute to the empowerment of people with disabilities rather than collude in their continuing disempowerment. In the U.K. some progress has been made in devising guidelines supportive of the emancipatory paradigm for funding bodies to follow when considering applications to undertake disability research. The tasks to be confronted break down into four areas.[2]

1. Defining disability

Funding bodies need to make explicit their commitment to a social, rather than a medical or individual, model of disability; that is, that they understand disability as the social restrictions confronted by people with disabilities living in a society that is not organized to take account of their needs. Defining disability in this way conceptualizes it as an equal opportunities issue; the funding body will need to draw up appropriate policies and practices to support this.

2. The funding body as an organization

Funding bodies need to practise what they preach. If they are to be credible in their funding of disability research, then they must get their own houses in order. This means that they must take positive action to employ people with disabilities on their staff and as advisers, ensure that they are represented on all decision-making bodies concerned with disability research within their organization and do whatever is necessary to enable equal access to all their activities.

3. The funding body as provider of resources for research and development

Applications from people with disabilities and organizations controlled by them must be explicitly encouraged. Appropriate support systems may be necessary to enable them to make successful funding bids. This may involve informal help and feedback from the first mooting of an idea for a potential project through the drawing up of an outline proposal to the production of draft and final applications. It may mean representatives of the funding body spending time with individuals and their organizations, helping them formulate their ideas and conveying them appropriately on paper. Providing small amounts of money to disability groups with good ideas but little experience in preparing funding bids will enable the groups to buy in expert help to prepare their application.

One major funding body in the U.K. recently earmarked funds for this purpose and, in addition, provided two separate days of on-the-spot advice to black and ethnic minority organizations so they could put together applications for funding for work on issues of concern to them. Another funder keeps a list of consultants with relevant expertise. When grassroots community organizations with innovative ideas but little experience in applying for funding approach them, the funding body pays for them to enlist expert help in thinking through their proposal and writing it up. A third funding body has been out visiting organizations of people with disabilities, checking out their ideas, seeking their views of what work should be supported in the future and encouraging applications in the areas identified by them.

Funding bodies need to keep a list of people with disabilities and their organizations who can be called upon to referee applications; people with disabilities and their organizations also need to be involved in the committees which advise trusts on which applications should be supported.

4. Criteria to be applied by funding bodies to organizations and individuals applying for support

Funding bodies, because they control the purse strings, are in a good position to exert a positive influence on those applying for funding. They can stipulate that organizations applying for funding must have equal opportunities policies and action plans and have people with disabilities in their employment. They can specify that all proposals to undertake disability research must involve people with disabilities and their organizations at all stages of the research process, as project directors, advisers and project workers, as well as research "subjects". They can make it clear that the costs of fully involving people with disabilities throughout a potential research project (including, for example, additional resources for facilitation, personal assistance, transport and interpreting) will be met by the funding body as a matter of course. They can require that all those applying for funding for disability research address issues of gender, race, class, age and sexuality within their proposals. They can make clear that preference will be given to applicants with disabilities and, where appropriate, individuals who apply for funding can be encouraged to work in partnership with organizations controlled by people with disabilities.

There are numerous implications for funding bodies in taking these kinds of measures. There will be costs: more time and resources for staff and others to offer help to applicants who need it; more money to meet the additional expenses incurred in involving people with disabilities and their organizations in research projects in a meaningful way. But the outcome will be that funding bodies can have confidence that they are supporting better research — research that is really relevant to the needs of those it purports to serve. And — what matters most — people with disabilities will be more likely to see funding for research that will help them in their struggle for empowerment.

Improving Relations between Disability Researchers and Those They Research

Within the positivist paradigm the relationship between researcher and researched is fundamentally unequal: research is carried out by "experts" on powerless "subjects". Within an emancipatory paradigm this has to change. Increasingly, people with disabilities are asserting their right to undertake research in this area and refining their skills to do so. The relatively small band of researchers with physical disabilities is growing in strength and numbers. Now people with learning difficulties are also successfully taking on the researcher's role.[3] But old habits die hard. People with learning difficulties are still disadvantaged by low expectations and limiting life experiences and treated as poor relations in the research process ...

1. The Research Family

There is little to commend in the upbringing of social science researchers. They have a staple diet of quantitative methods during their school career. They are socialized into borrowing methodologies from the bigger boys and girls and learn to devise research instruments with their help. Their patterns of speech become closely associated with those of their teachers. Their school education assists them in: refining their skills (and career choices); negotiating access to people and institutions; analysing and presenting information; and producing reports within a given time frame.

Universities, colleges and finishing schools specialize in applying for research funding and transforming sometimes very old studies and research findings into articles for refereed journals or, less prestigiously, chapters or articles for practitioner journals. The contribution of higher education to the prestige of social science researchers is considerable. They learn to believe that their published research accurately describes the existence of a neat and sequential pattern of research procedures, each step presupposing the completion of the preceding one. They learn not to question this model of reporting which creates an oversimplified and dishonest picture of research activities. They attend seminars where they regret that their findings have been bypassed yet again and they console themselves with submitting further research proposals and criticizing the endeavours of other researchers whose education, values and ideas are unlike their own. As they gather staff and students around them, they replicate their own educational experiences — send them on advanced quantitative methods and computing courses, compel them to give seminars for which they may be unprepared, fail their homework — and reflect to like-minded colleagues that it never did them any harm. They may recognize a case for giving staff and students time to explore procedures that will increase the applicability of their work, learn about new, more user-friendly paradigms and consider different ways in which findings can be presented — and offer cautious credit to them when they do so. But they are consoled that in an area of such limited expertise, favoured largely by newcomers, there is little danger of their label, "expert", being threatened.

2. *The Poor Relations*

There is little to commend in the upbringing of Poor Relations either. They have a staple diet of disadvantage which commences in infancy and continues into adulthood. In their segregated special schools they become accustomed to a narrow range of experience; if this is challenged by their parents, redress may be limited and late. Mostly, they do not benefit from friendships with local children. Although it is recognized in the U.K. that on average it is not more expensive to educate a Poor Relation in an ordinary school with support rather than in a special school for Poor Relations, and that the quality of the learning experience for Poor Relations in special schools is affected by a lack of pace and low levels of expectation, the Research and Professional Families are not convinced that the education of Poor Relations merits radical restructuring.

In the U.K. Poor Relations stay in the same special school and, even in their teenage years, will be getting ready for the bus home at 3:00 p.m. They are not encouraged to speculate about their future selves and they have yet to be emancipated from a *"day service"* assumption. Even though over 100,000 of them attend colleges on a part-time or full-time basis in the U.K., their student days are invariably segregated, long term and not geared towards employment. Even though Poor Relations share such familiar aspirations as friendships, intimate relationships, employment, money and their own homes, in special schools their prospects are less than enviable. They find it more difficult than young people in general to make friends beyond special schools and services, they enjoy fewer leisure activities outside the family home and young women in particular tend to have

more restricted or supervised lives in domestic seclusion than.
of young men. Poor Relations with a lot of service needs and th ꜱe
from black and ethnic communities are at a particular disadvantage.
They are much more likely to be home centred, even solitary, and
dependent on their parents for social activities.

The transition to adulthood of most Poor Relations is likely to be
prolonged or postponed indefinitely. Confiding in parents, especially
mothers, as opposed to other adults or special friends, is widespread.
Given this reliance on parents, it is unlikely that many young people
will ever be able to disclose sexual abuse which occurs at home.[4]

Poor Relations learn throughout their lives that their views can
be bypassed — apparently legitimately — by the Specialist,
Professional and Research Families. The reasons given include: their
limited or absent verbal skills; their speech, which is difficult to
understand; a tendency to acquiesce; difficulty in expressing
themselves in a consistent manner; and difficulties in making
judgements about whether an interviewer can be expected to possess
essential contextual information in order to make sense of responses
given. Layered onto this are two further disadvantages: being
socialized into believing that their views are not important since
those of others generally take priority; and living, working and
learning in settings that are not structured to enhance their capacity
for expressing views. Therefore, a great deal of information about
the lives and circumstances of Poor Relations is gathered by proxy
— usually from interviews with their parents and carers. Not
surprisingly, it yields few clues about Poor Relations themselves.

Though self- and citizen advocacy have proved powerful
vehicles for asserting their views and perspectives and changing
people's lives in positive ways that services cannot,[5] they still touch
the lives of relatively few Poor Relations. For them, middle age
drifts into old age without altered prospects in retirement because
their life cycle cannot easily be cut into the standard segments. The
practice of leaving work earlier, given impetus by mature pension
packages, is not an option as paid work has eluded most of them.
There is little room for grey power.

3. Towards honest interdependence

It may require a major feat of public relations to persuade Research Families to acknowledge that their credibility as experts is waning. But there are some signs that a reconsideration of the traditional relationship between them and their Poor Relations could be at hand. In opposition to traditional research practices where the voices of people with disabilities have been silent, some minority, counter trends are emerging:

Dominant Trends	Minority Counter-Trends
• The buccaneers of research funding defer to _experts_ to identify research questions and draft proposals	One or two funders have set this practice adrift (by involving people with disabilities in this role)
• Disability researchers feel no obligation to collaborate with people with disabilities	One or two funding bodies make this a requirement of funding
• Disability researchers have non-disabled advisers	A few disability researchers enjoy the benefits of advisory teams which seek equal representation of people with disabilities
• Disability researchers are largely non-disabled	Some disability researchers (both disabled and non-disabled) are now working in ways which incorporate the perspectives and contributions of people with disabilities and their organizations
• Traditionally, disability researchers have ignored the firsthand experiences of people with learning disabilities	Now some are exploring with people with learning disabilities better ways of gathering their views

At this point, amplification of the more hopeful counter-trends may be helpful. The few researchers who have sought to sidestep the persistence of the positivist research paradigm in favour of an emerging, emancipatory paradigm may outline the ways in which they have learned to overcome the obstacles to gathering people's views for example. They may describe ways in which children with limited communication skills have indicated their affection for, and preference to be with, certain people using photographs. (As long as care is taken to ensure that the children are not overwhelmed by too many photos, this is a very promising way of learning about the significant people in their lives.) Other researchers may summarize their learning about the use of drawings — they help many people to convey as much or as little about their lives as they wish. Diaries have been helpful in getting some sense of how people's days are structured. (A disadvantage is that the quality of the information collected is a function of the time, willingness and honesty of staff or family to complete the diaries.) Direct observation is a valuable means of understanding the activities and impacts of some services but it is an incomplete activity, particularly if the people who use or have used these services are not on hand to provide an explanatory framework.

The discussion comes of age when the abuse of power by disability researchers is acknowledged but that debate is set aside as both groups attempt to identify common ground. They both want to expand the research repertoire in ways that can produce useful and valid data and an altogether more satisfactory means of working together. The subject of satisfaction, recalled by people with disabilities as a weak concept painted with plenty of gloss by disability researchers is the starting point. Disability researchers acknowledge that they have not developed this adequately. Jointly they both list their dissatisfaction with satisfaction.

- "Satisfaction surveys" are hardly pertinent to people with disabilities who use services unwillingly.

- Measurements of satisfaction are neither standardized nor definitive and may never be so.

- Measurements of satisfaction for use with people with learning difficulties are experimental and developmental and may always be so.

- Satisfaction is multi-dimensional.

- Satisfaction is an inadequate indicator of service quality if people with disabilities are cautious in expressing their opinions because of their vulnerability to the goodwill of service providers.

- Satisfaction is an inadequate indicator of service quality for people who have become accustomed to impoverished services and whose expectations of these have reduced.

- Measures of satisfaction may mask the tendency of some people to report greater happiness, satisfaction or well-being than they really feel. This *surface* satisfaction may disguise distress, deep resentment and other emotions unlikely to be elicited in a brief interview.

- Dissatisfaction may be registered by people who are responding from positions of injustice, disappointment or deprivation. Without deeper probing, which may not be possible, it is impossible to determine what it is that presents as "expressed dissatisfaction".

- What should be essential features of services for people with disabilities, such as respect for their dignity and privacy, are unlikely to be adequately reflected in satisfaction measures.

The discussion casts a beam of light on new possibilities. The Poor Relations and the Research Family acknowledge the strength of their joint efforts. They are both hopeful, perhaps over-hopeful, of developing ways of working that meet their altered understanding of what is satisfactory as a matter of urgency. And they recognize that pooling their different experiences and expertise would make for better disability research in the future.

Making Disability Research Useful

If research is to contribute to the empowerment of people with disabilities, it needs, through its outputs, to do two more things.

- It must share knowledge, experiences and ideas with other people with disabilities, raising their consciousness, increasing solidarity and broadening the base of the disability movement.

- It must try to influence policy makers and practitioners to make changes in policy and practice that will work towards the empowerment of people with disabilities.

1. Sharing research findings with other people with disabilities

Most people are busy and have little time to read anything longer than a few pages. Most people with disabilities are poor and cannot afford to buy expensive books and research reports. Because of our inappropriate educational systems, a good many people with disabilities may find reading difficult. This will be particularly true of many people with learning difficulties and people with hearing impairments, for whom signing and video will be more appropriate media than the written word. Adopting an emancipatory research paradigm means paying special attention to how research findings can be shared most widely. Researchers must ask themselves: whom they are trying to reach; what their key messages are; and the best ways of sharing their findings.

The fundamental rules are to produce material that is brief, to the point, engaging, attractive and in as many formats as necessary—braille, large print, audio tapes, in a mixture of symbols and print and in minority community languages. Researchers need to ensure that adequate sums are put into research budgets initially to cover multiple dissemination formats. And funding bodies need to make it clear that their expectation is that researchers will produce materials in a variety of appropriate forms, and that they will be happy to meet these additional costs. The *Clear English Code* is a handy one-page reminder to any researcher of the do's and don'ts of writing as simply as possible for their audience.[6]

Making research findings and other information accessible to people with learning difficulties poses a particular challenge. At the Norah Fry Research Centre in Bristol, England,[7] an inventory of good practice in this area is being compiled, based on a survey of organizations with an interest in the field of learning difficulties. It indicates that various presentational techniques are helpful in communicating information — simplified vocabulary; clear language; symbols, pictures and signs (such as the Makaton sign and symbol system used in the U.K.); illustrations; cartoons; print style and so on.[8] Separate, simplified versions of materials have great value, but can still represent "them" and "us". Some researchers at the Norah Fry Research Centre feel that the separation between the actual documents used in the research world and those available to people with learning difficulties should be avoided, as another barrier to empowerment. One solution they have tried is a form of "parallel writing". This brings together the original research report and a simplified version as closely as possible. The two texts run side by side on the page, giving the reader access, with whatever help is necessary, to the information and arguments in the original form, in addition to a summary alongside. With the help of people with learning difficulties they have developed "parallel text" in this way and are producing a checklist, in pamphlet form, for others wishing to follow suit.[9] The Roeher Institute in Canada[10] has worked with people with learning difficulties to produce straightforward guides to research reports. These provide research findings in straightforward, accessible language.

Sometimes research findings are more easily digested when they are on audio- or videotape. There is accumulating experience now of ways of making audio- and videotapes in attractive, engaging formats. For people with hearing impairments, for whom signing is their first language, the presentation of research findings on video is a must. Since video is a more expensive medium than the written word, the costs for disseminating material in this form must be included in the original research budget that goes to funding bodies.

Of course, those conducting disability research also need to ensure that their findings are fed back to research participants and that they involve other people with disabilities in the decisions about how their material is best disseminated.

2. Influencing policy makers and practitioners

Policy makers and practitioners are unlikely to spend time reading lengthy documents. One solution, adopted by the Joseph Rowntree Foundation in England,[11] is to produce short, snappy *Findings* for each research project funded.[12] Two or, at the most, four pages in length, a summary of key findings on the first page, amplified with further detail on the reverse or subsequent pages, these are ideal for the busy reader. Accompanied by a press release, they also lend themselves to ready use by journalists who can produce an article on the research and its findings with little effort.

Many people with disabilities and organizations undertaking disability research have little experience in media relations, with few skills and even less confidence in this important area. Yet media expertise is vital if the messages of disability research are to be effectively conveyed. Accessible media skills workshops run by charitable organizations or progressive funding bodies will pay huge dividends in ensuring that research findings reach the audiences for whom they are intended.

At a fundamental level, an emancipatory research paradigm that aims to facilitate the empowerment of people with disabilities may cross the uncertain interface between dissemination of research findings and political activism. Any, perhaps most, funding bodies will draw a line at supporting campaigning or similarly "political" activities because of their charitable status. Nonetheless, they can certainly fund research that may, for example, identify discrimination against people with disabilities.[13] These findings may then be used by organizations in subsequent campaigns for anti-discrimination legislation.[14]

Funding bodies working to an emancipatory research paradigm will not be content simply to fund research, but will want to ensure that its findings are disseminated as widely and effectively as possible. In the U.K., the powerful findings of a research project on community care or independent living[15] (involving interviews with 50 people with disabilities now living in the community) were disseminated by the researcher (with the help of additional resources from the funding body) to the House of Commons All-Party Disablement Group, to other relevant MPs during a debate in Parliament on the Disabled (Rights) Bill and to local authorities involved in implementing new community care reforms. Key messages from the research were also taken to local authority practitioners during training days on "needs-led assessments", and presentations were given to organizations of people with disabilities throughout the country.

Within an emancipatory research paradigm, good research is not just research that is done well. It is research that is shared effectively. Research, even good research, is wasted if it does not reach those who need to be reached. What matters most is to ensure it does.

Conclusion

The seminar we described at the beginning of this chapter had a sequel, if not yet a happy ending. It prompted some leading disability researchers to approach a funding body known to have an interest in supporting more innovative disability research. A series of six seminars were held, involving disabled researchers, representatives of organizations of people with disabilities, other disability researchers and one or two representatives of relevant funding bodies. Each seminar explored a key aspect of disability research and the series culminated in a national conference and a special issue of the journal *Disability, Handicap and Society*, containing the papers presented during the seminar series.

The learning curve of those who participated in the seminar series — particularly the non-disabled researchers — was immense. We learned of the parallels and the differences between gender research, race relations research and disability research. We recognized that there may be conflict and difference even within the disability movement between men and women, and between people from different ethnic backgrounds.[16] There were sharp divisions between disabled and non-disabled feminist researchers on issues around people with disabilities and care-givers.[17] We acknowledged that a researcher with one impairment will not necessarily understand all that they need to understand about the circumstances of other people with different impairments but that, nonetheless, a researcher with a disability (particularly one involved with an organization of people with disabilities) is more likely to be sensitive to the issues confronting other people with disabilities than his or her non-disabled peers.[18] We recognized that the role of the non-disabled person in disability research (whether as researcher, supervisor or employee of a funding body) may be an uncomfortable one but that people with disabilities need non-disabled allies — provided that they know their place![19]

There is still a long way to travel before the basic tenets of an emancipatory research paradigm are accepted by many of those in powerful positions within disability research. As we were writing this chapter, a colleague who is a researcher and a mental health survivor told us of a recent experience. A group of mental health survivors had been asked by a respected organization for their comments on how best to measure "quality of life". Not surprisingly, the survivors' report included the recommendation that the researcher appointed should, by preference, be a mental health survivor. "Impossible," replied the organization, which is supposed to be developing good practice in this area. "We would want someone with research experience." (Do they really believe that there are no researchers who have had mental health problems?) "Besides, they would be biased." (Quite unlike the doctors who have undertaken mental health research in the past?)

Plus ça change...

Acknowledgements

Parts of this chapter draw heavily on the work of Mike Oliver and those involved in the researching disability seminar series, funded by the Joseph Rowntree Foundation, and reported in *Disability, Handicap and Society*, 7(2 and 3), 1992.

Notes

1. M. Oliver, "Changing the Social Relations of Research Production?" *Disability, Handicap and Society*, 7(2), 1992, pp. 101-115.

2. "Guidelines for Funding Applications to Undertake Disability Research", *Disability, Handicap and Society*, 7(3), 1992, pp. 279-280.

3. A. Whittaker, S. Gardner and J. Kershaw, *Service Evaluation by People with Learning Difficulties*, London: King's Fund Centre, 1991; J. Sullivan and P. Sullivan, *CCETSW (Central Council for Education and Training in Social Work) Research*, Halifax: Calderdale People First, 1993.

4. M. Flynn and M. Hirst, *This Year, Next Year, Sometime...? Learning Disability and Adulthood*, London: National Development Team and Social Policy Research Unit, 1992.

5. M. Flynn and L. Ward, "We Can Change the Future: Self and Citizen Advocacy", in S.S. Segal and V.P. Verma (eds.), *Prospects for People with Learning Difficulties*, London: David Fulton, 1991.

6. Words at Work, *Clear English Code*, Stockport: Words at Work, 1992.

7. The Norah Fry Research Centre, University of Bristol, England, carries out research on services for people with learning disabilities.

8. R. Townsley, *Presenting Information for People with Learning*

Difficulties: An Overview of Current Ideas and Techniques, Bristol: Norah Fry Research Centre, 1994.

9. L. Bashford, S. Mackenzie, R. Townsley and C. Williams, *Parallel Writing: Making Research Accessible to People with Learning Difficulties*, Bristol, U.K.: University of Bristol, Norah Fry Research Centre, 1994.

10. L'Institut Roeher Institute is Canada's national institute for education, information and the study of public policy affecting persons with intellectual impairment and other disabilities.

11. The Joseph Rowntree Foundation is an independent charitable organization supporting a large program of applied research and innovative development projects in the U.K. in the fields of housing, social policy, community care and disability.

12. Joseph Rowntree Foundation, *Drafting Findings*, York: Joseph Rowntree Foundation, n.d.

13. C. Barnes, *Disabled People in Britain and Discrimination*, London: Hurst and Company and University of Calgary Press, 1991.

14. British Council of Organisations of Disabled People, *Human Rights and Disabled People: Why Anti-Discrimination Legislation Is Essential*, Belper, Derbyshire: BCODP, 1992.

15. J. Morris, *Community Care or Independent Living?* York: Joseph Rowntree Foundation/Community Care, 1993.

16. O. Stuart, "Race and Disability: Just a Double Oppression?" *Disability, Handicap and Society*, 7(2), 1992, pp. 177-188.

17. J. Morris, "Personal and Political: A Feminist Perspective on Researching Physical Disability", *Disability, Handicap and Society*, 7(2), 1992, pp. 157-166; L. Keith, "Who Cares Wins? Women, Caring and Disability", *Disability, Handicap and Society*, 7(2), 1992, pp. 167-176.

18. C. Barnes, "Qualitative Research: Valuable or Irrelevant?", *Disability, Handicap and Society*, 7(2), 1992, pp. 115-124.

19. Morris, "Personal and Political", 1992 (see n. 17).

Chapter 3

Towards Inclusion: The Role of People with Disabilities in Policy and Research Issues in the United States — A Historical and Political Analysis

by Irving Kenneth Zola

Introduction

The Independent Living/Disability Rights Movement has, in the last two decades, become the voice to articulate the oppression of perhaps the largest disenfranchised group — people with chronic diseases and disabilities. To appreciate how far this movement has come as well as how far it has yet to go it is necessary to trace and contextualize its history. The history that this chapter will trace is the role of people with disabilities in regard to policies and research about them. The context is the ongoing web of political, social and economic forces. As recent historians of science and medicine have claimed, it has been traditional to analyze such institutions divorced from the society in which they are located. Consistent with the newer approach, this paper claims that definitions of disability as well as the services and research in response to its existence have *always* been influenced by the same forces that shape the rest of society. I will attempt in this chapter to trace this interaction through four historical periods in the United States.

The Defect with a Cash Value Period

The Civil War was the most devastating war in terms of casualties that the United States has ever engaged in, before or since. As a direct result of these casualties, there was the first pervasive governmental involvement in rehabilitation services and research. The efforts, by current standards, were crude and limited but the budgets of many states in the early post-war years were overwhelmed by large expenditures for prosthetic limbs for thousands of amputees.

Wars have always had a special place in the production of disability and they have produced medical advances in the saving of lives and, secondarily, in the rehabilitation of survivors. In turn, these survivors have often been seen as populations to whom the state and the populace owed a special debt. Social research has often been necessary for the sheer counting, measurement and legitimation of this "need".

Although war is a cyclical occurrence, from the mid-1800s on industrialization has had a more sustained effect on the production and management of disability in the United States. The progressive era harkened a new perspective on social responsibility and social reformers noted with alarm the growing number of people "crippled" by industrial accidents and occupational diseases. By the early 1900s that number reached 14,000 workers annually, with a cumulative figure of 500,000 in the working-age population. In its wake came such organizations as the Federation of Associations for Cripples, committed to publicizing "the problem" and proposed solutions.[1]

This issue was recognized in still another quarter. For industrialization also spawned the trade union movement. They in turn pushed for workmen's compensation legislation. The first law was passed in 1908 for civil employees and by 1920 almost every state had such legislation. The First World War transformed this steady flow of industrial diseases and accidents to a flood of injuries and disabilities. By May 1919, when American Expeditionary Forces returned, the number of casualties was 123,000.[2]

As a result of such foci, Frey has dubbed this era "the defect with a cash value period".[3] Although some research was devoted to rehabilitation services, the primary purpose of assessment tools was to measure loss of function. Since the latter was tied also to ability to return to work, it was not enough to assess merely some physical loss. To illustrate, at that time the loss of both eyes resulting in blindness was regarded as not only a total impairment but prima facie evidence of inability to work. But what of the loss of one eye? From the functional standpoint such a loss might not even necessitate a change of job. What needed to be measured was the loss of function in the context of the individual's actual work activity — an activity at that time perceived almost exclusively as male and remunerative.[4] No other losses were deemed worth compensating for.

"Rehabilitation Rather than Compensation"

Although the research and service issues of such an approach can still be found in policies even today, as an exclusive focus the approach had ebbed by the 1940s. By then what Frey has called the "rehabilitation rather than compensation" era was in full flower.[5] As with all eras, the forces pushing the blossoming were in place before the first bloom.

1. Demographic changes and perceptions were reflected in a Hoover Commission report of 1932. There a quite prescient sociologist noted that though there might still be occasional epidemics of influenza, the medical problems facing future generations would be the consequences of chronic diseases and the major health crisis would be the provision of long term care.

2. Industrialization had begun to require more and more skilled labour. The health needs of unskilled labour were not important to employers. If sick or disabled, they could

be easily replaced. Not so with more skilled workers and executives. And, therefore, an economic reason for rehabilitation was created.

3. In the mid-1930s the first major self-help movement took hold — Alcoholics Anonymous. Whatever its efficacy, it legitimated "fellow sufferers" as the primary source of support if not cure.

4. Although medicine, following advances in science and industry, became more high tech, there was also more talk of treating the whole person and of more "comprehensive" (read *not* exclusively biomedical) approaches. Psychiatry, the most holistic of medical specialties, was also gaining credence, becoming a specialty where the patient-client was a more active participant.

5. The Depression left its mark on the need for safety nets such as social security. And although Franklin Delano Roosevelt thought of, and then rejected, a national health plan, drawing on his own personal medical experience — adult-onset polio (and he was but the first of a long series of U.S. presidents to do so), he created the March of Dimes. This was the first national voluntary association devoted to research and service and had an almost "socialist" aspect, paying for the medical needs of a "polio victim" regardless of income. The service was his or hers by "right" of having had polio. The generation of polio survivors who experienced this program that gave help without hassles grew up with the strength, expectations and self-confidence required to provide leadership for a future consumer movement.

6. The only other disability group for which societal allowances have long been made are "the blind". No group has had a more ambivalent history from being considered the most tragic of punishments (Oedipus) to the most blessed inspiration (John Milton to Helen Keller). They

were the first to have their own schools; the only disability group to have a specific federal income tax deduction, a reserved job status (guaranteed vendor opportunities in buildings on federal property) and mail privileges (free matter for the blind); the first to have set aside state "financial and separate state agencies to serve them relief" funds and a long history of "designated codicils" in omnibus rehabilitation legislation.

7. Then, of course, there was the Second World War which again catalyzed medical advances. Some claimed that in its wake there was the "real" creation of rehabilitation as a "legitimate" medical specialty. Numbers were, of course, an issue but "restoration to the front line" for many skilled "workers" was also a stimulus. This "restoration" was enhanced by the development of multidisciplinary and psycho-socially oriented rehabilitation teams.

In terms of research there was a shift to issues of adjustment, adaptation and coping — away from exclusive focus on "the damaged body" to a need to understand the resulting behaviour. The research operationalization/instrumentalization of this approach came to be called "activities of daily living scales". These scales measured an individual's capacity to perform such "demands" of daily life as eating, drinking, toileting, dressing, bathing, walking and controlling bowels and bladder.

By 1958 the American Medical Association felt the necessity to more clearly differentiate between "impairment" and "disability".[6] The former was generally regarded as a medical judgement call whereas the latter was defined as an administrative issue relating to the "interaction between the impairment and a host of non-medical factors such as age, sex, educational level, economic and social environment". For Frey the implication was clear: "Understanding how these variables interact to limit one's abilities was outside the domain of the physician."[7] But questions of who was to determine these variables and in whose domain they would reside ushered in the next era.

The Recognition of Diverse Voices

Through the 1950s there was little widespread challenge to the notion that disability was an unmitigated "tragedy" to be contained as much as possible through rehabilitation services. The people so "afflicted" were, with rare exceptions, to be pitied. They were the object of study to be worked *on*, never *with*. Services consumers' attitudes towards themselves began to be acknowledged by the now diverse group of professionals providing treatment, but the importance lay mainly in the degree to which their feeling might affect motivation for prescribed treatment and improved functioning. The importance of their own decision making and expertise or the effect of other people's attitudes would not be widely recognized until the following decade. Still, another new age was dawning — one that, to use a 90s phrase, I call "the recognition of diverse voices".

Again a war played a major role but to me the greatest legacy of the Second World War was how it affected the people who participated — the surviving veterans and the general populace. Life would never be the same in the U.S. after the Nazi Holocaust and the atom bomb. There would be a questioning of almost every taken-for-granted issue and of every authority that claimed unquestioned legitimacy, as well as a more general questioning of the very meaning of life itself.

1. Scientific resources were shifted from the destruction of life to its preservation and enhancement in the enormous expansion of the National Institutes of Health.

2. While high tech medicine flourished, its very advances brought in ethical and social questions never previously addressed. When life began and when it ended became serious issues of debate.

3. Quantity of life lost its sacredness as a statistic and more difficult questions of the quality of life were being asked. Morbidity, chronic disease and disability statistics began to be more systematically collected.

4. University training programs for physical and occupational therapists and rehabilitation counsellors were being established and many had explicit, if not written, policies against accepting students with disabilities. The psychological wisdom expressed at that time was that such students would "over identify" with their *patient's* or *client's* problems and would thereby be rendered unhelpful to them. By the end of the 1960s, a few programs were allowing students with disabilities in but watching them closely.

5. By the 1970s rehabilitation researchers had begun to recognize the greater social complexity of adjustments, and measures of assessment followed suit. "The locus of assessment was shifted from concentration on the individual with a physical or mental impairment to the interaction between that individual and his or her surrounding environment".[8]

6. Self-help groups proliferated as did many disease constituency groups which, recognizing the benefits of mutual support, also clamoured for more resources and, occasionally, rights. The first cross-disability groups began to form, embracing ever wider non-categorical groups.

7. At the same time, people with disabilities requiring substantial support to live outside of family or institutional settings were beginning to apply to universities for education that might prepare them for competitive employment. The effort to secure such an opportunity by people such as Ed Roberts resulted first in the creation of "physically disabled student programs" and later in the first community-based independent living programs.

8. During this period a series of social movements, each claiming their place in the mainstream of American life and asking no longer for "good will" but civil rights,[9] emerged — most prominently blacks and then the second wave of feminism and the consumer movement.

Although in the late 1960s people with disabilities had a role in the passing of the federal government's, and later individual state's, architectural barrier laws, it was in 1973 that an obscure, almost unnoticed provision of a rehabilitation act, twice vetoed by President Nixon, built on all that had gone before and catalyzed a social movement. In reality there were several sections — but it was Section 504 that became known as the civil rights provision for people with disabilities. There were 50 words:

> No otherwise qualified handicapped individual in the United States as defined in Section 7 shall, solely by reason of his handicaps, be excluded from the participation in, be denied the benefits of, or be subjected to discrimination under any program or activity receiving federal financial assistance.

But it took three years for these 50 words and the equally brief following sections to be turned into thousands of pages of regulations for dozens of federal agencies. It was done under protest pushed by the sustained efforts of the first coalition of "disability groups". When, in 1977, Califano signed the regulations to the 1973 Rehabilitation bill, he also signed the regulations to the *Education for All Handicapped Children Act* (PL94-142 originally passed in 1975). This Act, although it paralleled in spirit the struggle for rights captured in Section 504, had a very different legislative, judicial and consumer history. Until the 1960s, elementary and secondary education for children was primarily a state and local activity. With the passage of the *Elementary and Secondary Education Act* (ESEA) in 1965, federal monies were to be allocated for educational materials based on the number of low-income children in each school district. Over the next decade, through a series of amendments and reauthorizations, funding for material and training were extended to special education teachers.

These pushes were part of a more sustained "parents' campaign" demanding an end to segregated education and the beginning of systematic "mainstreaming". To gain these ends parents took to the courts. In 1971 and 1972, two landmark decisions signalled the need for further, more encompassing legislative action. The first was *Pennsylvania Association for Retarded Children (PARC) v. Commonwealth of Pennsylvania.* In this case the plaintiffs, acting on behalf of 14 students with "mental retardation", brought a class action suit against the state of Pennsylvania arguing that the latter had violated their due process and equal protection rights. The resulting consent agreement required the state of Pennsylvania "to place each mentally retarded child in a free, public program of education and training appropriate to the child's capacity." The second case, *Mills* v. *Board of Education of the District of Columbia*, brought by the parents and guardians of seven "mentally retarded" children, charged that the defendant denied them publicly supported education. Given that this case was heard in a federal district court, its granting of these children "a free and suitable publicly-supported education" was thought to strengthen the legal foundations for a national mandate on mainstreaming.

Together these legislative, judicial and parental efforts resulted in PL 94-142, the *Education for All Handicapped Children Act*, which required states, as a precondition for receiving federal funds, to ensure that they provide a free and appropriate education to all children with handicaps. Most important, this legislation enshrined the concept of "least restrictive environment" and the necessity of a written and agreed upon Individual Educational Plan (IEP) negotiated by parents and educational administrators.

Most crucial for the solidification of these gains, for the translation of ideas into practice and for direct research implications was the passage of Public Law 95-602, the Rehabilitation Comprehensive Services and Developmental Disabilities Amendments of 1978. Now a movement was coalescing, coalitions were formed and specifics were added to the ideals of the 1973 provisions. For my purposes, three elements were important. Each pried the idea of disability further away from the medical model and medical dominion. Each in its own way helped to solidify a movement by creating and legitimating a cross-disease and cross-disability orientation and community.

1. Functional limitations rather than impairments got enshrined in the law.

2. Federal recognition was given to "independent living" services as a legitimate non-vocational goal of rehabilitation.

3. A National Institute of Handicapped Research was created, which gathered under its wing the already existing research and training centres, and had the right to create new centres as well as to sponsor field-initiated research. In further distancing itself from medical control, it was housed in the Department of Education. Also at that time, a number of social scientists allied to the disability community tried to establish a formal voice for people with disability in the setting and definition of research priorities. We lost and it would take nearly 15 years for this principle to be instituted at the renamed National Institute of Disability and Rehabilitation Research.

To some this seemed the last gasp of the Independent Living/ Disability Rights movement. The moneys allocated to independent living services and to research never reached the sought-for goals. And although there was now direct focus on disability and rehabilitation in a new institute, its title, the National Institute for Handicapped Research, seemed like an unconscious pun. The research aims and allocations were indeed perceived by some to be "handicapped", with a striving for legitimacy with other institutes often taking precedence over demands from the disability community. And finally, even as the laws were passed, the country was in the midst of a 25-year cycle of conservative cost-cutting (President Carter at the time of election was the most conservative of Democratic candidates) and federal deregulation.

The Age of Empowerment

The analysts and doom-sayers were wrong. The decade of the 1980s was one of digging in our heels, consolidating our constituencies and delineating our mission and our vision. Such events as the following ushered in the real age of empowerment.

1. There were long-term demographic trends coming home to roost. Not only was the general population aging but those over 85 were the fastest growing segment. Although there is not an inherent association between aging and disability, being old certainly put a member of that population at greater risk for physical changes and for being subject to a social-political-economic environment that was more likely to make those changes "disabling". The 1980s ushered in another epidemiological shift of profound significance. Every study, no matter what the measure, showed tremendous increases in both the general rates of disability and the specific rates of disability-related chronic disease conditions as well as the longer survival rates of anyone with an existing disability.[10] Moreover, three conditions were to "emerge" that would, each in its unique way, challenge traditional conceptions, measurements, service delivery and research: AIDS, Alzheimer's disease and learning disabilities.

2. Substantial, if not majority, consumer representation on directorial and advisory boards began to be required for functions as diverse as independent living programs in local communities to national research advisories. Such a body is the National Council on Disability, created by law for the primary purpose of overseeing the research activities within the Office of Special Education and Rehabilitation Services (OSERS) in the U.S. Department of Education.

3. A specific disability research constituency began to emerge with numerous special issues and special sections of academic journals, ultimately growing from a series of interest groups to a national society — The Society of Disability Studies. The society's intention was to influence the relevance and utility of disability research funded or conducted by public agencies. A greater intertwining of the disability and research communities calls for people with disabilities to shift from being only the objects of research and policy to partners in policy setting and research. "Participatory action research" and "consumer-oriented research and dissemination" are early attempts to designate the desired research topics and methods that are heavily influenced by those who are subjects of investigation or beneficiaries of the findings.

4. Voices of people with disabilities began to appear in anthologies and in full blown first-person accounts. Magazines for consumers of disability-related products and services as well as ones devoted to social and political issues also became marketable.

5. As previous social movements acknowledge, what one is called is more than a matter of semantics. Although no universally accepted terms have yet been established, there has been a shift away from pejorative associations (cripple, handicapped, lame, deaf and dumb) to more "people first" designations. Governmental agencies and private organizations have quickly followed suit.

6. In 1986 the Louis Harris Polling Service, with the backing of the National Council on Disability, conducted the first national attitudinal survey of people with disabilities about themselves, their treatment and their employment. It has become the standard and the most referred-to piece of research in disability policy debates. In the same year the

National Council on Disability issued its landmark report *Toward Independence.* This, with its follow-up report, *On the Threshold of Independence*, laid the basis for the early drafts of the *Americans with Disabilities Act* (ADA).

7. As Scotch has noted, during the 1980s the disability rights movement enhanced its relationship with other movements.[11] Although some alliances might have been expected with other opponents of Reagan-Bush policies (e.g., the liberal left, social welfare, the women's movement), disability advocates also found themselves joined with the pro-life movement. This was clearly an uneasy alliance but there was a joint agreement in the debate over the appropriateness of treatment to severely disabled newborns (the so-called Baby Doe cases). Therefore, in 1985 and 1986 disability rights leaders and researchers (including myself) willingly testified before two U.S. Commission on Civil Rights hearings that in general society did discriminate against people with disabilities.

8. Building on the more activistic stands of the anti-Vietnam War and other civil rights movements, disability protesters took more systematically to the streets and the TV screens. ADAPT (Americans Disabled for Accessible Public Transportation) became the most visible symbol when, in demanding access to mass transportation, they chained themselves to buses. (In the late 1980s and early 1990s their target shifted to the nursing home industry and to the demand for a national system of personal assistant services. To reflect this, they changed their name to Americans Disabled for Attendant Programs Today.) In the same period, the students of Gallaudet University in Washington, D.C., captured national attention for several days during their A Deaf President (for Gallaudet) Now campaign.

9. The political constituency of disability for the first time was recognized and incorporated into a political campaign. Presidential candidate Bush's remarks for bringing "the handicapped into the mainstream" was supposed to have shifted nearly a half-million voters.

These are but some of the events that led to an even more active movement and the political climate that led to the 1990 passage of the *Americans with Disabilities Act.*

The Future

The year 1992 was significant in many ways. It was then that the 1990 Act took force. It was also the year of another presidential campaign. This time the relevance of disability was not shown in a mere dozen words. The disability community, mostly through its now widespread media network, was intensely lobbied.

At research conferences such as the fifth annual Society of Disability Studies convention in 1992, the basic questions shifted far beyond reformulations of Activity of Daily Living scales to more basic questioning of the very definition and measurement of disability. There is a growing recognition that disability is multidimensional and must be measured that way. It is not a dichotomous status but a characteristic of individuals that varies through time. The number of people with a disability is not a fixed one but quite fluid. The magic number of "43 million" may be enshrined in legislation but not in any knowable reality. If we believe that disability is an interaction between an individual's physical/ mental condition, his or her resources and the socio-political economic environment, then we must cease measuring individuals exclusively and instead measure resources and "disabling" environments. And if, as some people claim, there is the possibility of disability culture and disability pride, then we must cease measuring or conceptualizing disability as an exclusively negative and undesirable characteristic or experience and, therefore, something to be automatically eliminated. These are truly radical forms of questioning "the nature of disability".[12]

Perhaps the most substantive indication of the intertwining of the independent living movement and the research community is the July 31, 1992, National Institute on Disability and Rehabilitation Research announcement of its proposed funding priorities for fiscal years 1993-1994 in regard to Rehabilitation and Research Training Centers. These centres were "established to conduct coordinated and advanced programs of rehabilitation research on designated rehabilitation problem areas and provide training to researchers, service providers, and consumers".[13] As such centres can be funded initially for up to 60 months and are renewable, they represent a considerable federal commitment. The set of five priorities reads like an agreed-upon agenda of the disability community.

1. Vocational rehabilitation and long-term mental illness.

2. Aging with a disability.

3. Disability statistics.

4. Personal assistance services

5. Independent living services for under-served populations.

Although each of the foregoing represents a greater intertwining of the disability community and the research community interest, it may not represent a real advance unless people with disabilities shift from being only the object of research and policy to a partner in both. This is what some have called participatory research.[14]

There have long been individual examples of participatory research; however, it was only in 1992 that we began to see a systemic effort to make it an essential element of research policy. We are now witnessing an attempt to make it integral to the very funding of research projects.

The 1992 amendments reauthorizing the *Rehabilitation Act* of

1973 included specific language to ensure that research supported by the National Institute on Disability and Rehabilitation Research (NIDRR) is relevant and responsive to the needs of people with disabilities, their families and those who provide services to them. During much of 1992 William Graves, then director of NIDRR, continually pronounced that active participation by constituencies in the NIDRR research process would become a central component of the agency's policy.

At the writing of this paper (1993), a draft document is being circulated by NIDRR in which it proposes to implement a policy on Constituency-Oriented Research and Dissemination (CORD). CORD is defined as "an approach to research, training, and dissemination in which appropriate members of relevant constituencies will participate in a meaningful way at key stages of the research process." The key stages are expected to include: identifying research needs; setting priorities; request for proposal development; the application preparation process; peer review; making awards; conducting projects; dissemination; and utilization and evaluations.

Such a list seems quite extensive. Its meaning will ultimately depend on the operationalization of such terms as "appropriate numbers of relevant constituencies". The proposal calls for the adoption of such a policy and the sponsoring of a national invitational conference of experts to refine the proposed policy, discuss implementation issues and present model approaches to constituency participation that have been used in the field. On the basis of this conference it is hoped that: 1) a formal policy of Constituency-Oriented Research and Dissemination be adopted for NIDRR; and 2) a CORD practice manual be developed.

Whether the foregoing is merely a symbolic act or the ushering in of a new era of a prominent role for people with disability in the formulation of disability-related research only time will tell. On the other hand, I feel compelled to make a final observation: prejudices and paradigms run deep — so deep that even a revolution will not overturn them in a single generation. Please do not interpret my observations as a call for gradualism; on the contrary I want full speed ahead. I am expressing rather a caveat about solution and about voice. If one has been oppressed for thousands of years, one does not gain a voice overnight. One of the features of oppression is the loss not only of voice but of the tools to find it. That is why teaching slaves to read and write was at one time a crime in the United States. The experience of disability has been for so long like death and dying, something that we denied could happen to us and when it did, it occurred out of sight and hearing. It will take us time to speak out, to learn what we have lost, to articulate what we need. But as I have tried to state here and elsewhere, the numbers trying to speak out are ever growing and the chorus of voices is increasingly diverse. All of you reading this chapter have just heard the overture.

Notes

1. Glen Gritzer and Arnold Arluke, *The Making of Rehabilitation: A Political Economy of Medical Specialization*, Berkeley, Calif.: University of California Press, 1985.

2. Ibid.

3. William Frey, "Functional Assessment in the '80s: A Conceptual Enigma, a Technical Challenge", in A.S. Halporn and M.J. Fuhrer (eds.), *Functional Assessment in Rehabilitation*, Baltimore, Md.: Paul H. Brookes Publishing Co., 1984, pp. 11-43.

4. Ibid.

5. Ibid.

6. Ibid.

7. Ibid.

8. Ibid., p. 24.

9. Richard K. Scotch, *From Goodwill to Civil Rights Transforming Federal Disability Policy*, Philadelphia: Temple University Press, 1984.

10. Irving Kenneth Zola, "Disability Statistics, What We Count and What It Tells Us - A Personal and Political Analysis", *Journal of Disability Policy Studies*, 4(2), 1993, pp. 9-39.

11. Richard K. Scotch, "Disability as the Basis for a Social Movement: Advocacy and the Politics of Definition", in Adrienne Asch and Michelle Fine (eds.), *Moving Disability beyond Stigma, Journal of Social Issues*, 44(1), 1987.

12. Zola, "Disability Statistics", 1993 (see n. 10).

13. Federal Register, Sept. 17, 1992.

14. Gary Woodill, *Independent Living and Participation in Research*, Toronto, Ont.: Ryerson Polytechnic Institute, 1992.

Chapter 4

Towards a Concept of Equality of Well-Being: Overcoming the Social and Legal Construction of Inequality

by Marcia H. Rioux

T he ways in which a society provides for people who, for one reason or another, are more socially and economically dependent throws into sharp focus the problems of equality as a political construct. The basic dilemma of social dependency is that of reconciling the responsibility of the state to ensure equality with the rights and needs of those who are dependent. The social, legal and economic policies in place at any given time in history reflect the ways that principles of justice have legitimated differential treatment. To study the case of intellectual disability,[1] therefore, is to reflect upon the legal microcosm of the struggle for social justice and the parameters of political obligation to ameliorate inequality.

This chapter identifies a number of major shifts in the framing and justification of state obligations in Canada towards persons with disabilities. We shall examine the way in which those with intellectual disabilities have been distinguished from other citizens to enable differential treatment and to justify fewer rights while purportedly upholding the central democratic tenet of equality. Although economic efficiency and effectiveness have historically taken precedence over equality in determining state obligations, recent conceptions of intellectual disability and the enactment of the *Charter of Rights and Freedoms*[2] have resulted in the demand for a more complex critique of whether state obligations can be limited according to these criteria within an equality framework.

Assumptions about the meaning and content of equality can be identified in the mechanisms for distributive justice applied to disability. In other words, equality has implications for resource allocation, but resource allocation also reflects certain notions of equality. The premises on which distributive justice is argued to be upheld may vary significantly depending on the underlying meaning of equality and the means adopted to achieve it. From a historical perspective it is clear that this is not a new dilemma. The understanding of disability itself has been shaped by political conflict about distributive criteria, including criteria concerning appropriate recipients of social assistance or support, and the nature of legal entitlements and of citizenship rights.

The theoretical constructs of equality fit into three general categories, each justifying different claims about entitlements and the legitimating criteria for differentiating or distinguishing people. One is the formal theory of equality[3] — that is, the equal-treatment model. The second is the liberal theory of equality,[4] incorporating both the ideals of equality of opportunity and special treatment. The third is the equality of outcome or equality-of-well-being[5] model.

What will constitute equality generally and equality with respect to intellectual disability in particular and which model of equality is most likely to ensure a just distribution of goods, services and support to individuals in achieving equality is yet to be resolved.[6]

This resolution will be particularly significant for persons with intellectual disabilities, because their differences tend to stem from a deficiency in those characteristics on which participation in the social structure and determination of equal status have been designed. The traditional assumption is that, having few of the needs or abilities considered to be intrinsic to citizenship or the capacity to exercise conventional legal rights, people with intellectual disabilities have had no basis for a claim to equality: only to the extent that they can approximate other citizens can they establish such a claim. This assumption raises three questions: 1) Do all classes of persons have the same needs and, if not, what are the criteria on which society may justly disentitle people? 2) Must one have the capacity to exercise a right to have that right? If not, are there other grounds for denying rights? 3) Is equality consequent on overcoming natural characteristics (and becoming as much like "the norm" as possible) or does it result from the equal value, benefit and rights of all irrespective of their relation to "the norm"?

The three models of equality reflect different assumptions of what constitutes equality. The models therefore draw the line between justified and unjustified distinctions at different places. A question remains as to whether the recent shift in legal direction found in the *Charter* is substantive or whether it will simply re-legitimize the prevailing inequalities founded on the values and assumptions of nineteenth-century liberalism.

The history of how disadvantage has been created and how inequality has been constructed and justified is critical to an understanding of equality as a principle of social obligation. This chapter argues that both the equal-treatment and equal-opportunity models of equality, as well as the type of redress they enable, are inadequate to address inequalities faced by those with disabilities. A more expansive notion will enable the underlying foundation of inequality and equality to be dealt with by focusing on participation and inclusion of victims of disadvantage rather than on particular actions or perpetrators of discrimination. Removing the barriers to equality, particularly for those with intellectual disabilities, means addressing the existing policies that represent and foster a dominant social agenda. Included among these barriers, particularly for those with intellectual disabilities, are practices that incorporate notions of efficiency and fairness in the context of merit.[7]

The question that surfaces in proposing the concept of equality of well-being is how to achieve a social agenda that can acknowledge difference (pluralism) without resulting in inequitable or unfair practices, while at the same time ensuring the benefits of integration (assimilation) into the economic and social structure. Assimilation has to be achieved without overlooking the unique needs faced by disadvantaged individuals and groups that must be addressed to realize those benefits.

Institutionalizing Inequality as Inherent to Disability

Western democratic ethos assumes that likes will be treated alike and that the rule of law will assure rational and fair treatment. The legitimization of the way of differentiating between people therefore became important, as a basis for entitlement and disentitlement and as a means of social control.

The conventional basis of social obligation to those with disabilities has been some notion of beneficence and charitable-privilege.[8] Reflecting its origins in the English Poor Laws, early Canadian policy aimed to protect society from those with handicaps and from the drain on social resources that they represented. If, however, it could be shown that there was a rational, objective basis for differentiating and limiting claims to rights and entitlements, then social justice could still be claimed even while some were disadvantaged.

The use of science and medicine (biological determinism and scientific positivism) as political legitimation for differentiation and unequal treatment of those with intellectual disabilities was supported by eugenics theory in the first half of this century and by the authority of medicine, the latter spanning into the second half of the century. Political inequality was justified on the basis of biological inequality demonstrated through IQ and merit. Biological determinism is purported to explain social and economic differences among social groups on the basis of inherited distinctions.

Accordingly, society simply reflects this inborn biological order in the distribution of rewards.

Worth can also be assigned to individuals and groups by measuring intelligence if it can be conceptualized as a single quantifiable unit. This became possible primarily through the development of intelligence tests, which purported to provide an "objective" standard by which persons could be placed in an intelligence hierarchy. Those below a certain point in the hierarchy were designated as intellectually disabled. Such an "objective" classification enabled law and policy to exclude or to treat differently those so designated.

Basic to psychometric science, mental measurement and testing is the concept of general intelligence, a major component of all forms of human excellence. The issue is not with the concept that intelligence or IQ is to some extent hereditary but with two other claims made by those who have used such tests for the maintenance of social ranks and distinctions. One is the fallacy of "reification", assigning to "intelligence" complex human capabilities that support "the importance of mentality in our lives and ... characterize it, in part so that we can make the divisions and distinctions among people that our cultural and political systems dictate".[9] The other dubious claim is the notion of "ranking" or hereditarianism, which equates "heritable" with "inevitable", downplaying or ignoring the role and range of environmental conditions in setting and modifying inherited characteristics. Ranking requires a criterion for assigning status in a single hierarchy; intelligence has been the principle tool for doing so. Although there is little empirical evidence to support the concept that human beings can be ranked from the "naturally" most able to the "naturally" least able, such ordering was, in the nineteenth century up to recently, argued to be practicable using standardized IQ tests. Psychometrics initially attracted eugenicists because it complemented their general view of the social order. As Evans and Waites point out:

[I]n the heyday of eugenics, high intelligence or "civic worth", was
considered to encompass all forms of moral and political wisdom, and
low intelligence was considered the cause of all forms of turpitude
and degeneracy, which the eugenicists sought to eliminate.[10]

The enthusiasm of the eugenicists and psychometricians for
finding a scale to measure innate difference was translated into
scientific evidence of inferiority and superiority. In the hands of
governments and law makers, the scale became a means to
differentiate and justify unequal treatment, including the restriction
of basic citizenship rights such as procreation, marriage, immigration,
education, property ownership and ability to contract. Hereditarian
theory reduced the state's responsibility for eliminating the
discrimination and inequalities that arise because scientific
legitimacy provided the basis for policy development. "Lower innate
intelligence" explained the lower achievement by designated
groups[11] and the complex phenomenon of social and educational
inequality was discounted.

When the source of inequality is located in the individual in
this way, there is a ready rationale for social inequality and limiting
social entitlement. The political and social strategies of such
technocratic rationality are then presented as value free. By
discounting the socio-political context of scientific inquiry and by
reinforcing it with the principle of "desert", measured by economic
and social self-sufficiency and independence, it is possible to
formalize inequitable social relations while still maintaining that
distributive justice is being upheld and the principle of equality
met. Because entitlement to social and economic benefits and the
level of benefit is argued to be based on social conformity, the
adjustment of the individual to the existing social system and
paternalism (beneficence), equal treatment and equality-of-
opportunity are achieved.

Legislation, including welfare law, has legitimized such a legal
status of civil disability — that is, of persons subject to state control
in exchange for state benefits and support. Therefore, the state is

relieved of all but minimal social obligation to those with intellectual disabilities and the debate on social justice, including the meaning of equality, is circumvented. The question of why the ethical principle of desert as a basis for distributive justice should hold sway over other ethical principles — including individual worth or some absolute notion of need — can be avoided. The principle of desert, based on scientific positivism and biological determinism, remains entrenched as the legal basis for differentiating people and for unequal treatment.

A major obstacle to the political equality of those with intellectual disabilities is the reification of the term (or like terms) itself. Groups within the scientific community have, to a greater or lesser extent, come to accept that the term is principally an administrative one. Hayman has pointed out:

> But the legal and political worlds continue to apply the label as if it had a validity independent of its sociopolitical origins. In accepting the reified construct of [intellectual disability], the law limits the permissible inquiry into the nature of the construct; it conceals the politics, prejudices, and now discredited scientific theories that have helped to create — and then re-create — [intellectual disability].[12]

Intellectual disability, unlike gender, physical disability or race, is not an objective condition. In many cases, the objective criteria on which to distinguish intellectual disability are weak.[13] For example, there is a vast number of conditions that might fall within the purview of mental handicap, yet might be classified as something other than mental handicap depending on external factors. People with learning disabilities have been classified as having intellectual disabilities in some situations but not in others. Individuals identified as intellectually disabled in some situations (e.g., at school) may not be so identified in other situations (e.g., at work).[14] The emergence of the definition has been driven, in part, by the need of individuals and agencies to classify people according to individual need or benefit.[15] The meaning of mental handicap is imbedded in entitlements and disentitlements, but reflects the weak objective definition. Arguably, the concept of inequality is inherent to the very classification. The "norm", by definition, precludes those labelled as having intellectual disabilities and the definition of intellectual disability presumes and legitimizes this inequality. If being unequal is one of the inherent premises of the concept of intellectual disability, then there must always be a class of citizens who are denied the ability to exercise citizenship.[16]

Remaining Neutral to Disability

The implications of *a priori* assumptions about the genesis and relative value of human characteristics are significant to the capacity to ensure equality. As important are the elements understood to comprise equality. First, if the status quo is assumed to be necessary for society to function and differences are defined as intrinsic to the individual, and in conflict with the status quo, then those who might make a claim for greater equality (that is, those with differences) have no grounds on which to challenge the designation of difference and its consequences which include inequality.

Second, if equality depends on sameness or on being similarly situated, then the fact of difference warrants unequal treatment. A concept of equality that requires that likes be treated alike and unlikes be treated differently presumes the impartial enforcement of legal and social rights. It makes no difference to attempt to clarify what makes people equal in particular circumstances or for particular purposes. There is no prescriptive element to the principle on which governments might base their decisions about which people are to be accorded the unequal treatment. The principle simply establishes the generally accepted rule of law[17] that *procedural* fairness must be applied for law to be legitimate. Neutrality in the application of the law and the absence of different treatment are presumed to result in equality.

For example, people who cannot fill out forms are denied the right to vote, while others, who can read and write, are afforded that right. The law is equally applied to all those who cannot provide the information; therefore, the fact that it has a differential impact on those with intellectual disabilities is insignificant. So are the extraneous causes for such a lack of ability: neither the systemic, legal exclusion of those with intellectual disabilities from the regular education system nor the means of eliciting the information, which is in a mode of communication less accessible to them than to others, are taken into account in determining justified and unjustified distinctions.

Another example is the legal denial, until recently, of the right to vote by people confined to institutions[18] — independent of their capacity to exercise that right. This disenfranchisement was justified on the premise that all persons in institutions were being treated equally. In that regard people who were similarly situated were being treated the same and justice was assumed to be safeguarded. However, the people who were being treated the same in this instance were being denied their vote on the basis of a false premise: that people in institutions were incompetent as voters.

In those circumstances where classes of people are identically situated with respect to opportunity sought, formal equality may perhaps lead to factual equality. In most cases, however, identical treatment leads to disadvantage or inequality the less a class of people approximates the advantaged group who sets the standards.[19]

Many laws affecting people with disabilities do, however, pass a test of formal equality. When the laws were implemented, people with intellectual disabilities were viewed as less than human. Therefore, no consideration was given to their being able to exercise the usual rights of citizenship, including the right to the rule of law or to procedural fairness.

In the case of people with intellectual disabilities, it would be difficult in many circumstances to argue that formal equality is not being achieved, as differentiations drawn between groups of people are justified according to an established set of criteria and are applied equally. Such formal equality, however, has led to situations that are discriminatory (in its pejorative sense) and unjust. For example, the law denying people with intellectual disabilities immigration to Canada could not easily be justified, even where the limited framework of formal equality was achieved.[20] The law specifically excludes those with intellectual disabilities on the grounds that those individuals are likely to become dependent on the state. There is no onus on the state to show that any particular individual with an intellectual disability will drain the resources of the state. It is only necessary to show that a person has an intellectual disability. In the case of minor children, even the test of formal equality is not being met. Other families applying for immigrant status are not required to prove that their minor children will not become a "burden" on society.

Critics of the formal principle of equality have argued that the rights achieved under this construct of equality may benefit some members of a disadvantaged class more than others. Andrew Petter, for example, argues:

> One of the dangers identified by critics of formal equality rights is that such rights, in addition to benefiting men at the expense of women, could serve to benefit extraordinary or elite women at the expense of ordinary women. The danger is a real one. While the guarantee of "equal treatment" serves to entrench the subordination of the majority of women who languish at the bottom of the social ladder, it promises tangible benefits for those few women who have ascended to higher rungs.[21]

The closer an individual can approximate the characteristics of the norm, the more likely they will benefit from an equal-treatment model. The black lawyer, the exceptional female athlete, the person with a mild intellectual disability, the professional who uses a wheelchair — all of whom might qualify except for a discriminatory regulation — are more likely than others who are black, female or who have a more severe intellectual disability to benefit from the equal-treatment model. Those who share fewer of the characteristics of the advantaged group do not gain, because the underlying, substantive inequalities are not addressed and resolved.[22]

Canada's failure in the 1940s to provide formal education for children with intellectual disabilities was argued by families who wanted services for their children to be unequal treatment. It is only in the past decade, however, that the separate education provided to remedy that unequal treatment has been raised as an equality issue. This follows from the arguments against "separate but equal" education for blacks in the United States, where it was accepted that the two terms were mutually exclusive and that the criteria even for formal equality could not be met within that formula.[23] Besides the understanding that dividing schools created a disadvantage for blacks, it was also argued that cultural discrimination resulted from such segregation. The objection to excluding people with intellectual disabilities from local schools stems from similar arguments.

The rationale for continuing to segregate students, based as it is on a judgement of whether a child has the capacity to learn, perpetuates the historical prejudice about people with disabilities and their abilities without considering the limitations of pedagogical theories or the general quality of education being delivered under the existing system. In other words, it excludes those with intellectual disabilities on the presumption that other students are able to benefit from the education system. Exclusion of this class of children also results in all children being deprived of affiliating, in the one case with non-disabled children, in the other with disabled children; arguably, both groups of children are equally harmed by such segregation on a number of grounds.

Formal equality theory, with its principles of homogeneity, individualism and interchangeability, has no entry point for those with intellectual disabilities seeking equality. Social dependency remains the justification for disentitlement to claims for even limited equal treatment.

Compensating Disability

Much recent discourse on equality, particularly since the enactment of the *Charter of Rights and Freedoms*, has addressed the inherent problems with a formal theory of equality by pointing to the substantive inequality between advantaged and disadvantaged groups.[24] Equality of opportunity[25] addresses some of the limitations of formal equality by taking into account and redressing historical conditions of inequality. It removes the necessity for the disadvantaged group to prove that they are "similarly situated" to a standard. However, it does not address all the fundamental differences that have conventionally provided a basis for disentitlement of those labelled intellectually disabled and it masks the significance of the "dilemma of difference."[26]

Attempting to establish equivalence between "the intellectually disabled" and "the mentally competent" reifies a material definition of difference.[27] A framework of equality that incorporates notions of difference, ideologically constructed and manifested in social and legal practices, can, however, provide the basis of a claim for equality. It recognizes the need to balance equality and privilege and assimilation[28] and pluralism.

Not only due-process rights but substantive rights have been recognized in recent court decisions on the meaning of equality,[29] the right to treatment, the right to refuse treatment, the right to vote,[30] and involuntary sterilization.[31] The *Charter* provides a basis for arguments that diverse group interests have to be recognized in achieving equality and that recognition of the fact and legitimacy of diversity must be taken into account.[32] In going beyond equality before the law and incorporating equality under the law, the *Charter*, at least in principle, recognizes a form of substantive equality.

Theories of compensatory justice within the model of equality of opportunity move beyond radical individualism[33] and formulate discrimination as a group phenomenon.[34] They attempt to delineate the basis of compensation or reparation, the nature of groups, and "the form and extent of their disadvantage". Broad guarantees of equality, as well as acknowledgement of the legitimacy of affirmative-action or employment-equity programs,[35] have led to the recognition of group rights as well as individual rights.[36] Because some groups have been unjustly disadvantaged, it can be argued that they have a legitimate claim to compensation. Preferential treatment is justified on the grounds that its ends are justified or that it is justified because of documented past injustice.[37] Affirmative action is justifiable, if not imperative, to provide equal opportunity to those groups who have been historically hindered and precluded from participation. To enable those groups to participate on an equal basis, government intervention is necessary.

A number of cases decided by the Supreme Court have recognized the legitimate claims of groups who have faced systemic inequality. Besides the *Andrews* decision,[38] a 1988 opinion[39] by Justice Bertha Wilson acknowledged the historical basis of women's experience of inequality. In the *Eve* decision, decided before section 15 of the *Charter* came into effect, Justice La Forest reflected a similar concern for the condition of women with intellectual disabilities and their right to assert their dignity and choice.[40]

Recognition of the historic and systemic basis of the inequality of groups underlying the equality-of-opportunity model can redress some of the persistent effects of discrimination; however, it is problematic as a model for cases (sex, religion, national or ethnic origin and physical or mental handicap) other than its paradigmatic case, racial discrimination.[41]

The major flaw in this model for enabling equality for people with intellectual disabilities is that their differences are not solely the result of historic circumstances. In most cases, they cannot overcome natural characteristics and become like the "norm", even with equality of opportunity, because it is based on the assumption that the aim of equal opportunity is to provide access to the competitive, individualistic market, not to such non-comparable goods as minimal nutritional and medical support. The basis for their claim to equality can be made only on their citizenship or on their humanness or on a general egalitarian value assumption — for example, that all people should be accorded equal respect by their government because they are persons,[42] not because of their ability to compete. Their claim on resources is to enable participation, although it will be unlikely,[43] even in the long term, that they will be competitive (within the existing social and economic climate) without some degree of ongoing support. It is not a claim for support to redress past discrimination or support to overcome particular barriers to participation (equality of opportunity). Instead, their claim is for redistribution of state resources and for ongoing systemic support to be able to exercise the same rights as others. This claim is not premised on the measurable social benefits (economic efficiency and effectiveness) foreseen to be achievable in exchange for additional state benefits, which is the case for other disadvantaged groups.

The unarticulated premises of the equality-of-opportunity model are homogeneity and interchangeability. Some feminist liberal equality theorists in the United States[44] have posited that one of the routes to overcoming the problems of the equality-of-opportunity model is equal recognition of identifiable, immutable difference, which they term the "special benefit rule". In the case of women, it is argued that lactation and pregnancy ought to be given special provision in the equality equation, as differences for which equality cannot be denied and accommodation provided. The effect, however, is virtually the same as that arising from the formal equality model with the addition that special status or priority are assigned for objectively definable characteristics. Where an objective distinction having a consequent systemic disadvantage can be identified, this may be marginally helpful. Given the wide diversity within the class of individuals who might be identified as "disabled", establishing such a constant is problematic. In any event, it does not address the underlying principle — the substantively male, non-handicapped standard, and the dominance and subordination of other groups. The organization of society around people with an intellectual disability is premised on an implied assumption that intellectual disability is an intrinsic inequality. The differentiation between intrinsic and extrinsic inequality is not made. As a result, inequalities arising from extrinsic factors, such as income, employment, housing and services, are presumed to arise because of factors intrinsic to the individual. Simply establishing that a class of individuals possesses a specific characteristic does not address such a problem. The weakness of this approach can even make disadvantage invisible[45] because it is difficult to identify anything but the most obvious intrinsic distinctions and subtler but pervasive issues of power in society that create disadvantage are ignored. It is true that the equality-of-opportunity model can recognize and address blatant prejudice; however, it is questionable whether people with intellectual disabilities are disadvantaged by inequalities arising from prejudice rather than from the much more extensive inequalities arising from how society is organized.

The Limits of Affirmative Action in Enabling Equality for People with Disabilities

Affirmative action has been widely advanced as a means for dealing with systemic inequality.[46] Its purpose is to identify and eliminate policies and practices that result in a group having less than its fair share of, or proper place in, the job market and other areas of opportunity. In other words, it sets out to address the systemic rather than the individual nature of inequality.

Affirmative action addresses inequality in a number of ways. First, it views the issue from a group rather than an individual perspective. The impact of practices on a designated group is identified by statistical evaluation of the discrimination effects of a given practice on the group. Second, unintentional discrimination is considered to be as problematic as intentional discrimination. And third, affirmative action is recognized as a necessary positive intervention for eliminating the inequality in outcome produced by existing structures. From this perspective it provides a working program for surmounting some of the most problematic aspects of both the equal-treatment and equality-of-opportunity models of equality.

The weaknesses in the application of conventional affirmative action to the case of intellectual disability[47] are, however, significant. Methodologically, the statistical comparison of participation creates some problems.[48] In addition, there are problems with the assumptions underlying the objective. The model generally assumes that barriers can be removed without substantially changing the nature of the work or of the provision of goods and services, but for people with intellectual disabilities participation in the workforce or in the community generally requires changing the nature of the work or activities. The concept of "reasonable accommodation", which has been incorporated into equal opportunity, does not extend to the systemic changes that would be required to restructure and redesign jobs and participation in the community. For example, the affirmative action model does not address the issue of job support that would enable access to the labour force for some people with intellectual disabilities. In most cases, "reasonable accommodation" has not been wide ranging enough to cover these circumstances even if it were to be implemented. Part of the reason for this is the continuing assumption that there are people who will never be assimilated into society and that they are provided for in other ways — the legacy of the "worthy poor" welfare principle.

In addition, affirmative action does not address the hierarchical division of labour nor the assumptions, first, that access to status, wealth, position and other economic assets, and even access to participation in the labour market and in political and social life, should be distributed according to merit; and, second, that measures of merit are impartial and value-neutral and tend to be measured in market terms. Qualifying for affirmative action, like qualifying for other socially valued goods, is based on measurements of the individual technical competence according to the normative meritocratic criteria of educational credentials and standardized testing. These criteria assume some basic level of ability or potential to achieve technical competence and that the talents used for recognition and reward are necessary for social efficiency and progress.

Meritocracy results in opportunity for those with superior intellect by making intellectual aptitude the criterion of social reward and by defining progress as excellence and efficiency in technology.[49] This leads to a competitive ethic that reduces the value of those with limited intellectual abilities by dismissing abilities other than intelligence.

Equality of opportunity (and its operational mechanism — affirmative action) become relevant only after the "natural" selection process of sorting on the basis of merit. Adjustments are then provided within the relationship of employer and employee (or service provider and service user) with common ends clearly in view, ends such as increased access to the labour market or gaining an education qualification. This may suit many cases of race or gender; however, it is problematic where disability is at issue. For example, barriers external to the individual-employer relationship create disadvantages that make it difficult for people with disabilities to establish merit. Therefore, the natural selection process does not become operative in the first instance for many. The goals that are to be achieved in the individual-employer relationship must be rethought if the individual and extrinsic circumstances render the achievement of typical goals difficult. Often, this means redefining the goal of, for example, work in ways that are foreign to market economy notions of work.[50] If commitment to such redefined goals is lacking, mechanisms such as affirmative action are likely to be ineffective.

As affirmative action is conventionally viewed as a means of redressing the legacy of discrimination and inequality, it is seen as a temporary measure. After it removes and eradicates past injustices it will no longer be appropriate. The underlying premise of redressing inequitable status is that there are no immutable differences between the disadvantaged group and the advantaged group; therefore, any mechanism that attributes differences in achievement to past discrimination will arguably lead to greater equality, thereby rendering the mechanism less and less necessary.

> What affirmative action is *not* is a program designed to create an adjustment to permanent differences (real or imagined) between [different groups].[51]

It therefore fails to take into account the inherent differences of the disadvantaged group. Equal outcomes in participation for people with intellectual disabilities require more than affirmative action. Adaptations can be accommodated within the framework of affirmative action, as they have for women, when immutable differences are taken into account in limited identifiable circumstances. It is more difficult, however, to stretch the concept for those with mental and physical disabilities, as the differences are less easily delineated and there are no characteristics that are shared by all members of the class. Equality for those with intellectual disabilities (or physical disabilities) requires long-term, *ongoing* means of establishing equal outcomes as well as a mechanism for removing persistent discrimination. No single uniform mechanism (such as the "special benefit" rule) will result in the permanent removal of existing and ongoing barriers to their participation and the exercise of their right to achieve their full potential.

Affirmative action does recognize the need for pluralism in ensuring equal outcome and does take into account some of the issues of permanent intrinsic barriers to participation. However, it is only helpful where there are identifiable, shared group characteristics. It would be difficult, at best, to determine what characteristics would be included in the case of people with intellectual disabilities. Moreover, even if one could make that determination, affirmative action would not necessarily lead to any greater equality of outcome, as it does not address the historically constituted relations of power and privilege and the assumption that social progress depends on the social order as it is presently constituted. Affirmative action does not have an impact on characteristics that limit the ability to participate in economic and social life without ongoing accommodation and support.

A question arises whether a coherent concept of equality that takes into account issues of disability can be framed within the context of a market economy. The only resolution may be a restructuring of the marketplace and of the fundamental values underlying the social contract. The presumption about equality underlying affirmative action — that it can be achieved through competitive individualization in the societal marketplace, with entitlement to social and economic goods based on merit — does not provide any greater advantage to those with intellectual disabilities than models of law that do not use equality as an ethical and legal basis for entitlement. Under affirmative action individual self-reliance and social efficiency remain the cornerstones of disentitlement and equality remains founded in the nature of discrimination rather than in the ethical imperative of equality as a valued end in itself.

Equality of Well-Being

The issue of equality for people with intellectual disabilities requires more than simply being treated alike ("formal equality") or provided equal opportunity to obtain access ("equality of opportunity"). Biological and sociological meanings of intellectual disability as a means of dividing a group from the rest of society are not addressed by these models of equality. The weakness of the formal and equal opportunity models of equality for disability could be overcome by a model of equality based on well-being as an outcome.[52] This concept of equality incorporates the premise that all human beings

— in spite of their differences — are entitled to be considered and respected as equals and have the right to participate in the social and economic life of society. Unlike the other models of equality, it would take into account the fact that the conditions and means of participation may vary for each individual, entailing special accommodation to make participation possible. Although the outcome — equality of well-being — would be universal, the programs or means to ensure equality could justifiably be targeted to enable those least able to achieve well-being to be supported on a temporary or long-term basis. Difference would both be acknowledged and be accommodated in ensuring the outcome. Political and legal decisions would have to take difference in the achievement of social well-being into account in the distributive paradigm of social justice.

Well-being has a number of components including equal achievement of self-determination, participation and inclusion in social life, and the exercise of fundamental citizenship rights. Equality itself would be an end not a means to meeting other social goals.[53]

Self-determination includes notions of choice, personhood and dignity. In its broadest sense this would incorporate Lukes' notion of a society with equal respect as one in which:

> [T]here are no barriers to reciprocal relations between relatively autonomous persons, who see each other and themselves as such, who are equally free from political control, social pressure, and economic deprivation and insecurity to engage in valued pursuits, and who have equal access to the means of self-development.[54]

It would recognize that, although people are not equal in talent, social usefulness or willingness to serve the community, they are entitled to make choices about how they want to live and what constitutes the good life for them, so long as it operates within the framework of the mutual recognition of others' self-determination.

Equality defined as the inclusion and participation of all groups in institutions and positions[55] makes clear the onus to include even those people who cannot meet the standards of economic self-sufficiency. This interpretation of equality shifts the basis for distributive justice away from economic contribution as the primary factor of entitlement and recognizes other forms of participation as valuable — including those non-market, non-productivity contributions that people with intellectual disabilities can make. The reproduction of the material and ideological conditions that benefit only one segment of the population would no longer be the primary rationale of social institutions, law and policy. Rather, the rationale of social institutions, law and policy would be to support the outcome of equality of well-being.

Equality of well-being would ensure the exercise of fundamental citizenship rights by all citizens independent of their economic and social contribution. The question would be how to determine which rights would be guaranteed to all citizens (that is, what is fundamental) and how to ensure that all individuals have the support to exercise those rights. Traditional limits that have circumscribed political obligation to ensure equality[56] become suspect when the meaning of equality incorporates the notion of well-being, with its implications for resource distribution.[57] Entitlement is based on a comprehensive notion of citizenship (that is, the intrinsic worth of the individual and on some absolute notion of need) not on one's status as a member of the class of worthy poor, or on inequality of talent or social usefulness.

As discrimination faced by those with intellectual disabilities is tied to traditional notions of worth, merely changing conventional definitions of discrimination may not by itself result in substantive equality. Structural changes are likely to be necessary on the political and legal levels. If the right to participate is to be recognized, the notion would have to be jettisoned that people with intellectual disabilities are members of a class provided with goods and services because they are worthy of care rather than by right of citizenship.

Unlike the two other models, equality of well-being starts not with an assimilationist view but with a pluralist perspective on how people with differences and similarities ought to see each other in a just society. It argues that formal barriers have placed groups in substantively different social positions (i.e., that differences have become sites of social disadvantage). Consequently, removing the barriers without also redressing associated disadvantage does not result in significant change. This model also assumes that systemic discrimination against groups is not a "mistake" but an integral part of policies fostering a dominant social agenda.[58] As such, it provides an alternative context for examining legal and social equality. To enable equality that takes into account immutable differences, differences must be accommodated in order to neutralize their effect as barriers to personal achievement and to entitlement as fully participating members of society — that is, barriers to personhood, dignity and self-determination. The emphasis is then on the means of reasonable accommodation, rather than affirmative action.[59]

A question that arises is: Can an equality of well-being model take difference into account through law and policy so that equality would be achieved for those with intellectual disabilities?

The inequalities faced by those with intellectual disabilities are substantively distinct from those of other groups and this affects the nature of their claims. For instance, a number of feminist theorists have argued for a political theory and practice that recognizes the pluralist nature of claims — one that values different cultures, experiences, and interests,[60] since annihilating or ignoring differences (the assimilationist approach) has been ineffective in addressing inequality.[61] However, if people with intellectual disabilities are to achieve equality of well-being, their claims have to be of both a pluralist and assimilationist nature. It is true that the point of similarity that disabled people share with racial minorities is that they are disadvantaged by the genetic supremacy claimed by proponents of segregation, but as well they share a point of similarity with women — the claim that they are entitled to consideration of their immutable differences. A means, therefore, has to be developed that incorporates both the assimilationist claims (i.e., participation and inclusion) and the pluralist claims[62] (i.e., accommodation) without losing the benefits of either.

The eradication of oppression against those with intellectual disabilities therefore requires a more fundamental alteration of the existing legal and social order than does the elimination of race or gender discrimination. However, people with intellectual disabilities have not received much consideration as intellectually disabled. It is true that certain benefits have accrued to them yet these benefits have resulted from their belonging to another category of deserving poor, such as persons in need or equality seekers.[63] Consequently, their particular equality claims have been circumscribed. A claim based on outcome would require that society surrender the basis on which power is distributed, not simply redress discrimination. An encompassing model of equality must confront intellectual differences, not ignore them. It is not a matter of irrational prejudice focused on superficial differences but the elimination of assumptions about the basis of legitimate claims to limited state resources for people with greater needs and dependencies than others, people whose salient differences will not diminish.

Claims, both of assimilation and of pluralism, are being made by disability advocates. They claim entitlement, for example, to public education within the regular non-disabled school system and access to employment opportunities in the regular labour market. Both are assimilationist claims. In both cases, however, they are also making claims to consideration of their differences and to additional resources, including personal supports, that will enable them to participate (to be assimilated) in spite of their differences.

Redress is also sought, as it is for minorities and women. To satisfy the equality claims of this group, redress must be found for both discriminatory impact as well as discriminatory form. Further redress is sought for claims about the basis for disentitlement. In other words, for those with intellectual disabilities the equality issue is not simply that they have not been fairly tested or evaluated in terms of their right to have a particular job but that classes of jobs have not been created for which they could legitimately qualify. It is not a matter of simply ensuring equal opportunities to compete for jobs and fair processes of determining qualifications (as is the case with race) or even restructuring existing jobs according to specific recognizable differences (as is the case for women), but entitlement to enter the job market itself, even if existing qualifications, determined to be fairly established, cannot be met.

Like women, people with disabilities have sought access to social benefits available to non-disabled persons without relinquishing the special benefits they have received in virtue of their disabilities.[64] In other words, they are attempting to achieve social benefits without giving away the basic human rights that have traditionally been their form of barter.[65] They are also facing challenges from non-disabled persons who want access to preferential treatment such as individualized instruction or support in the classroom,[66] just as men make claims for the special benefits claimed by women.

The premises of this model of equality are that all persons of distinguishable groups have the same needs for equality; that the capacity to exercise a right is not a distinguishing characteristic for the purpose of recognizing or denying that right; and that equality is consequent on the equal value, benefit and rights possessed in differences from the norm, not on overcoming natural characteristics and becoming as much like the norm as possible.

To achieve this form of equality would require the redistribution of state resources to actualize equality of well-being. Inequality would no longer be embodied in the concept of intellectual disability nor would intellectual disability be the basis for denying citizenship. The granting of entitlements could be attached purely by reason of an individual's being, independent of their potential to compete. This would refocus the concept of equality, both legally and socially, from the negative notion of "discrimination" to a positive means of integration. Distributive justice based on this idea of equality would require that social transfers were made, not just in financial terms, but on the basis of other needs as well, including support to participate.

This model makes irrelevant the question of similarly situated persons, which has established non-disabled as the normative model. It also addresses the issue of the white, male, able-bodied culture as the normative model and all others as deviations from that ideal.

Setting the equality standard as an outcome measure removes the need for each disadvantaged group to demonstrate discrimination. It replaces the capacity to compete as the basis for political obligation. It takes into account the social reality of the disabled and non-disabled as well as their biological differences. And it thereby makes the achievement of social justice dependent on a recognition of those differences that must be accommodated to achieve equality of well-being.

Acknowledgements

I would like to thank Ernie Lightman, Michael Bach, Cameron Crawford, and Jerry Bickenbach for their helpful comments on this paper.

Notes

1. Intellectual disability is used throughout this text. It includes individuals who have been variously labelled as mentally retarded, mentally handicapped, mentally disabled, mentally impaired, intellectually impaired, developmentally disabled and developmentally delayed and any other condition resulting in intellectual impairment.

2. Part I of the *Constitution Act, 1982*, being Schedule B to the *Canada Act 1982* (U.K.), 1982, ch. 11 [hereinafter *Charter*].

3. J. Sterba, *Justice: Alternative Political Perspectives*, Belmont, Calif.: Wadsworth Publishing Company, 1980; R. Nozick, *Anarchy, State and Utopia*, New York: Basic Books Inc., 1974; J. Rees, *Equality*, London: Pall Mall Press, 1971.

4. J. Rawls, *A Theory of Justice*, Cambridge, Mass.: Harvard University Press, 1971; B. Williams, "The Idea of Equality", in P. Laslett and W.G. Runciman (eds.), *Philosophy, Politics and Society*, 2nd series, Oxford: Basil Blackwell, 1962; W. Williams, "The Equality Crisis: Some Reflections on Culture, Courts and Feminism", *Women's Rights Law Reporter*, 7(3), 1982, p. 175.

5. R. Veatch, *The Foundations of Justice: Why the Retarded and the Rest of Us Have Claims to Equality*, New York, N.Y.: Oxford University Press, 1986; S. Lukes, "Socialism and Equality", in Sterba, *Justice*, 1980, p. 211 (see n. 3); C.E. Baker, "Outcome Equality or Equality of Respect: The Substantive Content of Equal Protection", *University of Pennsylvania Law Review*, 131(4), 1983, p. 933; R. Dworkin, *Taking Rights Seriously*, Cambridge, Mass.: Harvard University Press, 1977.

6. Under the *Canadian Charter of Rights and Freedoms*, people with intellectual disabilities ("mental disability") are specifically listed as a class of persons entitled to equality; that is, they have a *prima facie* entitlement to equality. The *Charter* also specifically excludes programs established to redress discrimination from being classified as discriminatory. In other words, special measures are deemed to be consistent with equality.

7. As Hutchison and Petter put it, the oppression and inequality that "flow from the seemingly natural operation of the economy." A.J. Hutchison and A. Petter, "Paradise Postponed", 1990 [unpublished].

8. That is, compassionate care, based on the notion that people with disabilities, although pitiable, are deserving of charity and benevolence. Within both the policy and legal framework, arguments are made that any different treatment of people with disabilities is justified because it is in the best interests of the individual according to some external set of standards. Differentiation has included the suspension of citizenship rights and the formalization of the dependent relationship of the individual to the state through legislation that provides unequal social and economic benefits.

9. S.J. Gould, *The Mismeasure of Man*, New York, N.Y.: Norton, 1981, p. 24.

10. B. Evans and B. Waites, *I.Q. and Mental Testing: An Unnatural Science and Its Social History*, London: McMillan Press, 1981, p. 188.

11. Implications of hereditarian thinking are as devastating for those distinguished as less equal by virtue of their race as for those labelled intellectually disabled.

12. R.L. Hayman, Jr., "Presumptions of Justice: Law, Politics and the Mentally Retarded Parent", *Harvard Law Review*, 103(6), 1960, p. 1248.

13. Generally, the criterion for being classified as intellectually disabled is that there is some significant intellectual impairment or developmental deficiency, the onset of which occurs in the early years of development (M.L. Batshaw and Y.M. Perret, *Children with Handicaps: A Medical Primer*, Baltimore, Md.: Paul H. Brookes Publishing Co., 1981). More recently, difficulty adapting to environmental circumstances has been added to the definition as a further criterion (American Association for Mental Retardation, *Mental Retardation: Definition, Classification, and Systems of*

Support, 9th ed., Washington, D.C.: AAMR, 1992). There are some specific objective conditions such as Down syndrome that have always been classified and continue to be classified as mental retardation; other conditions, such as epilepsy, were at one time classified as mental retardation but are no longer. Finally, the term has not conventionally included such conditions as Alzheimer's disease or senile dementia, because their onset is later in life. However, if the basis of distinguishing difference were competency rather than condition, these conditions would be included.

14. J.R. Mercer, *Labelling the Mentally Retarded: Clinical and Social System Perspectives on Mental Retardation*, Berkeley, Calif.: University of California Press, 1973.

15. The activities of medical and therapeutic professions reinforce this construction of disability and inequality. Theirs are not merely technical or commercial interactions but express the values of society generally. They operate as gatekeepers to the exercise and enjoyment of citizenship rights. The labelling of people as intellectually disabled is not therefore simply a technical medical "diagnosis". It affects the economic, social and legal interactions in which a person will participate and legitimizes political decisions concerning the relationship of that class of persons to society. The illusion that such decisions are "apolitical" has masked the practical political implications of the decisions and has enabled widespread discrimination and inequality without a political debate on procedural or substantive justice.

16. The definition of intellectual disability can always be applied to a segment of the population. This is because the definition is based on a relative measure. There will inevitably be a class of persons who are intellectually significantly less able in comparison to others and who have

comparative difficulty adapting to their environment.

17. W.S. Tarnopolsky, "The Equality Rights", in W.S. Tarnopolsky and G. Beaudoin (eds.), *The Canadian Charter of Rights and Freedoms: Commentary*, Toronto, Ont.: Carswell, 1982, pp. 399-401. For other discussions of the rule of law see International Commission of Jurists, *The Rule of Law and Human Rights: Principles and Definitions as Elaborated at the Congresses and Conferences Held under the Auspices of the International Commission of Jurists*, Geneva: ICJ, 1966; G. DeQ. Walker, *The Rule of Law: Foundations of Constitutional Democracy*, Carleton, Vic.: Melbourne University Press, 1988; A.C. Hutchison and P. Monahan, *The Rule of Law: Ideal or Ideology?* Toronto, Ont.: Carswell, 1987; F. Neumann, *The Rule of Law: Political Theory and the Legal System in Modern Society*, Leamington, Eng., and Dover, N.H.: Berg Publishers, 1986.

18. In this chapter, "institution" refers only to residential institutions for people with psychiatric or intellectual disabilities.

19. Feminist theorists have argued that the adherence to a formal view of equality (i.e., equality of treatment) perpetuates and legitimizes women's substantive inequality (i.e., equality of condition). G. Brodsky and S. Day, *Canadian Charter Equality Rights for Women: One Step Forward or Two Steps Back*, Ottawa, Ont.: The Canadian Advisory Council on the Status of Women, 1989; J.W. Scott, "Deconstructing Equality-Versus Difference: or, the Uses of Poststructural Theory for Feminism", *Feminist Studies*, 14(1), Spring, 1988, p. 33; J. Flax, "Postmodernism and Gender Relations in Feminist Theory", *Signs: Journal of Women in Culture and Society*, 12(4), 1987, p. 621.

20. Peter Westen argues that the notion of equality added

nothing to the determinations of proper treatment. His critique of the formal principle of equality as an empty idea reinforces the argument that equality could be achieved under that limited principle without the achievement of any substantive rights. "The Empty Idea of Equality", *Harvard Law Review*, 95, 1982, p. 537.

21. A. Petter, "Comment: Legitimizing Sexual Inequality: Three Early Charter Cases", *McGill Law Journal*, 34, 1989, p. 341.

22. The substantive inequality may even be legitimated by court decisions that find in favour of an equal-treatment model of equality because it can lead to advantaged groups winning their claims to scarce resources that are designed to remedy the acknowledged disadvantage.

23. *Brown* v. *Board of Education* 349 U.S. 294 (1955).

24. Brodsky and Day, *Canadian Charter Equality Rights*, 1989 (see n. 19); G.C. More, *Competing Conceptions of Sexual Equality in the European Community and Canada: Formal and Substantive Models*, Ottawa, Ont.: National Library of Canada, 1991; D. Gibson, *The Law of the Charter: Equality Rights*, Toronto, Ont.: Carswell, 1990; K. Swinton, *Advanced Constitutional Law: Equality Rights*, 1988-89 ed., Toronto, Ont.: Faculty of Law, University of Toronto, 1988-89; A.F. Bayesfky and M. Eberts (eds.), *Equality Rights and the Canadian Charter of Rights and Freedoms*, Toronto, Ont.: Carswell, 1985; K. Lahey, "Equality and Women's Specificity in Feminist Thought", 1983 [unpublished], cited in M. Mossman and D. Majury (eds.), *Readings for Law, Gender, Equality*, Toronto, Ont.: Osgoode Hall Law School, York University, 1989-90, p. 338.

25. Although there is no general agreement of the precise components of equality of opportunity, it generally

presumes that people of equal need and ability, desirous of a scarce resource not available to everyone, should have an equal opportunity to obtain it. In other words, extraneous social categories such as sex, race and disability are excluded from the consideration in determining who gets the scarce resource. See for example, Veatch, *The Foundations of Justice*, 1986 (see n. 5) and Williams, "The Idea of Equality", 1962 (see n. 4).

26. Martha Minow refers to the following question as the dilemma of difference: "When does treating people differently emphasize their differences and stigmatize or hinder them on that basis? and when does treating people the same become insensitive to their difference and likely to stigmatize or hinder them on *that* basis?" [emphasis in original]. M. Minow, *Making All the Difference*, Ithaca: Cornell University Press, 1990, p. 20.

27. Minow characterizes the traditional view that classifies people on the basis of mental incompetence, understood to be immutable and natural, as the "abnormal persons" approach. The assignment of difference is based on the person's basic or immutable nature and, in the law, the facts concerning a person's mental competence and capacity. Subtle differences are ignored: one is either normal or deviant. The mental capacity of those with a mental handicap is the determining factor in any case. Minow points out that this approach owes much to notions of fixed status relationships. M. Minow, "When Difference Has Its Home: Group Homes for the Mentally Retarded, Equal Protection and Legal Treatment of Difference", *Harvard Civil Rights/Civil Liberties Law Review*, 22(1), 1987, pp. 111-189.

28. During the 1960s intellectual disability began to be reconceived as a developmental issue rather than a

biological one or a matter of public threat. The concept of normalization ("utilization of means which are as culturally normative as possible, in order to establish and/or maintain personal behaviours which are as culturally normative as possible": W. Wolfensberger, *The Principle of Normalization in Human Services*, Downsview, Ont.: NIMR, 1972), developed during the 1970s, rested on the premise that persons with intellectual disabilities are entitled to some self-determination and freedom of choice in a context of assimilation. The goal was to break down the philosophical and material barriers between "normal" and "deviant" or "abnormal". Rights won in court and the concept of normalization had a powerful ideological and material impact in Canada, providing a crucial rationale for the efforts of those concerned with deinstitutionalization and development of community-based services. The limitation of normalization, however, was that it did not provide a theoretical basis that, in practice, gave much scope for pluralism.

29. In its first interpretation of the equality provisions of the *Charter*, the Supreme Court recognized that S. 15 protects against both impact as well as intent of disadvantage; that there must be an equality of both benefit and protection of the law; that difference in treatment will not necessarily result in inequality and that sameness in treatment may result in serious inequality. *Andrews v. Law Society of British Columbia*, [1989] 1 S.C.R. 143, 56 D.L.R. (4th) 1. In a 1988 opinion, Justice Bertha Wilson acknowledged the historical basis of women's experience of inequality. *R. v. Mortgentaler* [1988] 1 S.C.R. 30.

30. The Federal Court of Canada declared S.14(4)(f) of the *Canada Elections Act* unconstitutional in October 1988 on

the basis that "the assumption that a person suffering from any mental disability is incapacitated for all purposes, including voting, is simply a false assumption". *Canadian Disability Rights Council* v. *Canada*, [1988] Marie-Michele Bedard et al. and Her Majesty the Queen in Right of Canada, 3 F.C. 622, per Madame Justice Reed.

31. *Re Eve*, [1986] 2 S.C.R. 388.

32. Brodsky and Day argue that section 15 of the *Charter* should provide a basis for formal claims (process claims) as well as substantive claims to ensure that equality rights can be achieved. They point out that formal equality claims will in many cases compete with substantive equality claims particularly in cases of distributive justice. They propose that "section 15 [complaints] should be available for substantive equality claims by disadvantaged groups, and that members of advantaged groups who are disadvantaged only by virtue of their individual circumstances ought not to be able to bring substantive equality claims ... This would not mean that members of advantaged groups would be completely without equality rights, however. The process rights component of section 15 should be recognized and available to all. But it should be developed in a limited way to protect rights traditionally associated with the rule of law, such as access to the courts." Brodsky and Day, *Canadian Charter Equality Rights*, 1989, p. 197 (see n. 19).

33. See, for example, W.A. Block and M.A. Walker (eds.), *Discrimination, Affirmative Action and Equal Opportunity: An Economic and Social Perspective*, Vancouver: Fraser Institute, 1981. In this conceptualization of equality goals, the liberal values of competition, freedom and radical individualism are relied on to argue that there is no need

for government intervention. Competition in the marketplace is the equalizer in the sense that those who have been disadvantaged will cost less to employ and consequently the marketplace will regulate itself. Rights to autonomy and rights to freedom are conceptually linked to the fair play paradigm. See, for example, R. Nozick, *Anarchy*, 1974 (see n. 3).

34. See, for example, C.A. MacKinnon, *Sexual Harassment of Working Women: A Case of Sex Discrimination*, New Haven: Yale University Press, 1979; J.C. Livingston, *Fair Game? Inequality and Affirmative Action*, San Francisco: W.H. Freeman, 1979; L.C. Thurlow, "A Theory of Groups and Economic Redistribution", *Philosophy and Public Affairs*, 9(1), 1979, p. 25; A.H. Goldman, "Reparations to Individuals or Groups?" in B. Gross, *Reverse Discrimination*, Buffalo: Prometheus Books, 1977; T. Nagel, "Equal Treatment and Compensatory Discrimination", *Philosophy and Public Affairs*, 2(4), 1973, p. 348; J.W. Chapman (ed.), *Compensatory Justice*, New York: New York University Press, 1991; T. Nagel, "Equal Treatment and Compensatory Justice", in M. Cohen, T. Nagel and T. Scanlon (eds.), *Equality and Preferential Treatment*, Princeton, N.J.: Princeton University Press, 1977.

35. S. 15(2) of the *Charter*.

36. In ibid., s. 15(2), s. 23, s. 25, s. 27., s. 28, s.29.

37. Equality claims are framed by some as paramount to freedom claims. Macpherson claims that the premise on which equality of opportunity in liberal theory is based is "to provide the conditions for the free development of human capacities, and to do so for all members of society". He places this within the framework of serving the needs both of freedom and of equality — that is, "freedom of each individual from subservience to the wills of others

and equality in this freedom". While acknowledging the ethical significance of equality, this does not address the issues of history and nature. C.B. Macpherson, *The Real World of Democracy*, Toronto: Canadian Broadcasting Corp., 1966, pp. 58-59.

38. *Andrews* v. *Law Society of British Columbia* [1989] 1 S.C.R. 143, 56 D.L.R. (4th) 1.

39. However, *R. v. Mortgentaler*, [1988] 1 S.C.R. 30, was not decided on the equality issue.

40. In *Re Eve*, [1986] 2 S.C.R. 388, pp. 427-428, 434.

41. As Smith argues: "It is easy for most people to accept that the physical differences between the races do not matter and should be legally irrelevant. The equal opportunity model, in which justice is seen to be done when everyone is permitted to run from the same starting line, fits relatively well when the contestants differ only in the colour of their skins. (The problem, of course, is how to achieve the same starting line in a meaningful way.) However, there are physical differences between the sexes in relation to child-bearing and breast feeding which make identical treatment of the sexes unequal in some contexts. Running the race from the same starting line does not solve the problem of maternity along the way. Classifications based on sex may be legally relevant. Similarly there are differences between the able-bodied and the disabled and between young, middle-aged, and old people which can make identical treatment unequal. Simple equality of opportunity cannot conceivably produce equality of results in many of these situations. Such issues do not arise as squarely with respect to racial discrimination." L. Smith, "A New Paradigm for Equality Rights", in Lynn Smith et al. (eds.), *Righting the Balance: Canada's New Equality Rights*, Saskatoon: Canadian

Human Rights Reporter Inc., 1986, p. 365.

42. See K. Greenawalt, "How Empty Is the Idea of Equality", *Columbia Law Review*, 83(5), 1983, pp. 1167-1185.

43. As the classification "mentally handicapped" includes an enormous range of intellectual capacities, it is difficult to generalize claims.

44. A.E. Freedman, "Sex Equality, Sex Difference, and the Supreme Court", *The Yale Law Journal*, 92(6), 1983, p. 913; S.M. Wildman, "The Legitimation of Sex Discrimination: A Critical Response to Supreme Court Jurisprudence", *Oregon Law Review*, 63(2), 1984, p. 265; A.C. Scales, "Towards a Feminist Jurisprudence", *Indiana Law Journal*, 56(3), 1980-81, p. 375; Williams, "The Equality Crisis", 1982, p. 175 (see n. 4).

45. Brodsky and Day argue that the formal equality model, directed as it is to like treatment and different treatment, assumes that equality is a matter of sameness and difference under the law rather than dominance and subordination of groups. Brodsky and Day, *Canadian Charter Equality Rights*, 1989, p. 149 (see n. 19).

46. Canada, Commission on Equality in Employment, *Report of the Commission on Equality in Employment*, Ottawa: Supply and Services, 1984 (Chair: R.S. Abella). The concept was derived in large part from affirmative action in the United States, designed to deal primarily with racial inequality.

47. It also raises some similar problems for physical handicap.

48. W. Black identifies five specific problems with the statistical model of comparison in the case of disability. 1) Statistical comparisons require the identification of who is in the groups being compared. With disability it is difficult to determine who falls within the category because of the

wide variety and number of conditions. The impact of the conditions also may range from minor to very significant. 2) There is little data available about the participation rate in the general labour force of persons with disabilities. 3) Program targets established on the basis of current participation rates are a general problem with affirmative action because the rates set incorporate the effects of past discrimination. 4) The small numbers of persons with disabilities who have generally participated in the labour force mean that any statistical information is not reliable. 5) A statistical approach requires gathering of information about disabilities of employees, which raises problems of labelling or categorization which may be an infringement on the rights of those categorized and may reinforce stereotypes. W.W. Black, *Discussion Paper Prepared for the Manitoba Human Rights Commission: Affirmative Action for Persons with Disabilities*, Ottawa: Human Rights Research and Education Centre, University of Ottawa, 1990.

49. Livingston, *Fair Game?*, 1979 (see n. 34).

50. In the sphere of education, learning may be thought of as a means to other ends such as social status, employment, income and ethical behaviour. However, learning could also be defined as arriving at new insight — an end in itself. Pedagogical practice can be structured for these ways of looking at learning. Typically, however, the arrival at new insight is considered a less desirable focus of educational practice than promoting access to those other goals.

51. Williams, "The Equality Crisis", 1982 (see n. 4).

52. Variations of this model have been called "equality-of-outcome" or "equality-of-resources". R. Dworkin, *Law's Empire*, Cambridge: Harvard University Press, 1986, pp. 297-301; K. Neilson, *Equality and Liberty: A Defense of Radical Egalitarianism*, Totowa, N.J.: Rowman and Allanheld, 1985,

pp. 46-60; R. Dworkin, "What Is Equality: Part 1, Equality of Welfare", *Philosophy and Public Affairs*, 10(3), Summer 1981, pp. 185-246; "Part 2, Equality of Resources", *Philosophy and Public Affairs*, 10(4), Fall 1981, pp. 283-345; "Part 3: The Place of Liberty", *Iowa Law Review*, 73(1), Oct. 1987, pp. 1-54; "Part 4: Political Equality", *University of San Francisco Law Review*, 22(1), Fall 1987, pp. 1-30; P. Westen, *Speaking of Equality: An Analysis of the Rhetorical Force of Equality in Moral and Legal Discourse*, Princeton, N.J.: Princeton University Press, 1990; Canada, Law Reform Commission of Canada, *Report on Aboriginal Peoples and Criminal Justice: Equality, Respect and the Search for Justice*, No. 34, Ottawa: LRCC, 1991, pp. 9-12.

53. Equal treatment and equal opportunity in most of their formulations treat equality as a means to ensure fairness in achieving some other ends. Therefore, in the latter case, people of equal need and ability should have equal opportunity to obtain desired scarce resources not available to them.

54. Lukes, "Socialism and Equality", 1980, p. 218 (see n. 5).

55. Young proposes this as a characteristic of an equality of outcome and argues that it allows affirmative action to be seen not as an exception to the principle of nondiscrimination but a policy instrumental in undermining oppression. I.M. Young, *Justice and the Politics of Difference*, Princeton, N.J.: Princeton University Press, 1990, p. 195.

56. For example, as found in the Canadian adaptation of the English Poor Laws and in subsequent law and policy based on a status of civil disability, law and policy based on charity and paternalism, and law and policy based on equality of opportunity.

57. Resource redistribution necessary to ensure equal well-

being would require both the redistribution necessary to enable equal opportunity as well as the redistribution necessary to take into account unequal needs because of physical and mental differences. The equal treatment principle of equality, by contrast, supports deinstitutionalization and integration in the community — but not the provision of services to make this possible for those people with intellectual disabilities who might have trouble in a complex environment. The "special treatment" model, which is a form of equality of opportunity, supports the development of specially tailored assistance programs, but might also support institutional treatment.

58. See T.B. Dawson, "Equality Strategies — Legal Options and Approaches", delivered at the Human Rights Summer School, University of Ottawa, August 7, 1990; C. MacKinnon, "Feminism, Marxism, Method, and the State: An Agenda for Theory", *Signs: Journal of Women in Culture and Society*, 7(3), 1982, p. 515; C. MacKinnon, "Difference and Dominance: On Sex Discrimination", in *Feminism Unmodified: Discourses on Life and Law*, Cambridge: Harvard University Press, 1987; L.M.G. Clark, "Politics and Law: The Theory and Practice of the Ideology of Male Supremacy; or It Wasn't God Who Made Honkey Tonk Angels", in D. Weisstub (ed.), *Law and Policy*, Toronto: Osgoode Hall Law School, York University, 1976, pp. 35-73.

59. Fox and Willis suggest the significant difference between policy in the area of disability and other policy. "No other area of policy is precisely analogous to disability. An inexact analogy might be the mobilization of a country for modern warfare. Only in warfare have the people who make policy explicitly negotiated about who will be expected to work or to fight and then organized health and social services on the basis of negotiation." D.M. Fox and D.P. Willis, "Introduction: Disability Policy: Restoring Socioeconomic

Independence", *Milbank Quarterly*, 67(Supp. 2)(1), 1989, pp. 1-2.

60. I.M. Young, "Impartiality and the Civic Public: Some Implications of Feminist Critiques of Moral and Political Theory", *Praxis International*, 5, 1986, p. 382; M. Minow, *Making All the Difference*, Ithaca: Cornell University Press, 1990; I.R. Young, *Justice and the Politics of Difference*, Princeton, N.J.: Princeton University Press, 1990.

61. Herma Hill Kay concludes that it is necessary to preserve the comparative element of the anti-discrimination principle as the normal standard of measurement and make an exception only in those cases where legal problems are raised about reproductive sex differences. Wildman, "The Legitimation of Sex Discrimination", 1984 (see n. 44), has proposed that the comparative standard between men and women be discarded as a basis for the anti-discrimination principle. She argues that women have been the victims of sex discrimination not men, just as blacks are the victims of discrimination not whites. She argues for full societal participation to eliminate sexual discrimination against women. She does not accept the view of writers such as Kay, who posit that discrimination is practised against both men and women and that must instruct the legal model adopted. S.A. Law, "Rethinking Sex and the Constitution", *University of Pennsylvania Law Review*, 132, 1984, p. 955, offers a position that adopts both models. She would have laws regulating reproductive biology brought within the Fourteenth Amendment's guarantee of equal protection but not subjected to the anti-discrimination principle, while laws that made explicit sex classification would remain subject to the anti-discrimination principle. H.H. Kay, "Models of Equality", *University of Illinois Law Review*, 39, Winter 1985, pp. 35-88.

62. Scott and Minow argue that the framing of equality and difference as mutually exclusive terms misrepresents their relationship. Placing equality and difference in an antithetical relationship denies the way in which difference has figured in political notions of equality; it also suggests that sameness is the only ground on which equality can be claimed. Equality, as developed in the political theory of rights, is understood to mean the elimination of a particular set of differences at a particular time. Therefore, its starting point is the acknowledgement of a group of people as different. "[T]he political notion of equality thus includes, indeed depends on, an acknowledgement of the existence of difference" (Scott, "Deconstructing Equality", 1988 (see n. 19)). If individuals were "the same" there would be no need to ask for equality. Equality could be defined not as the elimination of difference but as indifference to difference. The political issue is, therefore, to find a notion of equality predicated not on sameness but on difference; Minow, "When Difference Has Its Home", 1987 (see n. 27); M. Minow, "Learning to Live with the Dilemma of Difference: Bilingual and Special Education", *Law and Contemporary Problems*, 48, 1985, p. 157; J. Flax, "Postmodernism and Gender Relations in Feminist Theory", *Signs: Journal of Women in Culture and Society*, 12(4), 1987, pp. 621-643.

63. They have also been disadvantaged by being subsumed within these categories.

64. Some special benefits have been provided by government such as the augmented welfare provisions and Vocational Rehabilitation for Disabled Persons program and special services. Others have been made available through charitable organizations.

65. M.H. Rioux, "Exchanging Charity for Rights: A Challenge for the 1990s", *entourage*, 6(2), 1991, p. 3.

66. There have not been any legal challenges of this nature in Canada, although arguments were made in the Robichaud and Rowett education integration cases (unreported) about the benefits received by the students (who had an intellectual disability) in special schools. There were also arguments about the effect of a student with an intellectual disability on the achievement of other students.

Chapter 5

Voluntary Disabilities and Everyday Illnesses

by Jerome E. Bickenbach

In March 1986, Darlene Ouimette missed three days of work at the Lily Cup plant in Scarborough, Ontario, Canada, because of asthma brought about by an allergic reaction to medication she took for a bout of flu.[1] A probationary employee, she was summarily fired. Since no one had complained about her work performance, Ms. Ouimette believed she must have been dismissed because of her illnesses. When she contacted the Ontario Human Rights Commission, they agreed: Lily Cup's probationary policy constitutes discrimination on the basis of handicap, contrary to Ontario's *Human Rights Code.*[2] Yet when the Commission brought the matter before a board of inquiry, headed by Dr. D.J. Baum, Ms. Ouimette's complaint was rejected. The asthma, Dr. Baum insisted, was brought about by her own "reckless negligence" and the flu is a transitory illness anyone can get, which does not produce substantial, ongoing limits on normal activities. Complaints like this one, Dr. Baum concluded, merely trivialize the important goal of preventing discrimination on the basis of mental or physical handicap.

Whether or not Dr. Baum was right to dismiss Ms. Ouimette's complaint, the reasoning he uses to reach this conclusion, I want to argue, is seriously flawed. And the flaw is not inconsequential; nor are the consequences restricted to the rarefied realm of human rights law. Dr. Baum's reasoning embodies and puts into effect two erroneous, indeed perverse, assumptions about disability that have historically distorted social policy for people with disabilities. If not confronted, they will continue to do so. These assumptions are all the more dangerous because they are seductively plausible.

Dr. Baum argued that the kind of asthma Ms. Ouimette acquired was "intrinsic" rather than "extrinsic" — that is, asthma brought about by her own actions. She was aware that the medicine she was taking for her flu might spark an attack of asthma but she took it anyway. So, it was her fault. In other words, and more generally, Dr. Baum believed that it is relevant to our judgement about the behaviour of Ms. Ouimette's employers that she had some measure of control over the onset of her disabling condition. I want to call this the "voluntarism" assumption, the view that if a disability is one's fault, in whole or in part, then the conduct of others with respect to that disability cannot be discriminatory.

Dr. Baum also denied that Ms. Ouimette's case of gastroenteritis, though an illness over which she had no control, qualified as a "handicap" as defined in Ontario's *Code*.[3] The flu, he argued, does not identify a discrete minority group. Moreover, as compared with diabetes mellitus, epilepsy, paralysis, amputation, blindness and other "genuine handicaps", the flu does not constitute, or bring about, a lasting, material disability. Dr. Baum made it clear that he was not concerned about the temporary nature of the flu — since, for example, heart attacks are episodic medical events that are disabling. His concern was that the flu is not serious enough; it is just an everyday illness.

But why did Dr. Baum come to the conclusion that Ms. Ouimette's complaint *trivializes* the social problem of discrimination against people with disabilities? Following a line of previous human rights cases involving disability,[4] he argued that the proper aim of human rights codes is to prevent employers, out of ignorance or irrational prejudice, from assuming that people with disabilities cannot perform jobs or tasks that they in fact can perform. And in those cases where the disability does affect the relevant repertoire of abilities needed for the job, these codes require, up to the point of "undue hardship", that "reasonable accommodation" be provided to offset the effects of the disabilities. A failure to provide accommodation is another instance of ignorance or irrational prejudice affecting an employment decision. In either event, when employers act upon these false and stereotypical beliefs, they deny equality of opportunity to an identifiable group of people. People with disabilities are not given a fair chance to show what they can do. This is discrimination.

Given that this is the rationale of human rights codes, the argument goes, when someone cannot do the job because of a voluntarily created disability or because of an everyday illness, then dismissal or demotion is *not* a violation of equality of opportunity and so not discrimination on the basis of a disability. It is not discrimination because, as one board of inquiry put it, the *Code's* definition of "handicap" does not "encompass every physical attribute or condition on the basis of which an individual is unfairly treated. The physical disabilities which the *Human Rights Code* protects against are in the nature of ongoing physical limitations which an individual cannot change and which are not relevant to ... employment potential."[5]

Although this argument may seem plausible, it is straightforwardly fallacious. It is absurd to think that one cannot be denied equality of opportunity (that is, discriminated against) on the basis of a self-created disability or everyday illness. Suppose, because of inexcusable carelessness on my part, I cause a car accident in which my leg is so badly damaged it has to be amputated. My employer then fires me because he believes that, with only one leg, I can no longer do my job as a computer programmer. Or suppose I go to work with a bad case of the flu and my boss immediately demotes me because he thinks flu causes psychiatric problems so severe that I can no longer be trusted. Surely, in both cases my employer has ignorantly or irrationally characterized what I am capable of doing because of my disabilities so that, by acting upon these beliefs to my detriment, I have been denied equality of opportunity.

Although fallacious, the underlying argument of the *Ouimette* decision is seductively plausible because *sometimes* the circumstances that led to a disability *may be* relevant to judgements we make about the person with that disability. The fact that I drove negligently and injured myself is germane to an assessment of my driving abilities. The fact that I came to work with a bad case of the flu may be relevant to whether I am sufficiently sensitive to the health of my co-workers. If my employer drew these conclusions about me and fired or demoted me on those grounds, then it would not be correct to say I was fired or demoted *because of a handicap*. To be sure, I could still legitimately complain that my employer did not have enough evidence to warrant these adverse judgements about my suitability, but this would not be a complaint of a denial of equality of opportunity on the basis of my disabilities.

Interestingly, even if one focuses on this kernel of plausibility in the argument, the *Ouimette* decision still cannot be justified. During the hearings, Dr. Baum accepted the argument that since Lily Cup's probationary policy *automatically* dismisses employees who have missed three days of work, for whatever reason, no one is dismissed because they have a disability. But this misses the point, since the policy is not neutral with respect to disability. People with disabilities sometimes cannot as easily avoid missing days of work as other probationary employees. Lily Cup's policy does not accommodate for disability and this constitutes a denial of equality of opportunity. The difference that disability makes is not rationally connected to what might be a *bona fide* basis for dismissing a potential employee — say, laziness or untrustworthiness — the basis which provides the only non-discriminatory rationale for the probationary policy.

My concern, though, is not shoddy reasoning but its diagnosis. The reasoning in the *Ouimette* case depends on the seductively plausible but highly prejudicial view that aspects of the circumstances of a disability are unfailing guides to our assessment of how others treat individuals with those disabilities. It behooves researchers in disability-related disciplines, and, in particular, analysts of disability social policy, to be aware of such methodological assumptions. Far from being inconsequential, these kinds of assumptions are often at the heart of discriminatory treatment of people with disabilities.[6]

Voluntarism: Blaming the Victim

Voluntarism is plausible because it fits neatly into a commonly held view about social obligations to people whose differences produce social inequality that result in them being disadvantaged. We believe deeply that social structures that systematically create disadvantage for people are unfair when people do not deserve such treatment. Moreover, we think that being disadvantaged because of a difference over which one has no control is the epitome of undeserved maltreatment. In other words, differential and adverse social treatment in terms of categories of immutable difference — race, colour, sex, age and disability — is morally and legally suspect because it is absurd to blame anyone for being so categorized.

In the case of mental or physical disability this reasoning is symmetrical. As a society, we have, over the centuries, agreed to provide for the "special needs" of those who have not earned these resources by their own effort in the marketplace. But, from the Roman *Code of Justinian* onward, a precondition of this charity has been absence of fault. The "worthy beggar" was poor, not because of idleness but because of disease or deformity, a condition over which he or she had no control.[7] This precondition for special treatment continues to this day in the form of complex eligibility requirements for disability programming.[8]

The assumption of voluntarism is, therefore, another facet of our culture's general approach to eligibility for "unearned" social resources. It is vital to notice, though, that voluntarism does not entail that self-induced, wholly voluntary disabilities do not qualify as disabling conditions. Nor could it, since, as a general matter, for nearly all of the relevant concerns involving mental or physical disability — the degree of dysfunctionality, the resulting repertoire of productive capacities, the needs that are created, the range of accommodations available and so on — the question of *how* the disability came about is utterly irrelevant. Voluntarism says nothing about what conditions are disabling; instead it makes a normative distinction between kinds of disabilities on the basis of the responsibility of the individual.

A useful and commonly accepted conceptual distinction will help to show the significance of this normative distinction.[9] A handicap might be defined as the social reception of a real or perceived disability — or, more correctly, the collection of disadvantageous social consequences that flow from that social reception. Handicapping consequences are, under this definition, unfair and unjustifiable; they are obstacles that stand between people with disabilities and equal participation in society. A disability, on the other hand, is a condition of mental or physical incapacity, identified by socially constructed expectations of what people ought to be able to do but grounded in a biomedically or psychologically recognized impairment of some sort.

Now, if we agree to use these terms as defined, a disability is not automatically a handicap. Rather, a disability becomes a handicap when the social reception of the incapacity is unfairly or prejudicially disadvantageous to the individual. Stigma, ridicule and stereotyping are obvious forms of handicapping; they are unwarranted, irrational and unfair social responses to disability. But, more pertinently, the failure to accommodate a disability at the workplace is also a form of handicapping, unless that failure can be socially justified. An individual who could successfully perform the tasks of a particular job, if the worksite were wheelchair accessible, will be handicapped by the disability if accessibility is not provided when, as a society, we agree that it should be provided. The moral and political foundation of social policy for people with disabilities can, therefore, be characterized as a matter of determining when the disadvantages a person with a disability experiences are handicaps and when they are unavoidable concomitants of disability that fall outside the range of misfortunes to which society has an obligation to respond. The assumption of voluntarism states, therefore, that self-inflicted or self-caused disabilities are not handicaps; they are, rather, misfortunes the individual must live with. Insofar as social policy is based on the proposition that society is not obliged to satisfy disability-created needs as of right, it can impose preconditions upon the distribution of these required but unearned resources. Voluntariness, historically, has been one of those preconditions. Given this central role in social policy, it should be apparent that voluntarism is a profoundly influential ideological tool. Its influence, in recent years, has greatly increased.

For example, a spate of U.S. and Canadian human rights cases involving obesity have held that people fired or denied jobs or promotions because of their weight, irrespective of their actual job-related capabilities, will have no remedy unless they can show that their condition is the result of an illness or other medical condition over which they have no control.[10]

Researchers agree that the primary rationale for linking a disability to a background illness or impairment has always been to insure against fraud or feigning.[11] Since obesity is not a condition one can fake, the only reason for demanding a background illness, as the cases say quite openly, is to deny remedy to anyone who, however unfairly they might be treated by their employer, could have lost weight if they had tried. Obesity cannot be a disability, in short, if it is remediable by will power.[12]

Recently in the U.S., voluntarism has been embraced by the highest court of the land. The *Traynor v. Turnage* case involves an appeal from a decision of the Veteran's Administration that two honourably discharged veterans could not take advantage of veteran's educational assistance benefits because of their "willful misconduct": they had been alcoholics.[13] The majority of the court, in effect, argued that when the legislature prohibited discrimination against people with disabilities they could not have had in mind the denial of benefits to people who "engaged with some degree of willfulness in the conduct that caused them to become disabled". The court, it should be said, at no point denied that these men had been disabled by their condition or that they were denied a benefit that other G.I.'s enjoyed. The point of the decision was rather that it was *their fault* that benefits were denied: as alcoholics, they deserved unequal and adverse treatment.

In some respects, this decision is consistent with a long history of U.S. government policy with respect to alcohol and drug dependency. Alcohol and drug abusers were expressly excluded from the protections of the *Rehabilitation Act* of 1973[14] and this practice is continued in part in the much-touted *Americans with Disabilities Act* of 1990.[15] Moreover, people who are HIV-serio-positive or who have AIDS were also excluded from these protections on the grounds that they had brought the condition on themselves and, in any event, posed a danger to others in the workplace. Fortunately, in both the U.S. and Canada, these highly prejudicial and irrational views about people with AIDS have been successfully rebutted and protections against discrimination have now been put in place.[16]

Although voluntarism has been a persistent theme in U.S. disability policy, its legitimation by the Supreme Court is particularly troubling.[17] And the danger of this assumption for people with *any* disability could not have been more eloquently expressed than by the dissent in *Traynor*, written by Mr. Justice Blackmun. We must keep in mind, Mr. Justice Blackmun argued, that what is at issue here is discriminatory practices founded on prejudices, stereotypes and other mistaken generalizations about disabilities and people with disabilities. That is, discrimination is a matter of handicapping, not disability. Voluntarism is precisely the kind of faulty generalization about disability that legislative protections against discrimination were intended to eliminate. We cannot, without violating equality, automatically conclude from the fact that a disability was "voluntary", that discriminatory treatment against that individual is justified.

But there is another reason to think voluntarism is dangerous. What are the limits of blaming? "Individuals suffering from a wide range of disabilities, including heart and lung disease and diabetes, usually bear some responsibility for their conditions," Mr. Justice Blackmun noted. "And the conduct that can lead to this array of disabilities, particularly dietary and smoking habits, is certainly no less voluntary than the consumption of alcohol." In other words, what victim of a car accident could escape the charge of partial responsibility? What person with a contagious disease could deny that, by radically altering their lives, they might have avoided the illness? Perhaps people with visual or other sense impairments should never leave their homes for fear that they will be held responsible for the risks they are taking. Indeed, perhaps all of us should lead the healthiest, most risk-aversive lives imaginable in order to escape the charge that we are to blame for our own ill health. However, even this is not enough to prevent the label "voluntary" since, in the end, voluntarism precludes anyone for blameless disability: by voluntarily not opting for suicide, everyone is in part responsible for their present or future condition of disability and the social needs it creates.

If this *reductio ad absurdum* argument is not persuasive, Mr. Justice Blackmun's first argument surely is. As a society, we are concerned about stigma and stereotyping because these persistent attitudes involve generalizations about people with disabilities that are highly prejudicial. But voluntarism is just such a generalization. The only protection against the distortions of stereotypes and generalizations is to avoid assumptions like this and insist that our social policy deal with people with disabilities, to the greatest extent possible, on a case-by-case, individual basis.[18] In short, to assume without proof that anyone who is responsible for their disability is untrustworthy, slothful, dangerous or unable to perform the tasks of a job is straightforwardly to deny them equality of opportunity and so to discriminate on the basis of a disability.

A measure of the tenacity of voluntarism can be seen in the fact that *Ouimette*, the obesity cases and *Traynor* were all decided against the background of law that expressly detaches the fact of discrimination from features or characteristics of the disability. That is, in nearly all of the jurisdictions in which prohibitions against discrimination on the basis of disability are in effect, the prohibition is expressed, not merely in terms of disabilities that people have but also disabilities they are *perceived as having*.[19] It is clear law that a person can successfully bring a case against an employer for discrimination on the basis of disability when the individual, in fact, has no disability whatsoever but the employer falsely believes he or she does. The rationale and justification for this feature of the law follows immediately from the distinction between disabilities and handicaps: discrimination is a matter of handicapping, the social reception or perception of a disability. However, that being said, one can just as easily be handicapped by the mistaken belief that one is disabled as by the correct belief.

Fortunately, from time to time, voluntarism loses its grip and the real question of discrimination is confronted head-on. In one recent human rights case involving obesity, the board of inquiry was wholly indifferent to whether the condition could be linked to some background illness over which the complainant had no control. Instead, and fully within the logic of the human rights code, the board asked whether the complainant was unfairly treated on the basis of the perception that he was obese and the resulting beliefs about how that condition would disqualify him for employment. Finding on the evidence that the complainant was the victim of misperceptions about his capabilities, the board concluded that he had been discriminated against on the basis of a disability, without ever finding the need to determine whether or not he was in fact disabled.[20]

Everyday Illnesses: Disability as Stigma

Why should we think that the flu, or any other everyday illness, is not the kind of impairment that may attract discriminatory treatment, so as to become a handicap as defined by anti-discrimination legislation? To recall, Dr. Baum in *Ouimette* gave two reasons for this view. "To state the obvious initially," he wrote, "it is difficult to identify the group for whom protection is sought. The Commission would include in that group all those who are subject to flu, even though literally everyone would be encompassed as the potentially handicapped." Presumably, the point here is that one cannot be discriminated against if one is a member of a group to which anyone could *potentially* belong. Secondly, the flu is transitory; "it lasts but a few days and then it is over." And when it is over — in the usual case — there are no ongoing disabling consequences.

On face value, neither consideration is a significant, or even a relevant, reason for thinking that people cannot be discriminated against on the basis of an everyday illness. Plainly enough, the class of people with disabilities *does* potentially include everyone so that, potentially, everyone could be handicapped. But then, how is the flu different from another disability? Secondly, as we have seen, the rationale of anti-discrimination legislation is to protect people against handicapping — stereotype, stigma and other groundless and prejudicial attitudes associated with disability. But handicapping is a matter of the social reception of a disability and social reception is in no obvious way shaped or determined by the etiology, the seriousness, the prognosis or even the existence of a background illness or impairment.

Dr. Baum's argument is therefore utterly spurious. But it retains an element of plausibility because it raises the concern that human rights protection for people with disabilities might be trivialized if just anyone can take advantage of it. This worry was put in a U.S. case which Dr. Baum cites: "The *Rehabilitation Act* assumes that truly disabled, but genuinely capable, individuals will not face discrimination in employment because of stereotypes about the insurmountability of their handicaps. It would debase this high purpose if the statutory protections available to those truly handicapped could be claimed by anyone whose disability was minor and whose relative severity of impairment was widely shared."[21]

The everyday illness assumption, in short, relies on the fear that frauds and malingerers will dilute or pervert the benefits provided by anti-discrimination legislation. As we saw, voluntarism too, although to a lesser extent, raises the spectre of the lazy schemer who would willingly bring about, exaggerate or fake a disability to take advantage of the state's largesse. In the U.S., these fears led to the legislative proviso, found in both the *Rehabilitation Act* of 1973 and the *Americans with Disabilities Act* of 1990, that a disability must involve, or be perceived to involve, an impairment that substantially limits an individual's major life activities.[22] Canadian human rights codes do not contain such a proviso but, as is evident from the *Ouimette* case, we can be moved by similar fears.

The question is, are these fears of fraud and fakery real enough to put up with the illogic of the everyday illness assumption? Not when such fraud as there may be could easily be dealt with in other ways. Certainly not, given how the concern about fraud is typically used in the human rights context. It is significant, that is, that at no point did Dr. Baum accuse Ms. Ouimette of fraud or any form of misbehaviour. On the contrary, he granted that she had been unfairly treated by her employer. His claim was different — that since the flu is an everyday illness it was not discriminatory on the part of Lily Cup *to assume*, without argument or even the possibility of rebuttal, that Ms. Ouimette was a fraud or a malingerer (and so, a bad risk as an employee). Like many other entrenched stereotypes, this irrebuttable presumption that Lily Cup enjoyed is a hidden, but pernicious, form of handicapping.

Outside of human rights law, the everyday illness assumption plays a similar role. We insist that eligibility requirements for disability insurance, social assistance or other forms of disability programming must capture the true "target population", those whose conditions of dysfunctioning are biomedically verifiable and "substantial" enough to disqualify the fraudulent and malingering. Doubtless, there are disabilities that, as a society, we can, fairly and reasonably, expect people to put up with. Yet whenever we rely on generalizations about disabling consequences of everyday illnesses, we take the very real risk of misrepresenting the range of disabling consequences that are possible. In other words, unless we insist on individualized disability assessment, administrative convenience, financial pressure or some other constraint will motivate us to force people to put up with disabilities we should not in fairness expect of them.

Taken together, the two handicapping assumptions that can be distilled from the *Ouimette* case show the need for disability researchers to scrutinize with care the received rationale and administrative rationality of our disability social policy. We need to be careful because these assumptions are plausible — in restricted and somewhat artificial contexts, they are even true. Moreover, these assumptions are not the products of intentional prejudice or hatred or *mala fides*. As a culture, if anything, we are motivated by a general and not well articulated sense of sympathy and pity for people with disabilities. We are concerned about frauds and malingerers because they do not deserve our sympathy, and there are others who do.

For many researchers in disability policy, it is becoming increasingly clear that sensible and fair social policy for people with disabilities must escape from the influence of sympathy and pity — especially when handicapping assumptions such as voluntarism are the direct products of these unproductive but otherwise benign attitudes. What is urgently needed is a non-distorting, non-handicapping normative and attitudinal foundation for our social policy, one which flows directly from the moral and policy value of equality.[23]

Notes

1. *Ouimette v. Lily Cups Ltd.* (1990), 12 C.H.R.R. D/19.

2. (1990) R.S.O. H-19. The case was argued under the general anti-discrimination provision, section 4, as well as the constructive discrimination provision, section 10(1), which provides that "a right of a person ... is infringed where a requirement, qualification or factor exists that is not discrimination on a prohibited ground but that results in the exclusion, restriction or preference of a group of persons who are identified by a prohibited ground of discrimination and of whom the person is a member."

3. Discrimination "because of a handicap" is defined in section 9(1)(b) of the *Code* as "any degree of physical disability, infirmity, malformation or disfigurement that is caused by bodily injury, birth defect or illness".

4. See *Cameron v. Nel-Gor Castle Nursing Home* (1984), 5 C.H.R.R. D/2170 and *Chamberlin v. 599273 Ontario Limited* (1989), 11 C.H.R.R. D/110.

5. *Ontario Human Rights Commission v. Vogue Shoes* (1991), 14 C.H.R.R. D/425, at D/437.

6. In my book, *Physical Disability and Social Policy*, Toronto: University of Toronto Press, 1993, I consider the historical sources and policy ramifications of several such handicapping assumptions and provide a sustained defence of the research methodology upon which this paper relies.

7. See Dominique Le Disert, "Entre la peur et la pitié : Quelques aspects socio-historiques de l'infirmité", *International Journal of Rehabilitation Research*, 10(3), 1987, p. 253.

8. This historical connection has been made by several researchers, as I have discussed in *Physical Disability and Social Policy*, supra n. 6, Chapter 4.

9. World Health Organization, *International Classification of Impairments, Disabilities and Handicaps: A Manual of Classification Relating to the Consequences of Disease*, Geneva: WHO, 1980. See also the more refined version found in the Canadian Association for the ICIDH, "The Handicap Creation Process", *ICIDH International Network*, 4(2), 1991.

10. In Canada see *Horton v. Niagara (Regional Municipality)* (1987), 9 C.H.R.R. D/4611 (obesity is not a handicap "unless there is evidence that it was caused by bodily injury, birth defect or illness"); *Ontario Human Rights*

Commission v. Vogue Shoes (1991), 14 C.H.R.R. D/425 (it is unreasonable to find that obesity, "a common condition, widely considered to be within an individual's control, is actually a handicap"); and compare *La CDP v. Heroux et al.* (1981), 2 C.H.R.R. D/388. In the U.S. see *Greene v. Union Pacific Railroad Co.*, 548 F. Supp. 3 (1981) ("plaintiff was not handicapped within the contemplation of such statutes by his 'morbid obesity' since obesity was not an immutable condition"); and, along similar lines, *State Div. of Human Rights v. Xerox Corp.*, 480 N.E. (2d) 695 (1985).

11. See Deborah Stone, *The Disabled State*, Philadelphia: Temple University Press, 1984, and Henri-Jacques Stiker, "Categories organisatrices des visions du handicap", in Jean-Marc Alby and Patrick Sansoy (eds.), *Handicap, vécu, évalué*, Grenoble: La Pensée sauvage, 1987, p. 163.

12. See the U.S. Social Security eligibility cases *Stone v. Harris*, 657 F. 2d 210 (8th Cir. 1981), and *Harris v. Heckler*, 756 F. 2d 431 (6th Cir. 1985). But see *Johnson v. Secretary of Health and Human Services*, 794 F. 2d 1106 (6th Cir. 1986), which held, against the current, that obesity cannot be presumed to be remediable.

13. 485 U.S. 535.

14. 29 U.S.C. 794.

15. 42 U.S.C.S. ss. 12101-12189; 47 U.S.C.S. ss. 225 and 611. Section 104 of the *Americans with Disabilities Act* provides, however, that this exclusion does not apply to current alcohol abusers or to drug abusers who are being, or have been, rehabilitated.

16. See J. Bickenbach, "AIDS and Disability", in Christine Overall and William P. Zion (eds.), *Perspectives on AIDS*, Toronto: Oxford University Press, 1991, p. 13.

17. See the use of the assumption in *Taub v. Frank*, 957 F. 2d 8 (1st Cir., 1992). And consider the case of *Terrebonne v. Butler*, 848 F. 2d 500 (5th Cir., 1988), where the court, upholding a Louisiana law making trafficking in heroin punishable by a mandatory life sentence without parole, rejected the claim that addiction should be a mitigating circumstance by citing *Traynor* and stating, "We think it would be poor policy indeed to attach benefits to a voluntarily assumed and voluntarily disposable (admittedly with effort) addict status."

18. This is the principal legal finding of the earlier Supreme Court case *School Board of Nassau County, Florida, v. Arline*, 480 U.S. 273 (1987), a leading case on the interpretation of discrimination on the basis of disability. For a similar position in Canada, see the Supreme Court of Canada decision, *Ontario Human Rights Commission and O'Malley v. Simpsons-Sears Limited*, [1985] 2 S.C.R. 536.

19. For example, s. 9(1) of Ontario's *Code* defines "because of a handicap" as "for the reason that the person has or has had, or is believed to have or have had ... any degree of physical disability, infirmity, malformation or disfigurement". The *Americans with Disabilities Act* defines "disability" as "(A) a physical or mental impairment that substantially limits one or more of the major life activities of such individual; (B) a record of such an impairment; or (C) being regarded as having such an impairment".

20. *Hamlyn v. Cominco Ltd.* (1990), 11 C.H.R.R. D/333. A similar decision was reached in *Davison v. St. Paul Lutheran Home of Melville, Saskatchewan* (1992), 15 C.H.R.R. D/81, but was overturned by a higher court ((1992), 16 C.H.R.R. D/83) on the grounds that the human rights code of Saskatchewan, unlike most provinces, does include "perceived to have a disability" in its definition of

discrimination on the basis of disability. For other "perceived" cases see *Foucault v. C.N.R.* (1981), 2 C.H.R.R. D/475, *Brideau v. Air Canada* (1983), 4 C.H.R.R. D/1314, and *Biggs v. Hudson* (1988), 9 C.H.R.R.

21. *Forrisi v. Bowen*, 794 F. 2d 931 (4th Cir. 1986) at 934. The court went on to deny that Mr. Forrisi had been discriminated against because, though his employer fired him because of his perceived impairment (acrophobia), the employer did not perceive that impairment to be a substantial limitation of one of Mr. Forrisi's major life activities. Arguably, this is a complete distortion of the point of the "perceived to be" category of disability.

22. See in particular Stone, *The Disabled State*, supra n. 11, and Claire H. Liachowitz, *Disability as a Social Construct: Legislative Roots*, Philadelphia: University of Pennsylvania Press, 1988.

23. See *Physical Disability and Social Policy*, supra n. 6, Chapter 7; see also M.H. Rioux, "Towards a Concept of Equality of Well-Being: Overcoming the Social and Legal Construction of Inequality", *The Canadian Journal of Law and Jurisprudence*, 7(1), January 1994.

Chapter 6

Quality of Life: Questioning the Vantage Points for Research

by Michael Bach

Formal and informal support systems have not, by and large, secured what is commonly referred to as "quality of life" for people with intellectual disabilities. Services and supports have historically resulted in their exclusion from the mainstream of society: from communities, work, social and political participation and a level of income necessary to meet their basic and disability-related needs. Consequently, there have been calls from the advocacy, service provision, research and social policy communities to evaluate policies and programs according to the extent to which they result in increasing and ensuring the quality of life of people with intellectual disabilities. Such calls for service accountability are laudable. They reflect a recognition that the ways we have organized our policies and programs are in many instances seriously misguided. These calls also suggest a need for some standard of quality of life if we are to ensure accountability of service providers to individuals and accountability to society for the significant level of public resources allocated to providing supports.

But how are we to strike such a standard? What is quality of life to mean? In what features of a person's life does the "quality" lie, or in what features should it lie? Quality of life research in the field of intellectual disability — the volume of which is increasing at a rapid rate — offers very different answers to the latter question.

Yet it is a question that goes to the heart of how we think about policy, program and service system reform. What features of a person's life should count in determining the quality of their life? What features require intervention in order to increase quality? I am reluctant to put the question in such stark and mechanical terms. However, when we undertake to design and carry out quality of life research we are undertaking to make visible certain features of a person's life that we, as researchers, believe should be the site of intervention. Therefore, when we engage in quality of life research we are engaging in an enterprise in which the stakes are of the highest order. It is an enterprise that offers public policy makers, public program officials and service providers a way of thinking about people and their lives, about what interventions should be introduced into their lives and about how these interventions should be managed.

The purpose of this chapter is to address this question — how are we to "strike a standard" of quality of life? — from the perspective of the research community.[1] The research community has an obvious role in assisting advocacy organizations, service providers and policy makers in designing and carrying out evaluations of the impact of policy, programs and services on the quality of life of persons labelled as intellectually disabled. But we also have a role to play in clarifying what standard of quality of life should be used in such evaluations. It is essential that the research community become more aware that this latter role needs to be played, that it is being played and that we encourage open debate about how best to play it. Landesman presented such a challenge to the research community in the intellectual disability field a few years ago:

> [T]he process of defining quality of life and personal life satisfaction is likely to be fraught with difficulties and disagreements. Similarly, any group-generated criteria are vulnerable to criticism and challenge. These problems are not unique to our field nor are they sufficient reasons to avoid confronting this extremely important topic. Until we are willing to struggle with these global concepts and to propose tentative guidelines to permit valid comparisons across programs and people, we will have the same old controversies without any hope of improving our understanding of what truly fosters better lives.[2]

This chapter is written not to resolve the debate but in recognition of the fact that the "struggle" is ongoing. The approach we use in defining the indicators or standards of quality of life sets the parameters for conceiving the possible — conceiving what the lives of persons labelled as intellectually disabled should entail. Depending on the approach we use, these parameters may be widened and more inclusive of possibilities. Alternatively, they may be constrained, limiting our expectations as to the standards our policies, programs and services should be judged against. My overall purpose in this chapter is to argue for a social well-being approach to quality of life research, one that can make visible the roots of the systematic marginalization of people with intellectual disabilities in our society. In doing so, I will distinguish the approach from other broad approaches to quality of life research, critically examining them in the process. The four approaches to be discussed are:

- client satisfaction

- the functionalist approach

- the ecological approach

- a social well-being approach.

Client Satisfaction

A "client satisfaction" approach to quality of life research is based on the assumption that the source for understanding quality of a person's life lies in that person's own subjective sense of well-being. A large body of literature on subjective well-being and its psychological indicators developed during the 1970s.[3] On the basis of this approach a number of "life satisfaction" scales have been developed to measure people's sense of satisfaction using "feeling measures", which typically range from something such as "bad" to "happy". By itself this approach is clearly inadequate for measuring, let alone understanding, the realities of exclusion and victimization in the lives of people with intellectual disabilities. Further, research that has examined the relationship between subjective indicators of a person's environment and objective social indicators of the same environment has not found a positive relationship between the two sets of indicators.[4] This is not to suggest that objective social indicators are the only valid indicators but simply that subjective assessments are one among many perspectives on quality of life. An approach to quality of life research that excludes other perspectives is not able to expose the broader conditions underlying the person's status and relationship to his or her society.

Although there are few who would now advocate an exclusive reliance on client satisfaction indicators of quality of life, it is still essential that the perspective of the subject whose quality of life is in question appear in the research. The question is how. A client satisfaction approach tends to construct the person as a consumer of services, as a passive recipient of their environment and as a meter of feelings and responses. The strategy of the research in this approach is simply to "read the meter". A person's agency, his or her interaction with the environment and larger society and the different perceptions about who the person is — perceptions that structure the delivery of funding and services — do not serve as sources for understanding the quality of a person's life.

As an exclusive approach to quality of life research, then, the client satisfaction approach raises some insurmountable dilemmas. The lens of this approach is wide enough only to read a meter of subjective responses. It is unable to see a whole person and the conditions structuring his or her life. Therefore, the conception of quality of life rendered is at best unacceptably relativistic in ethical terms and at worst a denial of what are known to be basic conditions of quality of life, conditions that a client satisfaction approach may not make visible.

The Functionalist Approach

The limitation of the client satisfaction approach, the reduction to a singular perspective, is the same limitation found in the set of approaches to quality of life research that views the person from a so-called objective standpoint of "normal" social roles, "typical" behaviours or "basic" needs. This broad category encompasses within it many approaches to quality of life research and these approaches are unified in the sense that there is assumed to be an objective set of standards that the research community can construct to guide research.

The concept of the person represented in this approach is radically different from the previous approach but just as limited. Where the client satisfaction approach assumes that the person defines him or herself by virtue of his or her feelings, the objective approach is based on an assumption that the person is defined entirely by socially established categories of role, behaviour and needs. This draws its logic and its justification from functionalist social theory in which valued social roles, behaviours and needs are evident: they are required for a well-ordered and functioning society. Indicators of quality of life can then be objectively defined, not from the perspective of the individual whose quality of life is in question but from some other transcendant, so-called objective standpoint.

Philosophers and policy analysts who work within the boundaries of this tradition hold out for the possibility that there is a list of objective roles, behaviours and basic needs, the fulfillment of which would count as minimum indicators of quality of life. They reject a "preference" or subjective approach to defining need, as is the case with the client satisfaction approach. In contrast, objectively determined basic needs, or what Braybrooke has defined as "course of life needs", do not depend on preferences. Instead, according to Braybrooke, "People have a need for exercise regardless of whether they wish, prefer, want otherwise, or choose. They have the need even if they do not much care to live or be healthy."[5]

131

What does the history of society's relationship to people with intellectual disabilities tell us about so-called objective roles, behaviours and needs. They have been a ruse. They have been used to exclude certain groups from economic, social and political life. The underlying limitation of this approach is that certain actors and certain processes are given the power to define the needs of others, or their appropriate place in society, in accordance with certain assumptions that are never made fully explicit. Conceptually, this approach makes some advance over the client satisfaction approach. It moves beyond indicators of quality of life that are based simply on subjective "feeling" measures. But it raises as many problems as it solves. Who is to define need? Who is to have the power to define need? From where are we to obtain our guidance in constructing indicators of quality of life?

A variation of strictly objective methodology in constructing quality of life indicators is to use what have been defined as "community standards".[6] A community standards framework does not begin with an outside, imported standard but with the standards that relevant communities themselves articulate. A community may be a service delivery agency whose mission statement and strategic plans provide a "community" consensus about what are to serve as standards. A number of sources may be drawn upon to construct these standards including government statutory frameworks, the policy and program guidelines of funding agencies and the goals articulated by consumers being served, their friends and families.

This framework can draw its philosophical roots, to some extent, from the communitarian approach in moral and political philosophy. To the extent that our community standards accord with the valued traditions in our community is the extent to which the standards can be justified. Although they do not deal with quality of life research in the field of intellectual disability, proponents of a communitarian philosophy, such as MacIntyre and Sandel, point towards communitarianism as a corrective to the "shallow liberalism" that underlies approaches such as client satisfaction where "anything goes".[7] The basic argument is that, without some appeal to community traditions, we are in danger of slipping into an "ethical relativism" where one conception of quality of life is as good as the next. Yet we know at an intuitive level, as MacIntyre and Sandel know, this is not the case. Some conceptions *are* better than others.

The danger, however, with a communitarian approach, as many have pointed out,[8] is that the traditions of communities cannot always serve as a standard because it is precisely those traditions that have been used to justify the exclusion and marginalization of certain groups. The history of society's treatment of people with intellectual disabilities, whether we refer to institutionalization or to conflicts over placement of group homes in the community, is a case in point. If we go beyond geographical communities and think about communities of interests, the same problem applies when it comes to appealing naively to community tradition as a source of standards. Within the movement of organizations advocating for people with intellectual disabilities and the system of service and support providers to people with intellectual disabilities, there can be diametrically opposed assumptions about what constitutes quality of life and the services required to achieve it. Simple appeal to community tradition or community consensus about what is to constitute quality of life seems entirely inadequate in the face of what we know about the relationship between communities, however defined, and people with intellectual disabilities. Communities have been parochial and exclusionary in the past. They will likely continue to be so in the future.

There are fundamental dilemmas, then, with the client satisfaction and the functionalist approach to quality of life research. The former renders a conception of quality of life that does justice, possibly, to the standpoint of the individual who is the subject but can in the process pay little attention to conditions of quality of life such as income, education and adequate housing, the importance of which we would all accept. In attempting to correct the limitations of the client satisfaction approach, the functionalist approach, which is defined by an emphasis on normal social roles, typical behaviours or basic needs, dismisses the standpoint of the individual in favour of some transcendant standpoint. The latter is obtained either by the definitional fiat of an objectivist and positivist methodology or by community standards. In either event, this standpoint becomes vested with the power to define the normal, the typical and the basic. However, the roles people want to play and the needs they have cannot be determined *a priori*. These roles and needs are the subject of struggle, conflict, adaptation and ongoing interpretation.[9] "Normal" and "typical" quickly become "realistic", "acceptable" and "required" — categories that become the basis of service delivery decisions and are written into policy. It is by proceeding through such a logic that policy and service delivery have come to secure exclusion rather than an acceptance of difference and the inclusion of people with intellectual disabilities.

The Ecological Approach

There has been a substantial body of quality of life research in the field of intellectual disability that draws on what has been termed an "ecological" approach.[10] The ecological approach seeks to address the dilemmas raised when either the subjective perspective of the person *or* the objective assessment of the environment are drawn upon exclusively to investigate quality of life. In this approach, quality of life is seen as the degree of "fit" between a person and his or her environment, between a person's expectations in his or her environment and the resources that environment provides to the person. "Environment" in an ecological approach has been defined in a number of ways to include the social supports in a person's life, the settings in which he or she lives and works, and the broader policy environment that regulates the provision of supports and services.

In recognizing that a person cannot be separated from his or her environment, this approach makes substantial advances over the client satisfaction and functionalist approaches. However, it provides no way of judging what the relationship between a person and his or her environment or society *should* look like, because it is not founded on an ethical framework. It rests squarely on a naive positivism in which it is assumed that degrees of positive and negative person-environment "fit" or environmental "stressors" can be measured and that this information will provide a basis for designing environments. There are ecological studies that critically examine the residential and other environments in which adults with an intellectual disability are supported, from ethical standpoints such as that of self-determination.[11] But the importation of ethics into the ecological approach is at odds with its exclusively positivist foundations. The ethical standpoints are not constituted as part of the methodological framework of the approach. Therefore, there is no basis within the methodology for guiding the selection of ethical standpoints to judge the person-environment relationships being explored.

This is the risk the ecological approach runs. It takes seriously the person-environment relationship, but provides no way of judging whether or not some environments, regardless of the ways in which people are able to "fit" into them, are acceptable from an ethical standpoint. We could have very well-run institutions for people with intellectual disabilities, very efficient segregated schools and sheltered workshops that provide intensive vocational training. If in carrying out quality of life research we seek to examine these and other environments from an ethical standpoint, as Bercovici does, we have moved beyond the ecological approach, even if we draw on some of the methods it furnishes. We have moved to what we might term a social well-being approach.

A Social Well-Being Approach

In the sections above I have critically examined different assumptions about what constitutes the "quality" in a person's life.

Does a person's quality of life reside in their experience of satisfaction, of feeling good: the higher the "feeling good" quotient, the higher the quality of life? Does it reside in their adaptation to certain "objective" standards of roles, behaviours or needs? Is it in the degree of "fit" with the environments in which they happen to find themselves? In exploring the quality of life of persons with intellectual disabilities, all these assumptions contribute something to a valid approach. However, when used exclusively to guide a methodological framework for quality of life research, each has limitations that bring into question the research methodologies based upon them.

A fourth approach is to consider "quality" as inhering in or residing in a person's social well-being — that is, in the nature and the quality of the relationship of a person to the society in which he or she lives. This goes beyond the person-environment "fit" of the ecological approach to quality of life and it goes beyond an examination of social relationships, social networks, personal relationships and other psychosocial indicators.[12]

How do we *do*, conceptually and methodologically, a social well-being approach to quality of life research? In adopting this approach we are asking about *social* well-being, about the relationship of persons to their society and about the "wellness" of this relationship. As a result of asking the questions in this way we must acknowledge that we are entering the territory of legal and ethical principles, simply because there are very different ways in which persons can be related to their society. What the relationship should be is, fundamentally, a normative question. To ask about quality of life within a social well-being approach, then, is to ask a question that cannot be divorced from ethics.

So we need an ethical framework. At the end of the 20th century, in what ethical framework do we situate ourselves to examine the relationship of persons to society? We are in an era where liberal democracy is increasingly the guiding political vision globally and liberal justice is one of the central, guiding moral visions. However, our current liberal democracies and standard conceptions of the liberal moral vision seem ill-equipped to respond to the challenges posed by growing social differences and diversity of social identities organized along the boundaries of ethnicity, language, gender, race, class and disability. Why are they ill-equipped? It is due to the fact that liberal democracies and liberal justice have relied to a large extent on an inadequate conception of the person and an understanding that society only has a residual responsibility to ensure the conditions of quality of life for persons. The 20th century has seen a sustained challenge to these ideas, to what might be called "shallow liberalism". The labour movement, the civil rights movement, the women's movement, the disability movement and other new social movements have challenged the notion of the "rugged individual" on which our liberal democracies, to a great extent, have been built. They have challenged the notion that the person is essentially separate, independent of the claims and relationships others wish to have on him or her; a self-determining being whose personhood rests in an instrumental rationality, where everything and every being beyond the person exists simply as a means to his or her ends. These movements of people and ideas have also challenged the idea that society's responsibility to enable self-determination must be cast inevitably as a very limited responsibility.[13]

The claims of these movements have often been misread. It is often assumed that in attacking shallow liberalism they are attacking the core principle of liberalism, the self-determination of the person. Often they are attacking instead the lack of conditions available to different groups to realize their self-determination — whether this be adequate income, access to education or protection of the right to be free from discrimination. These movements themselves have also attacked liberalism but, as Dunn has written, these critics "are fundamentally undecided as to whether they have come to destroy liberalism or to fulfil it."[14] The women's movement is a case in point. In advocating for free abortion clinics the movement is challenging the current institutional arrangements for delivering health services but doing so in the name of realizing the principle of self-determination: access to free abortions as a condition of women's right to control their own bodies.

If we adopt the moral framework of liberalism as a guide to selecting an ethical standpoint, how are we to think about social well-being or the relationship that persons *should* have to their society? One could trace the many sources of the moral vision of liberalism, a task undertaken by others. However, serious philosophers of liberalism and community in the 20th century agree on basic points. These points have received their most influential elaboration in the 20th century in the work of John Rawls.[15]

First, self-determination of the person is a core principle and value and it should be expressed not as an end in itself. People should be self-determining with respect to their life plans — that is, people should be able to make choices about what will be significant in their lives and about how they will go about living out their lives. There are important debates among libertarians and communitarians about the extent to which individuals are free to choose what will be of significance to them, given their ties to community, cultural and specific historical epochs. However, that people should be free to have life plans with significance for them is a point of agreement in these debates.

Second, people are not able to develop or realize their life plans — plans that are a mark of their self-determination — without certain conditions, or what Rawls has referred to as "primary goods", such as basic human rights, needed goods and services and responsibilities to others. Philosophers, policy makers and social movements are in continual struggle over the definition of what constitutes the conditions or primary goods necessary for persons to live out their life plans. There is, however, agreement on one point: governments have a responsibility to ensure that the basic conditions are in place.

Third, when self-determination is conceived as the realization of a person's own life plans, it cannot be conceived apart from social justice; hence, liberalism is also about social justice. In particular, it is

about ensuring a just distribution among individuals and g₁
the goods or conditions they require to realize their life plans. Alth   ₁
justice may be a virtue of individuals, in the context of the moral and
political vision of liberalism, social justice is an attribute of society's
institutions. Governments are not only responsible for ensuring that
the conditions of self-determination are in place, they are also
responsible for ensuring that the institutional arrangements that make
these conditions available result in a just distribution of the conditions
among individuals and groups.[16]

In summary, self-determination as the development and
realization of freely chosen life plans, societal responsibility for
ensuring conditions to realize life plans and justice in the distribution
of these conditions are elements of a social well-being approach to
examining quality of life. In what features of a person's life do we
assume that quality lies when we use a social well-being approach?
The quality lies in the presence in a person's life of a set of conditions
for developing and realizing a life plan of his or her own choosing.
The level of quality of life depends, then, on the degree to which
the conditions necessary for a person or group of persons to develop
and realize life plans are distributed to them in ways that accord
with principles of social justice and just distribution. Therefore, our
conceptions of quality of life are intimately connected to our
conceptions of justice. If we do not formulate our questions from
the standpoint of justice, we run the risk of entrenching and
justifying, through quality of life research, the immense injustices
people with an intellectual disability face in society today. This is
the risk run by the three approaches to quality of life research
outlined above.

Moral philosophy aside, what does this social well-being
approach mean for doing quality of life research in the domain of
services and supports to persons with intellectual disabilities? Most
importantly, this approach suggests an alternative line of research
questions to guide quality of life research, questions that flow from
each of the three elements of social well-being outlined above.

Self-determined and "authentic" life plans

There is a whole avenue of questions to pursue with respect to life plans. Policies, programs and delivery of services to people with disabilities have latched onto the idea of individual planning and programming in the past 20 years. But this has usually been an exercise carried out within the context of the first three approaches to quality of life discussed above. If people seem "happy" where they are, or do not seem to resist what is happening, a plan to keep them where they are regardless of whether or not they are confined to an institution can be justified. If people's behaviours do not accord with "adaptive behaviour" standards, they should receive a plan that lays out the adaptive behaviour as the goal and includes the strategies that will be adopted to get there — regardless of whether or not the adaptive behaviour reflects a person's life plan and regardless of whether or not the strategies to get there are "aversive".

A community standards approach has also been used to circumscribe the life plans of people with disabilities and people with intellectual disabilities in particular. This is evident, for instance, in the vocational training area where vocational counsellors or providers determine the boundaries of the "realistic" vocational goals that people will be supported to pursue. "Realistic" depends on assumptions about the local labour market and the prevailing assumptions about the place of people with intellectual disabilities in the labour market. As a consequence, these goals usually consign people with intellectual disabilities to, at best, life-long training programs in sheltered workshops and, for the lucky few, poorly paid entry level jobs.[17]

In a social well-being approach, the status of life plans differs substantially from these approaches. A life plan is not a technical exercise managed by an interdisciplinary team of professional care-givers. A life plan is a narrative of a person's past and present circumstances and future hopes, a narrative that is a condition for a coherent self. The concept of self as narratively structured, coming into being only within the context of a story woven of past, present and future, is gaining increasing credence in moral philosophy,[18] social psychology[19] and medical ethics.[20] In this vein, Joan Didion has written about feeling as though she had mislaid her "script" when she experienced the onset of multiple sclerosis:

> I was supposed to hear cues, and no longer did. I was meant to know the plot, but all I knew was what I saw: flash pictures in variable sequence, images with no 'meaning' beyond their temporary arrangement, not a movie but a cutting room experience ... We tell ourselves stories in order to live ... [With the onset of multiple sclerosis I] began to doubt the premises of all the stories I had ever told myself.[21]

As Carolyn Heilbrun has suggested, the narrative structure of the self means that we can reflect critically on the "scripts" by which we have lived and write new ones, new scripts of possibility.[22] This narrative approach to the birth of the self suggests that the life plan, central to realizing the ideal of self-determination, can be seen as the narrative that people put together about their lives (or that is put together for them), about who they are, where they have come from and what they want. How this narrative is put together and the choices it reflects is then a central issue for a social well-being approach to quality of life.

From the wide-ranging body of literature cited above one can see two key ethical principles that could be useful in framing research questions about life plans in the context of quality of life research in the field of intellectual disability. These two principles can be referred to as the "ethic of authenticity" and a "narrative ethic". Taylor articulates the sources of what he terms the ethic of authenticity in philosophers who fashioned the liberal vision and its implications for a view of individuals as self-determining beings. These are philosophers such as Descartes, Kant, Rousseau, Locke and John Stuart Mill. To be authentically human, according to Taylor, is to acknowledge that:

> [t]here is a certain way of being human that is *my* way. I am called upon to live my life in this way, and not in imitation of anyone else's ... This is the background understanding to the modern ideal of authenticity, and to the goals of self-fulfillment or self-realization in which it is usually couched.[23]

There are a number of issues surrounding what choices within a life plan can be considered *authentic*. This is where philosophers working in the communitarian tradition, such as Taylor, have made a major contribution to the theory of liberalism. It is a contribution suggesting that unless the traditions, values and issues that are present in our historical context, that transcend our individual person, are taken into account in conceiving of the self-determining person, we will have a shallow liberalism, one in which any "self-choice" is as good as another. As Taylor writes:

> [U]nless some options are more significant than others, the very idea of self-choice falls into triviality and hence incoherence. Only if I exist in a world in which history, or the demands of nature, or the needs of my fellow human beings, or the duties of citizenship, or the call of God, or something else of this order matters crucially, can I define an identity for myself that is not trivial. Authenticity is not the enemy of demands that emanate from beyond the self; it supposes such demands.[24]

Communitarian philosophy provides a way of thinking about self-determination that does not necessarily slide into an ethical relativism where any choice of action can be considered as valuable as the next. This understanding of an authentic life plan within a framework of social well-being substantially challenges the claims that people with intellectual disabilities could make authentic life plans to live in institutionalized forms of support that cut them off from the bonds of community and the duties and opportunities that come with citizenship. The parameters within which we exercise our self-determination are not entirely open ended.

The notion of a "narrative ethic" has emerged as an approach within medical ethics[25] to deal with difficulties in medical decision making, especially when it comes to medical decisions related to the withdrawal or refusal of treatment. A patient's narrative that is defined by a history of diagnoses, medical decisions and treatments — the narrative form usually produced through the health care system — obliterates the personal history, relationships and hopes for the future that are the stuff of a narrative of a past and future self. When people are viewed by the health care system through the former narrative structure, they lose their particularity, their particular life histories. The process of labelling, through diagnoses and a history of treatments, is a process of fitting the person into a general framework of categories through which the health care system can frame an appropriate response. In such a scheme, the standard for appropriate medical decisions is related to whether the treatment corresponds to the person, not as an individual with a particular narrative history and future, but as one instance within a generalized category of diagnosis. Miles suggests that a narrative ethic "shifts the weight of the standard for evaluating ethics problems from 'well-reasoned solutions' to 'well-lived lives.'"[26]

A narrative ethic makes visible that there is not only one narrative of the person, there can be many and these narratives can be conflicting. This is clearly the case in the provision of services to people with intellectual disabilities. In some quality of life research in the field, the point has been made that capacities, needs and behaviours of persons, and their past and future hopes, can be seen in very different ways depending on who is producing the "story" about the person: professional care-givers; government social workers; family members; or the person him or herself.[27] Very different consequences can result depending on whose story is given recognition in the service system.

These two ethical principles, the ethic of authenticity and the narrative ethic, generate a number of useful questions for quality of life research within a social well-being framework. Which narratives of the person are produced and given recognition? Do any of these narratives approximate an authentic life plan for the person? What is the framework of options a person is supported to experience and from which they are supported to express preferences? What are the expectations of those around people with intellectual disabilities, in terms of the person's needs and possibilities for the future? To what extent does the standard of authenticity drive the ways in which people come to know the person labelled as intellectually disabled? To what extent is an authentic narrative of the person a guiding force in funding and service delivery? The list could go on. The point here is to suggest a line of questioning for quality of life research that does not emerge from the other approaches outlined above.

There are a few examples of research in the field of intellectual disability that focus on quality of life and life plans. Brown et al. identify "the building of life plans" as an important quality of life outcome. In a study of rehabilitation agencies, the researchers suggest that this outcome resulted from changes in the way a set of vocational rehabilitation services organized the provision of their service. The changes included encouraging workers to support persons within the "orbit" of a person's family, community and wider interests outside of the segregated vocational settings that had been the previous model for provision of support. These connections expanded people's options for choice and responded to vocational interests that persons had not expressed or been able to pursue within the segregated vocational settings. Life planning was not a technical exercise managed by the agency. Instead, the fact that persons were beginning to build their own life plans became evident in their comments after the reorganization of services. They had, in other words, begun to produce alternative stories about themselves which did not, according to the researchers, "necessarily lead to a quieter life for others in the person's life; it [could] bring greater noise and anxiety."[28]

The conditions for developing and realizing life plans

Rawls has defined the set of primary goods necessary as conditions for realizing life plans as rights and liberties, opportunities and powers, income and wealth, and a sense of one's own worth.[29] As indicated above, the task of defining the conditions for which there is social or governmental responsibility to create availability is never completely fixed. Our understanding of what the conditions are is based on an understanding of the kinds of life plans people make. These plans change depending on the "horizons of significance", as Taylor refers to them, that appear in different regional, cultural and historical contexts. One of the tasks of quality of life research, then, must be to continually examine the fit between the life plans people develop and the conditions that are required to enable their development and realization.

In this regard, Kymlicka has argued that in our era, where there is an increasing pluralism of cultural groups seeking recognition of language and cultural rights, we must recognize cultural structure and cultural membership as a primary social good within the Rawlsian framework. This is because:

> [t]he processes by which options and choices become significant for use are linguistic and historical processes. Whether or not a course of action has any significance for us depends on whether, or how, our language renders vivid to us the point of that activity ... [Cultural structure] is a [primary] good in its capacity of providing meaningful options for us, and aiding our ability to judge for ourselves the value of our life-plans.[30]

Similarly, there is a growing recognition within the intellectual disability field that people labelled as intellectually disabled, and their families, may require information, decision-making assistance and advocacy support if they are to formulate plans, identify needed supports and negotiate appropriate service packages.[31] As such, an argument could be constructed that such supports are primary goods when it comes to people with disabilities. Our task as researchers in quality of life, committed to social well-being, must include critical reflection on the indexes of social indicators that are available. If we seek to do justice to the circumstances of people's lives, and to their hopes and possibilities, we must continually investigate the life plans that people are choosing and the conditions necessary to realize these plans.

A just distribution of conditions

A third area of research we must pursue within a social well-being framework has to do with the determination of appropriate principles or criteria of just distribution of the conditions necessary for developing and realizing life plans. This is an area of considerable debate in moral philosophy and social policy. Should goods or conditions be distributed according to criteria of equality, need, merit or some other criterion? For our purposes as researchers into quality of life and intellectual disability, this is not an insurmountable problem. We can enter the shifting terrain of moral philosophy and the debates about what *should* constitute valid principles of justice. There has been recent work on what justice requires when it comes to people with disabilities and the argument has been made that justice must be seen as equality.[32] As researchers we need not enter the shifting terrain of moral philosophy to justify certain kinds of principles over others. We can look at our own societies and governments and ask what principles of just distribution have been institutionalized in our constitutions, in our statutes, through case law and in policy frameworks. Our role is not to develop principles of justice. It is to apply existing principles to the distribution of conditions or goods in society and to make this application from the vantage point of people with an intellectual disability.

This is not to suggest that the task of identifying existing criteria of justice is a simple one. On the contrary, it is made difficult by the conflicts over interpretations of valid criteria, conflicts that exist within governments, between governments and the courts and between both of these and different social movements. What this means is that there is no transcendant, objective, scientifically "pure" standpoint from which to make judgements about people's quality of life. The standpoints from which we must make these judgements are rooted in history, in the principles we have adopted in constitutional, statutory and case law and in the daily struggles over what social justice requires both in terms of basic conditions and in terms of the distribution of basic conditions. Hence, in a social well-being approach, quality of life research cannot be carried out in a policy vacuum. As researchers we can draw on interpretations of what justice requires, interpretations being put forward by advocacy movements, the courts and so on to challenge dominant interpretations. We can examine the degree of fit between the criteria of justice and the actual circumstances of people's lives.[33]

In summary, the meaning of quality of life is at the heart of current debates about the service system and about how people should be supported to participate in all aspects of social, economic, cultural and political life. I have argued that the prevailing approaches to quality of life research in the field of intellectual disability have missed some critical questions — questions that must be asked if we are to make visible the systematic marginalization of people with intellectual disabilities in our society. I have suggested that a social well-being approach, rooted in a moral vision of liberalism that is committed to self-determination, the possibility of authentic lives and social justice, provides such an approach.

However, in adopting a social well-being approach we are moving into new territory, both in terms of the intellectual roots of the field of disability (those in moral philosophy and ethics) and in terms of the demands such an approach will make upon us as researchers. No longer can we assume that the test of validity of our research questions and approaches lies in taking up some transcendant, objective, scientifically pure standpoint. In order to examine the quality of life of persons from the perspective of their social well-being, we must enter the fray of history. We must be attuned to people's own vision of the "good life". In carrying out our research we must deploy ourselves to the courts, to the legislatures and to the disability and other human rights movements in order to gain a better understanding of the struggles over what justice is to mean and what its requirements are. If we must enter these struggles and take a position, because of our own commitments, so be it. We are often better able to understand the nature of these struggles when we see them from the inside looking out. Finally, quality of life research, at its best, should be about public policy. It should be about the ways in which society organizes and distributes the conditions for people to lead authentic lives.

Notes

1. A version of this paper was presented at the Ninth Congress of the International Association for the Scientific Study of Mental Deficiency, Australia, 1992.

2. Sharon Landesman, "Quality of Life and Personal Life Satisfaction: Definition and Measurement Issues", *Mental Retardation*, 24(3), 1986, pp. 141-143.

3. For a review of this literature see E. Diener, "Subjective Well-Being", *Psychological Bulletin*, 95(3), 1984, pp. 542-575.

4. S. Lewis and L. Lyon, "The Quality of Community and the Quality of Life", *Sociological Spectrum*, 6, 1986, pp. 397-410.

5. See David Braybrooke, *Meeting Needs*, Princeton, N.J.: Princeton University Press, 1987, p. 32.

6. Peter Penz, "Normative Issues in Social Needs Assessment: A Theoretical Overview", *Faculty Research Papers*, Toronto: Faculty of Environmental Studies, York University, 1987.

7. See Alisdair MacIntyre, *After Virtue*, Notre Dame: University of Notre Dame Press, 1981; Alisdair MacIntyre, *Whose Justice? Which Rationality?*, Notre Dame: University of Notre Dame Press, 1988; M. Sandel, *Liberalism and the Limits of Justice*, Cambridge: Cambridge University Press, 1982.

8. See Will Kymlicka, *Liberalism, Community, and Culture*, Oxford: Clarendon Press, 1989.

9. That "needs" are not fixed and immutable entities, but rather the outcome of a social, political and cultural process has been argued by social scientists and moral philosophers alike. See William Leiss, *Limits to Satisfaction: Needs and*

Commodities, London: Boyars, 1978; Selya Benhabib, *Critique, Norm and Utopia: A Study of the Critical Foundations of Society*, New York: Columbia University Press, 1986.

10. See S. Landesman-Dwyer, "Living in the Community", *American Journal of Mental Deficiency*, 86, pp. 223-234; K.S. Keith, R.L. Schalock and K. Hoffman, "Quality of Life: Measurement and Programmatic Implication", *Region V Mental Retardation Series*, Nebraska City, Nebr., 1986; S.A. Murrell and F.H. Norris, "Quality of Life as the Criterion for Need Assessment and Community Psychology", *Journal of Community Psychology*, 11, April 1983, pp. 88-97.

11. See, for example, S. Bercovici, *Barriers to Normalization: The Restrictive Management of Retarded Persons*, Baltimore, Md.: University Park Press, 1983.

12. The concept of social well-being as an aim that defines the basic ethical commitments of a society, and the implications of this concept for public policy analysis, has been developed in a series of papers by l'Institut Roeher Institute. See L'Institut Roeher Institute, *Social Well-Being: A Paradigm for Reform*, North York, Ont.: Author, 1993.

13. See Iris Marion Young, *Justice and the Politics of Difference*, Princeton, N.J.: Princeton University Press, 1990.

14. J. Dunn, *Western Political Theory in the Face of the Future*, Cambridge, Mass.: Cambridge University Press, 1979, p. 28.

15. See John Rawls, *A Theory of Justice*, Cambridge, Mass.: Harvard University Press, 1971.

16. Ibid.

17. For an examination of how employment-related policy works to ensure this form of exclusion and these consequences

see L'Institut Roeher Institute, *On Target? Canada's Employment-Related Programs for Persons with Disabilities*, North York, Ont.: Author, 1992.

18. See MacIntyre, *After Virtue*, 1981 (see n. 7); Benhabib, *Critique, Norm, and Utopia*, 1986 (see n. 9); Charles Taylor, *Sources of the Self: The Making of the Modern Identity*, Cambridge, Mass.: Harvard University Press, 1989.

19. See, for example, Jessica Benjamin, *The Bonds of Love: Psychoanalysis, Feminism, and the Problem of Domination*, New York: Pantheon, 1988.

20. See, for example, H. Brody, *Stories of Sickness*, New Haven: Yale University Press, 1987; Eric Cassell, "Recognizing Suffering", *Hastings Centre Report*, 21(3), 1991, pp. 24-31; Carl Elliot, "Literature and Psychiatry", *Current Opinion in Psychiatry*, 4, pp. 753-757.

21. See Joan Didion, *The White Album*, New York: Penguin, 1979. Cited in Carl Elliot, "Literature and Psychiatry", *Current Opinion in Psychiatry*, 4, 1991, p. 753.

22. Carolyn Heilbrun, *Writing a Woman's Life*, New York: Ballantine, 1988.

23. Charles Taylor, *The Malaise of Modernity*, Concord, Ont.: Anansi Press, 1991, pp. 28-29.

24. Ibid., p. 39.

25. See especially S.H. Miles, "The Case: A Story Found and Lost", *Second Opinion*, 15, 1990, pp. 55-59.

26. Ibid.

27. See, for example, L'Institut Roeher Institute, *The Power to Choose: An Examination of Service Brokerage and Individualized Funding as Implemented by the Community Living Society*, North York, Ont.: Author, 1991.

28. Roy Brown, Max Bayer and Patricia Brown, "Quality of Life: A Challenge for Rehabilitation Agencies", *Australia and New Zealand Journal of Developmental Disabilities*, 14 (3 and 4), pp. 189-199.

29. Rawls, *A Theory of Justice*, 1971 (see n. 15), p. 92.

30. Kymlicka, *Liberalism, Community, and Culture*, 1989 (see n. 8), pp. 165-166.

31. See L'Institut Roeher Institute, *The Power to Choose, 1991* (see n. 27); Brian Salisbury, Jo Dickey and Cameron Crawford, *Service Brokerage: Individual Empowerment and Social Service Accountability*, North York, Ont.: L'Institut Roeher Institute, 1987; Ontario, Ministry of the Attorney General, *You've Got a Friend: A Review of Advocacy in Ontario*, Toronto, 1987.

32. See, for example, Marcia H. Rioux, *The Equality-Disability Nexus* (forthcoming).

33. L'Institut Roeher Institute in North York, Canada, has carried out a number of research studies that explicitly examine the degree of fit between a set of ethical standards related to self-determination, autonomy and equality, and the actual policy arrangements and outcomes in the lives of people with disabilities. Studies by The Institute in this vein include: *Income Insecurity: The Disability Income System in Canada*, 1988; *Poor Places: Disability-Related Residential and Support Services*, 1990; *The Power to Choose*, 1991; and *On Target?*, 1992.

Chapter 7

Naming and Renaming Persons with Intellectual Disabilities

by Fred E. Stockholder

Introduction

I wrote this chapter for two audiences:

1. the people who form and execute social policy in practical ways — administrators, government officials, members of community organizations and ordinary citizens who are drawn into the process of social change; and

2. scholars, researchers, and students who are interested in the problems of social movements.

The central question I am trying to examine and answer is, "What do I call a person who is said to be 'mentally retarded'?" The answer here is that it depends primarily on the state of the public mind. For the people who must make practical language choices, I offer advice on how to name. This advice is drawn from the long tradition of language discussion. The use of language in public life has always been problematic. None of the advice given here can make language less problematic. People will always find their own methods of changing language, making their own choices as they speak and write. I hope to give readers useful thoughts about the nature of language change and naming.

A Theory of Names and Naming

Modern philosophers refer to words, names and utterances of some length as "speech acts". When we use an old speech act or when we create a new one, we are concerned with its definition, its reference and its more expressive existence in social exchanges. Speech acts live in complicated aggregates of meaning. Any single act may have a history of which the users are aware. The context of the speech act creates and alters the dictionary and historical meaning. Therefore, when the words "moron" and "retarded" became speech acts, when they moved into conversation and print, when they entered children's street and school yard encounters and when they were spoken in lawyers' arguments and reformers' pleadings, the words accumulated ugly meanings which named and formed new social relations. "Moron" and "retarded" began their lives as clinical terms introduced by physicians, administrators and reformers who wanted to create humane conditions for people who, labelled with earlier names, would have endured lesser lives. Despite these good intentions, the new names became terms of abuse. Today, "retard" is a form of insult without clinical meaning. "Moron", which originally meant a person who had a low IQ, came to be a mislabelling of a group as sexual degenerates.

How are we to understand these alterations of meaning? One group of language theorists talks about the result of language limits. Benjamin Lee Whorf and Edward Sapir noted that we are limited in what we can think by the available language. People who live in the Arctic, they observed, have as many as 18 words for snow. We, who have fewer, are unable to think about snow with as much complexity. The Hopi people have fewer words related to time than people living in industrial cultures. The Sapir/Whorf thesis concerning Hopi people asserts that they are unable think about time in the various ways Europeans do so easily. The outcome in Hopi/European relations is a series of misunderstandings about time.

The Sapir/Whorf thesis almost explains what happened to the word "moron". The clinical word for low IQ was precise and polite language, but it did not quite support the thoughts of many people about a person with a low IQ. In speech acts, unexpressed thought was brought into play and the word carried the new load of meaning. Ultimately, the Sapir/Whorf thesis breaks down in this kind of speech situation because the thesis is customarily used to discuss language in stable and slowly changing social orders. The theorists believed, furthermore, that the word limited thought about the conception behind the word, that language imprisoned thinking inside the words. This notion can only be partially true because what happened to the word "moron" shows that something else is going on.

Goddard, the inventor of the term, believed that people labelled as "morons" were criminal, sexually deviant and generally evil. Many people shared his belief. The Sapir/Whorf thesis accounts mainly for speech situations in which the conceptions behind the words are fixed. The word "moron" was designed to give a scientific limit to meanings attached to the word. According to their thesis, those who had the designation were supposed, thereby, to be protected from cruelty. The belief system behind the word, unlike that behind the Hopi words for time, was filled with the punishing hostility found in 19th-century social engineering. That is why when we examine the limiting powers of language (the Sapir/Whorf thesis), we must also examine the ideological character of the thought found in speech acts and examine the thoughts behind and beyond the language.

Ideology is central to the problem of naming. The Hopis, as we just noted, have a slowly changing social formation. The fixity of basic assumptions in Hopi thinking is very different from thought in modern industrial societies. The intellectual systems of modern societies seem unable to last the 20-year span by which we measure generations. The resulting intellectual life shapes itself ideologically: we all reason with idea systems which, however fervently we hold them, tend to be temporary. They are temporary because the intellectual life in a dynamic society constantly reveals the errors of our beliefs.

Sometimes ideology is called false consciousness, but here I am including in the term other meanings introduced by thinkers such as Erik Erikson. Erikson talks about the ideology necessary in late adolescence if a youth is to move into coherent maturity. The adult may abandon the belief system of his youth but during his or her psychological growth that system makes sense of the world. Therefore, we can understand that Goddard created the word "moron" within an ideological frame. Although we see the frame to be a false construction (people with low IQs labelled "morons" usually have ordinary sexual impulses with as much deviance as is found in the rest of the population), Goddard's ideological naming was part of his effort at developing a true understanding of his clients' mental states. Later in life, he did abandon his belief that "morons" had evil natures. Therefore, when we explain naming, we must be aware of ideological snares. Sapir/Whorf are, in part, right because names sometimes do limit our thought. The dynamics of modern life often break these limits but we cannot count on that. When we make new names, we have to be aware of the ideological issues in the naming situation.

We are trying to understand the honest shaping and reshaping of consciousness in which language is an instrument. For example, the treatment of child factory workers in Victorian England will help us see the word "child" in motion. In the 1830s and after, parents sold their children into factory apprenticeships. Before then, children often worked in family cottage industries, weaving and doing other jobs. Some Christians marched the children from the factory to church on Sunday then marched them back to complete a 12-hour work day. The parties to that social performance were not, usually, liars or hypocrites. They were inside a set of values that meant the role performances of childhood and child care were differently defined than they are in late 20th-century Canada. Today we mean different things *systematically*, although the naming words and the value concerns for "suffering the little children" are the same. The Victorians who participated in the industrial revolution, who subjected the children to these conditions, were often the ones who reformed the condition of childhood. The parents who sold children and the Christians who marched the children also pressured the government to pass the *Factory Acts*. They created the conditions that now enable us to think differently with the same words.

Now, we think about children in terms of a network of caring agents and agencies, parents and kin, courts, social workers, physicians and so on. In the Victorian period, a very different network conditioned the meaning of the word "child". The state played a smaller role in child care. There were fewer hospitals, no vaccinations, no publicly supported day cares and fewer schools. The main supports for a child were family, factory friends and administrators, the church and the social reformers' efforts at ameliorating the suffering of the poor. The word may be the same and even its dictionary meaning is the same but the context is so altered that the word is now very different.

In recent history, the words surrounding other contested social roles had more turbulent changes. The words associated with gender, race and nationality exist in areas in which the contending people are not diverted by rationalization. When blacks, Jews and women attacked the language associated with their subordinated status, they did so from zones of misery in which the names of the role identities themselves were expressions of abuse. There was considerable brutality towards children in the 19th century but the role of childhood itself reached a new height in public esteem. In the cases of women, blacks, Jews and gays, their roles were entwined with major social changes such as the end of slavery, colonial wars and rebellions, a new formation of nationalism and the women's suffragette struggles. All the parties in these were articulate and the plane of language itself was understood to be part of the substantive ground being claimed in the various contests.

Therefore, during the struggles in the early part of this century, blacks were named in various ways: abusively as "niggers" and "blacks"; and genteelly as "darkies" and "coloured". Black intellectuals such as Carter Woodson and W.E.B. Dubois campaigned to be named Negro (with a capital letter). Both these activists were influential in establishing Negro History Month. With considerable agility, Dubois supported several different names. He was for some years an important figure in the National Association of Colored People and the author of *The Souls of Black Folk*. In the years after the Second World War, he backed the Pan-African independence movement that supported the attribution "black". In the community of those we are currently asked to call African-Americans, the debate was heated up. Many felt that the use of the word "black" burdened the group with the onerous meanings generated by the traditional Christian symbolism regarding white and black (good and evil).

The decision to use "black" despite symbolisms was and is a remarkable one. In her study of psychological defences, Anna Freud called this kind of tactic, "joining the aggressor". The black movement culture frequently uses this gesture in shocking ways. Richard Wright, in his novel *Native Son*, creates a heroic figure who robs, rapes and murders. The social type, the "mean nigger", is a nightmare monster born in slavery and resident in American mythology. To present that figure as a hero was important because an aggressive agent is a better source of social power than the victims found in *Uncle Tom's Cabin*.

Humour is used to control the force of this language tactic. Dick Gregory, the comedian, regularly employs "nigger" in comic routines. He entitled his autobiography *Nigger* and he says to black audiences he likes being called nigger by blacks but when a white person uses the word it is objectionable because he does not know how to pronounce the word. In Wright's sensationalism, in Gregory's comedy, in terror, in humour and in naming, black writers have sought to convert racial stereotypes into devices against racism.

The feminist strategy of naming is opposite to that of the black power movement. The situation of women during the growth of their rights movement had a different order of development. The abusive naming of women violated the polite culture in which women were socialized to perform their roles. Bohemian women, intellectual women and lower-class women could use obscene language but when women's movements formed, they sought to voice their aspirations in civil speech. Valery Solanas did form a feminist organization called SCUM (Society to Cut Up Men), but the membership was never large nor influential.

"Girl" and "lady" were originally terms of respect for female members of society. "Girl" was applied to young females marking only age. "Lady" was applied to respectable members of middle or upper class society. Later, "lady" applied sometimes to the respectable moral status of a woman without regard to age or class position. At this point, the names "lady" and "girl" began to be applied indiscriminately. Often used condescendingly, these names came to represent strict feminine roles that included restrictive character traits: passivity; politeness; and emotional and intellectual incapacity. The women's movement has had involved discussions about these names and with a few exceptions has decided not to "join the aggressor". They chose to remove the word "lady" from polite language and to make "girl" stand only for young females.

In a current debate, feminist theoreticians have divided over the meaning of "women". Some observed that in naming females "women", the word means more in speech acts than its dictionary definition. "Women", for example, were formerly excluded from Olympic marathon events; "women" were excluded from combat roles in the military; and "women" were and are excluded from various jobs. These exclusions were supposedly the result of the "biological fate" included in the meaning of the name acted out but only vaguely spoken. For Simone de Beauvoir and other "essentialists", a "woman's" biological fate is necessarily the source of female tragic experience.

Other feminists such as Jean Bethke Elshtain believe this reasoning is misguided. They argue that traditional feminine roles are historically and ideologically formed, but they are also dependent on the actual biology of the two sexes. This group of thinkers argues that women have a cultural heritage associated with the name we might properly think about as essential womanliness. The argument is that not only women are interested in peace and child care but that women are historically and biologically interested in those important social causes.

When the citizens who apply names came to rename the "mentally retarded", a similar debate took place. The name "mentally retarded", like "woman", is a biological and an ideological category. In so far as the term "mental retardation" was ideological, its loss has been welcome. The biological content of the term, in its original sense, is now outdated. Intellectual disability is now understood as various kinds of mental condition. The discarding of the old term was part of the literal liberation from confinements. One result is that the various mental conditions are now open to new understanding, because free people appear to grow and learn better than those in confinement.

Just as the language strategies of blacks and women are useful in the pursuit of an appropriate language for a mental condition, the homosexual intentions in naming, particularly the names "gay" and "lesbian", are also instructive. The male term "gay" is another instance of "joining the aggressor". Originally it was a name given to female prostitutes and later became a cant word used only by homosexuals to refer to members of the community. Its use by them and later by members of the straight community was sometimes abusive. The conversion of the name into a term of pride was a political act much like the adoption of the name "black" in slogans such as "black is beautiful".

"Lesbian" began life in the golden-age mythology promulgated by homosexuals. The romanticized archaic communities found in Plato and in Sappho (she lived in a community of women on the island of Lesbos; hence, Lesbian) were used by 19th-century gays and lesbians as honoured antecedents. The function of such naming connects the life of an abused community to history and to an enlarged existence that includes the archaic cultural heritage and its rights, honours and power.

The Long March through Names

The language strategies of blacks, women and gays arise out of each group's particular history. Persons with intellectual disabilities are found in these groups and, therefore, directly share the problems. All these groups indirectly have similar problems, but the historical situation of people with intellectual disabilities with regard to naming is closer to that of the oppressed children we have described above. In the past, they were not given the chance to speak or name for themselves.

The naming of intellectual disability has a complex history. There are four stages of that history: the archaic or classical; the medieval; the Enlightenment; and the modern. This history does not disappear. The old forms of reasoning about names are not discarded. They are present in new discussions, sometimes disguised, sometimes integrated into modern reasoning where they still haunt us.

The framework of assumptions around mental life is older than that around race and somewhat younger than that around sexual and gender identities. The basic assumptions concerning men and women and homosexuals begin in primitive societies. The basic assumptions about race begin in the late 18th century. Race is a scientific category and racism is an ideological outgrowth of it. The earliest understandings about mentality, however, appeared in primitive cultures; the notions we assume to be parallel or similar to those found in primitive groups appear in preliterate cultures today. These are not scientific understandings, though they are sometimes fairly sophisticated. The Iroquois, for example, make intellectual use of dreams. They see dreams, as many modern psychologists do, as part of the human reasoning process.

The first full-fledged theories of mind appear in Aristotle and Plato. There, the whole of being is ranked in what we have come to call the great chain of being. In that ordering, the more material elements of being are judged to be inferior to spiritual elements. The stuff of mentality — ideas — exists in the spiritual realm at the top of the chain of being. There we also find the virtues: the good, the true and the beautiful. The implication, for Plato, is that those men who think and reason are spiritual in action and dwell in the purest area of virtue. The lower orders of virtue are found in the practical realm of necessity where craftsmen, women and slaves dwell.

Women and slaves in archaic social ordering take care of material needs (low ranked) to allow free men to engage in the mental life (high ranked) connected with the public life of the state, in politics. This social structure is the source of many values in the modern world. In most industrial societies, the division of the work force into manual and intellectual labour duplicates the archaic rank ordering. We live in a world where political, economic and social life are rewarded according to intellectual merit. Aristocracy is changed into meritocracy, a social order dominated by the most powerful mentalities. In the treatment of people with psychiatric disabilities and those with intellectual disabilities, the platonic view strongly influenced early Christianity and modern therapies and social rankings. Plato saw people who had psychiatric disabilities and intellectual disabilities as outside the realm of freedom — along with women and slaves.

Medieval Christianity, despite its platonic character, altered this archaic view of mentality in two ways. First, it remystified the working of the psyche by objectifying evil; demonic forces were entered into the account of the disordered mind. Then mental anomalies were understood not merely as self-created chaos — the person suffering from them was a victim who was properly the recipient of care. And second, victim and care-giver were elevated in status. The person who was ill, the women and the slave or worker were all doing God-like work, comforting suffering people. Through this work they entered a more democratic and spiritual existence without being mentally superior.

The Christian view of mental disorder was, nevertheless, dual; a mental disability was both sacred and profane. One central Christian method for dealing with evil and the profane is separation.

Therefore, just as demons were exorcised (one treatment for madness), so too people considered mad or foolish were thrust out. The ships of fools, the separate community in Belgium at Gheel and Bethlehem (now Bedlam) in England are benign anticipations of modern asylums.

When asylums were established in the second millennium, there was a well understood distinction between the people considered mad and those otherwise mentally impaired. The word "mad" is derived from the old English word "gemaed" meaning fool. On ships of fools and at Gheel, the residents are both the people considered insane and those considered fools. The word "fool" originally meant unknowing and ignorant, as it does today, but it also had another sense. The medieval phrase, "the fool of God", described a moral ideal, the good man who would act morally even if it violated his own interest. He is the person who would turn the other cheek. The medieval moralist understood the fool as a person with a special order of knowledge; his foolishness marked him as man touched by divinity.

Shakespeare's fool in *King Lear* had a special wisdom and was, therefore, free to speak unpleasant truths to the king. The king was free to whip the fool when truths became too unpleasant. In the century following the death of Shakespeare, European thought changed radically. Medieval conceptions concerning "simple-mindedness" and "madness" were mixtures of natural and magical elements. The word "lunatic" was part of astrology; it derived from the French word "lune" and indicated that form of insanity or intellectual disability caused by the moon. The word "silly", another designation for intellectual disability and insanity, also retained its original meaning: fullness of soul.

In the 18th century, the supernatural meanings were less important. They were displaced by the materialist and quantitative views of scientists and a substantial commercial class that merged with royalty and clergy as the intellectual leaders of public opinion. This meant there was new reasoning behind the names of intellectual disability.

In the 18th century, there was also a period of renaming. Few new words were entered; most of the new terms were older words revived, but there was a new frame of understanding. "Half-wit", a new name, did two things. It separated the "simple" from the "insane", and it renamed them with a quantity as well as a quality of wit. "Witless" served earlier to make this division, but the newly added prefix was part of the new attitude towards mentality.

Some of the older terms also moved into this frame, such as "simple" and "natural". With these names, the 18th-century thinkers developed euphemisms hiding new harsher attitudes. The older medieval names contained some charitable respect for their bearers. The "lunatic", because he is moonstruck, is a significant figure in an enchanted universe. The new terms moved beyond enchantment. Today, charity towards these victims means giving money to help them. The old meaning of charity, a selfless giving, is replaced by self-aggrandizing giving found in high-society fundraising balls. These transformations of language — the reduction of "wit" and the debasement of "charity" — have a connection to the changes in the treatment of the "insane" and the "simple". The institutions housing them have grown harsher and more punitive.

When the 18th century ended, the reformers arrived — Pinel, Tuke and others. However, the terms of reform are now conditioned by the modern concept of "wit". During medieval times, "wit" served conceptually, as "intelligence" does today, to name intellectual endowment. For the medieval, however, an act of wit was to see into the supernatural or the platonic realm of ideas — the enchanted universe. The 18th century was an age of wit (in the sense of intellectual comedy) but that wit had little magic, less spiritual content and no charity. The mean spirit of this period is an expression of the worst characteristics of the modern world.

In the revolutions of the 17th and 18th centuries, new hierarchies were formed. The commercial classes based on wealth entered into the established order with a quality that displaced the breeding of royalty and the courage of soldiery. Shrewdness of mind justified their new power.

When we read Jonathan Swift, one of the greatest spokesmen of his age, we are struck by his powerful intellect. What is also striking when we compare *Gulliver's Travels* to any Shakespeare play is that Swift's depiction of the world is so lonely. In the Enlightenment, a cruel God is substituted for the traditional one, a mental God who comes disguised in wit, simplicity and naturalness. When we examine how those attributes and virtues were used to justify the cruelty with which people with intellectual disability were named, we see how an awful chain of language was fashioned.

The scepticism that secularised the world in the 18th century created an intellectual climate that enabled more people to think scientifically. The arguments about the treatment of people with psychiatric and intellectual disabilities were tested, henceforth, within the milieu of science. That milieu, including the pure sciences and the healing arts of medicine, produced a vocabulary heavily freighted with ideology. Looking back now, we can easily see how quirky and even dangerous the early efforts at psychiatry were; mesmerism, phrenology, cranial measures, facial expressions and racism constituted scientific studies. They were important in the 18th and 19th centuries and persist even now in serious science. Gobineau's race theories persist largely in disreputable science. However, Darwin (with facial expression) and Freud (with hypnotism) developed their work from those peculiar origins.

All science must be critically examined to reveal how its naming commits us to orders of existence outside of science. Ethical, social and political formations use scientific names as they shape and reshape themselves. The great achievement of 18th-century science was in the field of classification, which made it possible, in the 19th century, to show the variety of conditions that were formerly lumped together. By the end of the 19th century institutions were formed for all kinds of social ailments that were given separate confinements; the "simple" were parted from the "insane" and so on. Although in this century, to paraphrase T.S. Eliot, there was time for revisions and decisions which needed to be reversed and the reformers, Pinel and Tuke, sought to remove straitjackets and other restraints, other caring and confining institutions multiplied. They were seen as necessary because the kinds of people who were dangerous to the social order were multiplying: workers; slaves; the colonized; criminals; foreigners; sexual deviants; racial minorities; wayward women; the poor; and the hungry. In addition, this was an age in which the new factory economy generated more innocent victims: orphans; alcoholics; widows; and the sick. Millions were overworked, starved, beaten and killed. George Bernard Shaw called this the most disgusting century in human history.

One question preoccupies historians and social thinkers: why did people accept this maltreatment so passively? One important answer is that many did not accept it, although the great majority did. Why? One element was their belief that the widespread injustices were either necessary or somehow the result of social choices made by the victims. Moreover, social commentators convinced many that the victims were intrinsically inferior because they were subhuman, unfit for survival or not human at all. For example, some said that widows deserved their impoverishment because their deceased husbands were careless in providing for their survivors. The blatant injustice of this reasoning had an underpinning in a widely held set of assumptions forming a new ethic that, to some degree, has persisted in the 20th century. Though challenged by many, Social Darwinism became the main justification for inequality and its attendant miseries.

Much of the naming and reordering of names for intellectual disability in the 19th century is formed in the web of assumptions found in Darwin's theories and Social Darwinism. Social Darwinism proposes that it is right for the rich to be rich and the poor to be poor because the rich are more fit than the poor. Their success is said to be ethically right and inevitable because Darwin's mechanism for evolution, the law of the "survival of the fittest", makes it so. In Social Darwinist theory, the conflicts among nations, classes and individuals are said to be much the same as the struggles among species. When men, women and children were victimized, the biological naturalness of it all made it appear good.

The persuasive power of Social Darwinism rests on its similarity to older religious notions: Darwin's facts about the struggle among animals suggest an older allegory of good and evil — Adam, Eve and the snake. When the new science of psychology developed, it used the species categories in a new Darwinist allegory. Dr. Down divided people with intellectual disabilities into types which he named after racial groups, succeeding in one intellectual move in demeaning both the races of the world and people with intellectual disabilities. Sir Peter Medawar, the late anglo-Indian biologist, joined with other Asians in a successful request to the *London Times* that its style sheet disallow the term "mongolian idiot" and replace it with Down syndrome. That Down believed his taxonomy to be science — unprejudiced, pure knowledge — gives a clear measure of how unaware intelligent thinkers can be in the naming process.

Sir Medawar's example, his successful renaming, is an important case of rebaptism. It takes place 100 years after the original naming, when the status of Asia has been transformed after Indian independence, the Chinese revolution and the Japanese rise to extraordinary economic power. Sir Medawar's change of the name became possible after a world system had substantially altered.

Goddard and his colleague, Fernald, engaged in naming under the auspices of the American Association for the Study of the Feeble Minded, named in 1907. The association was originally formed in the 19th century as the Association of Medical Officers of American Institutions for Idiots and Feeble Minded Persons. It was renamed again, in 1933, the American Association on Mental Deficiency. In their naming system, Goddard and Fernald concentrated on the degree of intellectual disability, their core terms being "moron" (50-70 IQ), "imbecile" (20-50 IQ) and "idiot" (20 IQ and below). This rank ordering of persons by intelligence combines the taxonomic science of the 18th century with a social science fetish of statistics. The result was to create a way of labelling that allowed medical staffs to imprison those who now had numerically determined fixed identities. The early work of Fernald and Goddard also continued the Christianized form of Social Darwinism; they not only believed the law of the survival of the fittest worked in human society, but they also tried to prove the rightness of the law by showing that people with intellectual disabilities were sinners, specifically in sexual deviance and in petty criminality.

One of the more comical oddities in Fernald's writing about the sins of persons with intellectual disability occurs when he accuses them of licentious behaviour. He rounds it off with a charge that they are socialists. This wild charge shows the attitudes of conservative American medical administrators from the 1880s to the 1920s. Waves of fear swept through American society during this 40-year period. Indigenous Americans saw immigrant labour pouring into the country in the same way Fernald saw persons with intellectual disabilities, as ignorant, dirty, sexually profligate genetic contaminators and socialists. Soap sales went up, the temperance movement flourished and confinements of all kinds grew more numerous: insane asylums; prisons; reform schools; homes for people with hearing impairments and intellectual disabilities; and unwed mothers' shelters.

This was also a period when barriers against people considered inferior were created. Universities and professional schools put in quotas limiting the entry of racial, religious and national minorities. Feminist organizations joined this great cleansing of America; they supported prohibition and eugenics. But women, too, became targets in much the same way as did people in minority groups. The most important example of this is the movement to sterilize women deemed to be unsuitable parents. Many women with intellectual disabilities, along with a smaller number of men, were sterilized. During this period, the terms "feeble minded" and "moron" had the implication of sexual danger. In this context, it is easy to see that naming had the purpose of validating the Social Darwinist belief in the unfitness of people with intellectual disabilities, particularly those who were women and members of minorities.

In Canada, Social Darwinism was and is more powerful than in the United States. According to Simmons, the word "idiot" in the

1840s in Ontario meant someone who was close to being incurably insane, whereas in the United States an "idiot" was a human who needed care.[1] The altruism found in United States institutions came largely from the early feminist reform movements that overlapped with the abolitionist movement. The strong movements against racism and sexism in Canada developed after 1945 and it is probably more than a coincidence that many other social movements mobilized then as well.

The humane scientists in Canada and the United States developed the powerful name "mentally retarded" in the middle of the 20th century. This term was a breakaway from early IQ-based theorizing in one crucial way. It does not, as the term "idiot" does, rest on the concept of fixed character. The name "retardation", conceptually, describes someone who is a victim of a growth disorder. This concept and this naming refer to a different sequence of social acts than the concept behind "idiot". The persons named "retarded" have many different conditions. They are expected to have various careers as they pass through institutions. With appropriate attention, they can expect to be released from institutions or avoid them and have "normal" development.

Critics find other reasons to complain about the term. Its social and legal implications have made it disliked among people who have an intellectual disability, their parents and social reformers. Socially, the persons labelled wear a stigma that causes other "normal" people to treat them as less than human. The implications of danger found in the "myth of the menace of the feeble minded" have fallen on people labelled "retarded". In colloquial language, to be a "retard" is to be labelled abusively.

The legal consequences of the label were different in different jurisdictions. It often meant, in mid-century, being confined or being put in the care of health institutions that made dependents out of their clients. If the client tried to avoid some forms of care, it sometimes meant being cut off from financial support. The web of relations built around the term trapped the client.

My contention here is that the past is still present in the social order in which we live and name. Persons with intellectual disabilities are still subject to classical, medieval and Enlightenment thinking along with modern scientific reasoning. A historical perspective of naming enables us to realize how difficult it is to construct just social realities. It is a long march. Naming is only part of the effort. We name persons or groups so as to put them in a place that is part of a larger organization. Naming is not arbitrary or accidental. If we are to change the conditions of persons called "mentally retarded", the name change is only part of the undertaking. We shall, furthermore, have to change many things about the way persons with intellectual disabilities are treated before the newly named can live out the relations symbolized in the new name.

Naming Strategies

To recommend a policy with regard to language strategies can be unwise and even futile. The current struggle over naming is filled with parables for the unwary. The situation around "political correctness" is instructive. Political correctness, as the name of a naming phenomenon, covers a multitude of vices and virtues. Before political correctness became the name of a movement or movements, it was first simply a phrase with literal meaning. In the 1960s, it became a term used by social activists who criticized companions who were influenced by dogmatic Marxists. The Marxist dogma being most criticized was the notion that one could make absolute statements about the political future — that is, be correctly clairvoyant.

By the time George Bush became President of the United States in the 1990s, the cold war had ended and Marxism was less threatening without the military power of the Soviet Union backing it. Political correctness was Bush's baptism of all social movements seeking change and using renaming practices in that process. He was famously racist, not much help to feminists and certainly inactive with regard to gay issues (AIDs research was underdeveloped during his administration).

The behaviour of social activists is not uniform, but it is clear that George Bush found a vulnerable target in the behaviours of many social activists. Naming and renaming is an aggressive act and the power found in words is often painfully delivered by social activists. The pain of being called a racist, a male chauvinist or a homophobe is unpleasant to persons being asked to change their behaviour. It is more so to those who are falsely so named, particularly when they actively participate in decent actions. The current economic situation has filled North American politics with rancour. The guns of language are out and firing. Abusive naming is widespread.

Group conflicts are like war parties; the arguments are about possession and not about the means of getting possession. The sides have agreed to use violence. Social movements, particularly the large sweeping ones, are usually coercive but, unlike makers of war, their strategies and tactics are not necessarily violent. That is why naming and other language issues are so important. Language is a major instrument of non-violent action for those with grievances. And as the example of George Bush shows, all sides are involved in naming and renaming. Listed below is a wide set of possibilities, not complete by any means, with suggestions as to how they might be appropriate now. This material should be seen as a pragmatic exercise worth going through as policies are being formed. None of these comments should be understood as "correct". Social movements exist in a shifting terrain in which, as Hamlet says, "the readiness is all".

1. Use of new knowledge

As thinkers and researchers develop knowledge, they coin new words to describe new understandings. All who participate in this process — persons with an intellectual disability, parents, teachers, sympathizers and scientists — together create this "social construction of reality" which includes naming. As they do this they should keep in mind that changes in language and realities have consequences. The development of eugenics, with its association with racism in the first half of the century, shows how scientific research can take an unwanted ideological turn.

2. *Extremes*

It is possible for interested parties to do nothing or very nearly nothing about language. Classical rhetoricians advise speakers to be careful about multiplying terms. If you introduce too many new names into your persuasive speech and writing, you can lose the support of your listeners and readers in their irritation and confusion. New names may not be as good as the old-fashioned appeals for sympathy; sometimes begging and pleading might work better than changes in vocabulary. The other extreme, a variant of this same language strategy (no new names), is an attack with verbal and physical violence using old names. People with physical disabilities in the United States have done this with sit-ins and mass lobbying. In this way they successfully moved legislators to pass laws protecting the medical care provided by the federal government. Both of these extremes are best approached cautiously. Sometimes people find themselves forced into extreme passivity or extreme action. Both radical change and conservatism are effective, but the cost is often high.

3. *Militant encounters*

Non-violence is a political technology perfected by Ghandi. In language struggles and political conflicts, this mode can become revolutionary because it sometimes provokes violence. The gay movement, among others, employed this recently. In peace demonstrations, some gays have carried signs saying, "Queers for Peace". Some women wear large buttons on their shirts announcing, "Dyke". This is verbal skirmishing for public recognition and for the legitimacy of individual sexual preference. A routine by Lenny Bruce shows what is at stake in these speech acts, this "joining with the aggressor":

Are there any niggers here tonight? ... That's two kikes and three niggers and one spic ... Two guineas, one hunky funky lace-curtain mick. That hunky funky boogey ... The point? That the word's suppression gives it the power, the violence, the viciousness.[2]

Lenny Bruce's analysis seems slightly incorrect. It is not the suppression that gives it the power, it is possession of the word that signals the possession of power. The acquisition of obscene power demonstrated by Bruce in his act has often been employed by blacks, gays and feminists as noted. Here, we can imagine a sign at a peace demonstration, "Retards for Peace", or large buttons with the proud self-identification "Geek". It could work if appropriately organized and if many were prepared to wear the button, as the Danish king and his people wore yellow stars to protect the Jewish Danes who were forced to wear them by order of the Nazi occupation authorities during the Second World War.

4.   *Bridge building and negotiating*

The major difficulty with strategies 2 and 3 is that they are uncompromising; the opposition must yield or else live in an uncivil set of relations. Sometimes that works well but even if you have the power to win the day, you may find the field abandoned with an undesirable change. The most obvious recent instance of this is the deinstitutionalization of insane asylums: people with psychiatric disabilities were dumped onto the welfare system that often had few resources to support them. Consequently, large numbers of people with psychiatric disabilities are now homeless. The anti-psychiatry movement did not intend that outcome. They did not anticipate that so many governments would gladly abandon people, to leave the stage on which the argument had been conducted.

A good example of bridge building is found in Wolfensberger's *Normalization.*[3] That author used a term which the least demanding reformers were beginning to find too conservative. "Normal" and "abnormal" are terms associated with adjustment therapies and punitive imprisonment. The critics of normalization have seen the term as an ideological fiction that establishes conformities. Furthermore, it is an impediment to the realistic understanding of pathology in human behaviours. There is a growing list of behaviours formerly thought to be "abnormal" that are now seen in new ways (not including "normality"): homosexuality; learning disabilities; hyperactivity; and so on. When, however, Wolfensberger applied the term to people with intellectual disabilities, he performed a major act of reconciliation with the powers that controlled institutions.

Wolfensberger's negotiating strategy enabled reformers and civil servants to find common levels of sympathy as they improved the lives of people with intellectual disabilities. Agreement about the nature of human realities was then unimportant. The price for quiet changes, the ones resulting from negotiation, is probably not as high as noisier ones. There are, however, drawbacks. The main one in Wolfensberger's strategy emerges from a leftover issue. How are people with disabilities to develop lives in a world antipathetic and uncaring about their differentness. In the movie, *Children of a Lesser God*, the heroine, who has a hearing impairment, asks of her hearing lover that he enter her realm of silence and not ask her to be "normal". That realm of silence is analogous to the different mentality of people with intellectual disabilities.

That different mentality has often been mythologized; the "wisdom of the fool" and the specially licensed fool in Shakespeare's *King Lear* are cousins, often with similar powers, of the equally mythological prophetic madman. In a critical understanding of these myths we can separate the fiction from the important truths in them. Not all fools have wisdom, any more than do other people. Knowingness, however, often gets in the way of the wisdom that is the knowledge of important things. The parable of the child who knows and says the emperor has no clothes shows something of the actual nature of the wisdom found in people with intellectual disabilities. Their mentalities, however, are often judged and measured on the scales of intelligence. With a little consideration, we can see that intelligence is a measure linked to a particular form of life. Adam Smith describes this form of life:

But finally, we must realize that in the knowledge-intensive late 20th century, Confucian — and Calvinist — characteristics pay off. We knew them once; we may have to learn them all over again.

That means we have to pay attention to hard study and hard work. American industry is already beginning to learn these lessons. But American industry is receiving recruits who cannot always read and write with skill. The answer is not merely government policy — though government can help with consciousness-raising. School policy is determined on the state and local level by voters — and parents — and too many parents have the same goals of athletic prominence and social success that their children do. We do not need to go to the extent that Asians have in their disciplined work and study but we have to move in that direction. We have to have some "Japanese Jewish mothers" or some "Chinese mothers" who make sure the child has a desk and that the TV is turned off. It may be curious to think that the industrial future of our country depends on such things, but this is how we got to preeminence in the first place.[4]

The narrow chauvinism of this statement is clear when we study the lives of people with intellectual disabilities. They have a contribution to make to the preeminence of the United States and Canada, but that preeminence has to be understood outside Calvinist and Confucian ethics. All persons, not only people with disabilities, want more than disciplined work and study. They want work and study with a content and a form that express deeper values than work and study for itself alone.

Good though work and study may be, all persons have internal orders of accomplishment that need expression outside industrial necessities. The "wisdom of fools" is other than the "received wisdom" of Adam Smith. It contains patterns of culture found in the several thousand years of pre-industrial society. Other cultures have made poetry and the arts, athletics and caring relations central products in which all take pride. If normalization becomes the central goal for people with intellectual disabilities, we may all find ourselves in cramped lives.

5.   *Forms of consciousness raising*

The general rejection of the name "retarded" has led to the proliferation of terms: intellectually disabled; mentally fragile; general learning disability; mentally challenged; mentally handicapped; and so on. As the new terms appear, they seem to attract criticism or ridicule. For example, "handicap" has been turned into a mildly abusive name. Some words seem to be euphemisms, at best pleasant masks for reality or at worst sentimentalities. Often critics find the names faulty. "Mentally handicapped" came under a pall because the original meaning of "handicap" referred to the deferential tug at the forelock or cap as a sign of respect by the lower for the upper classes.

The large number of terms being generated everywhere does point to an ideological fluidity. Many seem unable to arrive at an understanding of intellectual disability that enables those concerned to join together in a common cause with agreed-upon names. Sometimes parents have difficulty naming a child and they delay for a while. The desire to rebaptize infants with intellectual disabilities comes from a sense that naming will make things better. That can only be so if the name can attract followers who persuade the public to live in a new way.

That type of social action is a complex event, often triggered by many things such as forms of public education. Schools, universities and mass media are effective mediums of social action but the most important form of political education in the second half of this century grew in small group discussions. We have come to call this consciousness raising; in churches, in black soul sessions, in feminist consciousness raising (they named it) and in psychological encounter groups, citizen education was raised to a fine art and the public mind was rescued from the destructive power of television.

Such groups have many means for handling problems:

- Soul sessions: These are particularly useful when issues are puzzling to groups in the midst of difficult actions. In moments of failure or success, new directions are hard to establish. The deepest feelings and thoughts of the participants gain from sharing and deliberation. In moments of puzzlement, groups can sometimes find leadership, solutions or simply the will to go on. Most importantly, in the naming process the group can review possibilities.

- Struggle sessions: In the midst of conflicts, groups need to regroup, gather strength and eliminate weakness. Identification and naming can be a useful form of self-analysis. The resolution of struggle sessions frequently includes the development of the group's understanding of itself in its name or renaming.

- Deliberative discussion: In this kind of group gathering, the group agrees to gather regularly in order to meet experienced people or experts or to read and research together. Here the group makes itself into a school. This enables it to approach the forefront of knowledge and to test that knowledge in its experience. For example, one group of persons with intellectual disabilities began to examine attribution theory. This theory observes that naming preconditions the way an individual or a group will be perceived and treated. As a consequence of their understanding, they called for the elimination of the labelling attached to them. They decided to name themselves "People First". That renaming, a public assertion, asks the public to think in a new way about them.

Unfortunately, the president of the organization found he was not allowed to cross the border into the United States after the renaming. The U.S. Immigration Service refused him entry because he was "mentally retarded". The newspaper articles about the incident, however, featured the name People First and the next time he went to speak, the authorities let him through.

Conclusion

The theory of names is necessarily double:

1.   names are only conventions; and

2.   names are important instruments in the construction of social reality.

In 1928, W.E.B. DuBois defended the naming of black people "Negroes" to a young man in this way:

> [W]ithout the word that means us, where are all those spiritual ideals, those inner bonds, those group ideals and forward strivings of this mighty army of 12 millions? Shall we abolish these with the abolition of a name? Do we want to abolish them? Of course we do not. They are our most precious heritage.

And then he concluded his letter:

> Get this then, Roland, and get it straight even if it pierces your soul: a Negro by any other name would be just as black and just as white; just as ashamed of himself and just as shamed by others, as today. It is not the name — it's the Thing which counts. Come on, Kid, let's go get the Thing![5]

Notes

1. Harvey G. Simmons, *From Asylum to Welfare*, Downsview, Ont.: National Institute on Mental Retardation, 1982.

2. Quoted by Art Spiegelman, "Mightier Than the Sorehead," *The Nation*, 258(2), January 17, 1994, p. 45.

3. Wolf Wolfensberger, *The Principle of Normalization in Human Services*, Downsview, Ont.: National Institute on Mental Retardation, 1972.

4. Adam Smith, "Are Asians Really That Much Smarter?", *Esquire*, 108(3), September 1987, p. 100.

5. W.E.B. DuBois, "The Name 'Negro'", in *W.E.B. DuBois*, New York, N.Y.: The Library of America, Viking Press, 1986, pp. 1221-1222.

Chapter 8

Knowing about Knowing: Margin Notes on Disability Research

by Aileen Wight Felske

Margin Notes

"It's still a wonderment about what's out there." (formerly institutionalized man now living in the community)

"[What I like about living in a home is it's] ... not lumping everyone together." (women labelled intellectually disabled)

"I want to learn more reading and writing so I can make more choices ..." (woman labelled intellectually disabled)

"I want to play in a band." (man labelled intellectually disabled)

"My goal is to marry, have a family, somewhere I'll belong..." (man labelled intellectually disabled)

"He makes simple decisions such as what he wants to eat, wear, who he wants to spend his time with, when to make his bed, some activities or chores about the home." (a parent)

"His personal budget is so low he must live with two other men, wear secondhand clothes, restrict his outings that depend on transportation." (parent/guardian)

"It is discouraging because government staff are paid more for doing the same job ... no one has had an increment or raise in the four years I have been here." (a community living worker)[1]

Introduction

An epistemology is a theory of knowledge. It answers questions about who can be a knower, what tests beliefs must pass in order to be legitimated as knowledge, what kinds of things can be known and different ways of knowing.[2] People with a disability and, in particular, people who have been labelled intellectually disabled and their families are marginalized as knowers. Their voices are not included by the "body politic" of disability research.[3]

Disability research is based implicitly or explicitly on particular epistemological paradigms. Depending on the paradigm in which it is rooted, the research process legitimizes certain people as knowers and producers of knowledge and identifies certain objects as worthy of study over others.

A scan of disability research for epistemology notes three widely differing paradigms underlying the construction of research agendas: positivism; interpretative social science; and critical social science. These contrasting theoretical frameworks generate divergent standpoints for the study of disability.

This chapter traces the differing realities of disability, and in particular intellectual impairment, through the research literature drawing out the epistemological assumptions of the three paradigms. The method for this chapter is an analysis of the different stories of the same man, someone labelled as intellectually disabled. The stories are drawn from this author's participatory research program evaluating change in funding arrangements for individuals with the label intellectual disability who are living in the community. The same story is told twice in order to illuminate the differing epistemological standpoints that lie in its construction.

A Positivist Paradigm

In disability research the positivist paradigm has operated on the assumption that disability is a deficit, a problem in the individual who must be rehabilitated. This view of the individual in need of medical "fixing" holds whether the impairment is physical or intellectual, temporary or life long. The positivist view holds that there is only one true reality and a careful application of the rules of observation, comparable to the methodology of the natural sciences, will produce the necessary theoretical constructs to predict and control events, to produce a "cure". Positivists argue that research must be objective or value free.

In the following story, the view of an individual with an intellectual impairment or "deficit" is presented. A mechanistic view of individual learning as one of an organism responding to the environment represents the positivist view of disability research.[4] It is, unfortunately, the "norm" for information contained in case files of rehabilitation agencies for persons labelled intellectually disabled and the perspective taken by many researchers as a way of knowing. The following story is written from this positivist perspective.

Story 1: Deficit-based description

> Mr. Smith has the mental age of an 18-month-old infant. His intelligence quotient tested in 1990 is 18; he is severely and profoundly retarded. Severe impairments are shown in adaptive behaviour. He has a severely limited verbal ability and an inability to comprehend abstract concepts. He has a severe seizure disorder and is medicated. Mr. Smith is a "behavioural" client. He has been documented regurgitating over 1800 times a day. There is no day program. A restrictive behavioural intervention program, based on limited food intake and using a helmet, is recommended. There is no family involvement. Public guardianship is held.

Positivist researchers believe in "objective" research, in measuring the world quantitatively and testing hypotheses statistically. Behaviourism in the social sciences has most successfully emulated the rules of natural science observation and replication. Early individual program planning adopted the behavioural model of remediating deficits.[5] Intense efforts to establish skill sequences for adults with intellectual disability labels, using a behavioural framework, resulted in vocational workshops teaching repetitive "non-work" tasks. Research in the treatment of behaviour disorders adopted the behavioural paradigm of punishment for control. Only recently has the community living movement begun to successfully challenge this oppression.[6]

Program evaluation models drew heavily on the positivist assumptions of objective evaluation. These evaluation models, adopted by service delivery organizations, were soon judged irrelevant by people with disabilities. One example of this phenomenon has been social role valorization.[7] Although offered as a theory of the social constructs of disability, it is still criticized as a theory of deviance at the micro level. PASSING, the evaluation tool drawn from social role valorization, has applications to the evaluation of current service delivery systems, yet its language of discourse limits its understanding and application. Its lack of sensitivity to ethnic diversity and gender has been noted.[8]

The research results of the positivist paradigm have contributed to a theory of intellectual impairment valued mostly by academia and dismissed by the "labelled" people and their families. They are critical of the methodological dependence on irrelevant quantitative subject descriptions drawn from psychometric test scores. The traditionally presented intelligence quotient is an example. The usefulness of this construct is strongly questioned by the advocacy movements. Its primary outcome has been one of exclusion rather than inclusion. Even the concept of adaptive behaviour is questionable since it has led to rehabilitation interventions dominated by deficit lists that must be overcome to achieve separation from segregated programs. Adaptive behaviour scores are the tool of "readiness" ghettos. These measures of success are "tied" to the kingdom of "dis"ability, passports to its entry but not to its exit.[9] Peck comments that it often seems we measure it because we know how, not necessarily because it is relevant.[10]

People with intellectual impairments and their families are also limited in access to research findings. Moving from research to practice has been slow. It has been hindered by academia that felt no responsibility to disseminate findings to consumers in ways they could understand and use. Peck has examined the connection between social policy development and the research process. He concluded that "we are told we must wait until research data have been collected and analyzed before we can know what policies to support and what practices to implement."[11] This situation seriously under-represents the sources of knowledge that are relevant to decisions about policy and practice.[12] Oliver, who describes this paradigm as "research as alienation", may have written an appropriate epitaph for it.[13]

Interpretative Social Science Paradigm

Interpretive social science is an alternative paradigm underlying disability research. Although more slowly adopted by social scientists doing research into disability than by those in cross-cultural anthropology or the sociological study of other marginalized groups, it is now commonly accepted. Interpretive social science focuses on the study of socially meaningful or purposeful social action. This research strives for empathetic understanding: how people feel, create meaning and their reasons or motivations for understanding the social act.[14] It accepts that there are many realities and researchers embrace a variety of approaches: hermeneutics or ethnomethodological or phenomenological examinations of peoples' experiences. The interpretive social science paradigm recognizes the social realities of people and their multiple roles in society.[15]

The interpretative social science paradigm has created a "story telling" view of disability — the voices of individuals sharing their lives. In the last decade the number of publications based in an interpretative social science model has increased exponentially. The interpretive approach is idiographic. It provides a symbolic representation. It is also inductive; a more general statement is built up slowly after immersion in specific observations of social life. Generalizations emerge out of the specific details of observation. This is grounded theory, rooted in the specifics of social life.[16] Early examples of research in this paradigm are Matthew's *Voices from the Shadows* and Bodgan's *Inside/Out*.[17] More recent anthologies such as Atkinson's and Williams' *Know Me as I Am* have been widely distributed.[18]

The interpretative researcher's rules of research production are based on ethnographic research methodologies such as interviews and participant observation techniques to measure outcome. These methodologies record community events and interactions from which new understandings can be created. Using this methodology, O'Brien has outlined five new community living parameters for measurement: community presence; participation; choice; roles; and competence.[19] These outcome measures reflect the interconnectedness of people as a framework to measure quality of life. The social relations of research production, however, although muted, are still based on the traditional power differential between researcher and subject. The precursors for a further paradigm shift came from this new view of disability and its emphasis on social context. As the wealth of stories of people with disabilities has grown, creating an everyday book of life and disability, the pressure from persons with intellectual impairments, their families and advocates for a critical analysis has increased.[20] With the growing public recognition of these stories, there has developed an awareness that research could be employed as a form of social action.[21]

Critical Social Science

This awareness paved the way for the emergence of the third

paradigm: a critical social science of disability. Newman defines critical social science as:

> a process of inquiry that goes beyond surface illusions to uncover the real structures in the material world in order to help people change conditions and build a better world for themselves.[22]

Research is recognized in this paradigm as a legitimization of knowledge and a source of power. People are defined as powerful in society, not only in societal resources but as producers or participants in the creation of knowledge, in "ways of knowing" themselves and the social structure in which they live. In this perspective, disability is defined as a societal issue of discrimination in attitudes, access to services and social policy. Therefore, it is assumed that through research the central tenets of life for persons with a disability — economic marginalization and a continuing struggle for citizenship — can be addressed.

Two assumptions regarding this new "way of knowing" and of carrying out research are made:

1)   inter-subjectivity, an authentic dialogue between all participants, respected as equally knowing subjects, is the basis of the research process and of knowledge production; and

2)   an examination of people's social reality in a framework of rights analysis is the context in the research process.[23] Rather than divorcing "facts" and "values", it is recognized that "facts" are always known only from a value orientation.

Critical social scientists increasingly recognize that disability research questions are drawn from the society that produces disability. People with a disability and, in particular, people who have been labelled intellectually disabled and their families, are marginalized in terms of economic resources[24] and as citizens holding a multitude of roles in society. The devaluation and exclusion by disability is compounded when individuals hold roles in other marginalized groups: women with an intellectual disability; Aboriginal people who have a disability; people with ethnic minority memberships; and elderly persons. Traditional researchers have ignored the role of gender or cultural group membership in their research on disability. For example, "most literature on disabled persons ... [is] genderless", yet the social reality for women with disabilities is a marginalization due to their disability and denial of their roles as a woman (nurturer and child bearer).[25]

Critical social science also leads to a recognition of the need for an inclusive analysis of race and disability.[26] The current approach to service delivery for persons with intellectual impairments is described as:

> color blind ... experiences, circumstances and needs of black and ethnic minority children and adults with learning difficulties and their families are ignored, or assumed to be the same as those of their white peers.[27]

Cocking and Athwal, in their analysis of services, are critical of the failure of services to meet the needs of black and ethnic people with learning difficulties in the United Kingdom.[28] For women with disabilities who belong to minority groups, this disadvantage is compounded yet again — a triple jeopardy.[29]

The critical social science paradigm moves beyond social reflexivity, the "knowing of individual realities", to a framework of citizenship and social policy analysis that accounts for these multiple identities. As stated by one participant in a recent Women and Disability Forum:

> The point of research is not only to document the conditions of ... lives (people with disabilities) ... it's [also] a starting point. We want to change the conditions, we want to radically restructure society ... [to] improve our lives.[30]

The profile of disability as a rights issue is increasingly recognized worldwide. The philosophy of social justice is delineated by three parameters: citizenship; inclusion; and equalization of opportunities. The DPI (Disabled Persons International) Manifesto defines equalization of opportunities as:

the process through which the general systems of society such as the physical environment, housing and transportation, social and health services, educational and work opportunities, cultural and social life, including sports and recreational facilities, are made accessible to all.[31]

The discourse on disabilities in the critical studies paradigm has become one of citizenship. Therefore, the research questions are related to poverty, violence, social reform, alternative housing models and inclusion of people in social systems such as the inclusive education movement (school reform) and employment initiatives.

It is in the context of this paradigm that the story first told by positivists is now retold from an epistemological standpoint that departs substantially from that of the positivist.

Story 2: A human rights perspective

Tom Redbird is in his early twenties. He has always lived in a large institution in central Alberta. Recently, as a result of the government's adoption of deinstitutionalization as a policy, he moved to a government-operated group home. Tom is bored and angry; he has begun regurgitating his food. Except for a formal observation and recording procedure he is left on his own by the unionized staff most of the day. The kitchen has been blocked off so that Tom cannot get into it.

Tom has had a new guardian appointed for him under the *Dependant Adults Act* in Alberta. When the government residential staff applied to the restrictive procedures committee of the agency for permission to implement a restrictive program for Tom's regurgitation, they found the guardian was active in her role supporting Tom in his right to a quality life. She visited the home and, concerned for his life, went outside of traditional social services to find support. Because Tom was a First Nation (treaty status) Aboriginal, he was eligible for money from the Department of Indian and Northern Affairs. Individualized funding ($2,200 CAD a month) was applied for by a monitoring agency and two new community support staff members met Tom and began to spend time with him. The restrictive program was rejected as a violation of human rights.

The new support workers found Tom to be friendly, with good non-verbal communication. Together they went for walks and car rides and, at Tom's request, began to go to the public swimming pool regularly. Tom's regurgitation dropped to almost nothing. There were some frictions as support workers parallelled their more highly paid government counterparts. A half-day segregated program outside the group home was arranged when community living workers could not be with Tom. His room was decorated with personal possessions, using his own money from social allowance, and the symbol of his native band was hung on the wall. Leaders from the band were contacted and a visit from an uncle and two other band members occurred. Tom and his support worker were invited to visit a drop-in centre operated by the Band Council.

The community living workers employed through individualized funding would like to help Tom move into his own home, possibly with friends. At present he is a captive in the government facility, due to the high cost of 24-hour staffing and even his access to individualized funding is at risk as the government has decided he is being double funded. The cost of Tom living in his own home would be somewhat less than the government facility costs. Ironically, if the restrictive procedure had been implemented Tom would likely have died.

The importance of paradigms for researchers is highlighted by Blatt: "Some stories enhance life; others degrade it. So we must be careful about the stories we tell, about the ways we define ourselves and other people."[32] Critical social science researchers in the community living movement have chosen the second story on which to base their methodologies. Their research is driven by new questions and new approaches to evaluating possibilities for people. They have an increased appreciation of the facts of interdependence and the values of interpersonal cooperation.[33] This is the *new* story for people with a disability. Its truth depends on the power of the community living movement to establish a human rights context for perceiving people with disabilities. The researcher creates the reality as it is studied, recorded and shared with others.[34]

The emergence of new researchers to alter the paradigm in disability research is predictable from an understanding of other areas of study. In his analysis of the structure of scientific revolutions,

Kuhn illustrates how paradigms dictate world views or ideologies in the physical sciences and how researchers become resistant to change.[35] Paradigm shifts or "radically different ways of viewing the nature of reality" are often led by new researchers holding different ideologies than their predecessors.

Critical social science researchers are creating a totally new research methodology. The choice of research partnerships, research questions and research rules of an emancipatory paradigm are evolving. New rules of research production on the road to critical social science research include:

- the involvement of "persons with disabilities as respondents ... [which asks] about their perceptions of support, [and] their desire for intervention by the human services system;"[36]

- research questions are generated by, for and with people with disabilities;[37]

- the role of the researcher in an emancipatory methodology is one of partnership in the production of research as a tool of liberation;[38]

- researchers share the same value base as the participants;[39]

- guidelines for funding research clearly shift the balance of power in research partnerships to people with disabilities, their organizations and their alliance groups;[40]

- the new critical social science paradigm draws on both quantitative and qualitative data;[41]

- the new paradigm expands the venues of research dissemination.[42]

The challenge for researchers from and of the margins is to develop an emancipatory methodology in which research is organized in a fundamentally different way — by and with the people it is ultimately supposed to benefit, where expertise is a resource available to all rather than a form of power for a few.

Conclusion

This chapter argues that a new epistemological paradigm for disability is emerging. Through it research can become a useful process in the arguments for a fairer distribution of societal resources. Critical social science recognizes research as having a political agenda. People with disabilities, elderly people, women, Aboriginal people and members of ethnic minorities have been marginalized in terms of their material goods, their memberships and roles in the social sphere and in their ownership of knowledge. Their experiences, although different in origin, share an increasingly recognized commonality: they are all without power. Disability research must move from a medical model of individual deficit to a recognition of disability and marginalization as a human rights issue and an awareness that poverty, housing, violence, income reform, education and employment are the issues of disability research.

If marginalized people are to participate in research as a valued "way of knowing" their experiences, and if they are to use research as a tool in the struggle for social action, the fundamental nature of the epistemology must alter. In this chapter a critical theory of disability is traced through positivism and an interpretative social science to an ethical framework of social justice. This evolution is "praxis": the creation of a critical studies paradigm in disability. Critical studies in disability uses a framework of citizenship and social justice to raise questions of policy reform as it affects individuals, families and social systems. A new network of researchers, having adopted this paradigm of critical social science, are challenging epistemological foundations regarding disability and society.

Notes

1. These statements were drawn from the interviews of people who have been labelled intellectually disabled and were excluded and denied the experiences of citizenship for much of their lives. They are now living in the

community. This is the social reality of disability — "margin notes" on the new paradigm in disability research. Through their voices we share some sense of their experiences on the margins and their efforts at improving their situation.

2. S. Harding, *Feminism and Methodology*, Indiana: Indiana University Press, 1987.

3. S. Kirby and K. McKenna state that part of what it has meant to live "on the margins" is to be "required to perform a kind of doublethink/doublespeak in order to translate ... experience into the concepts and language of the status quo". S. Kirby and K. McKenna, *Experience, Research, Social Change, Methods from the Margins*, Toronto: Garamond Press, 1989.

4. B. Skinner, *Science and Human Behaviour*, New York: Free Press, 1953.

5. See G. Martin and J. Pear, *Behavior Modification: What It Is and How to Do It*, 2nd ed., Englewood Cliffs, N.J.: Prentice Hall, 1983; and L. Meyer and I. Evans, *Nonaversive Intervention for Behaviour Problems: A Manual for Home and Community*, Baltimore, Md.: Paul H. Brookes Publishing Co., 1989.

6. L'Institut Roeher Institute, *The Language of Pain: Perspectives on Behaviour Management*. Downsview, Ont.: Author, 1988.

7. W. Wolfensberger and S. Thomas, *Program Analysis of Service Systems: Implementation of Normalization Goals (PASSING)*. Downsview, Ont.: National Institute on Mental Retardation, 1983.

8. H. Brown and H. Smith, "Whose 'Ordinary Life' Is It Anyway?", *Disability, Handicap and Society*, 4(2), 1989, pp.

105-119; and A.L. Chappell, "Towards a Sociological Critique of the Normalization Principle", *Disability, Handicap and Society*, 7(1), 1992, pp. 35-51.

9. A. Wight Felske, "Postcards from the Margins", paper presented at the Ninth World Congress of the International Association for the Scientific Study of Mental Deficiency, Brisbane, Australia, 1992.

10. C. Peck, "Linking Values and Science in Social Policy Decisions Affecting Citizens with Severe Disabilities", in L. Meyer, C. Peck and L. Brown (eds.), *Critical Issues in the Lives of People with Severe Disabilities*, Baltimore, Md.: Paul H. Brookes Publishing Co., 1991, pp. 1-5.

11. Peck, "Linking Values", 1991 (see n. 10).

12. M. Oliver and G. Zarbe, "The Politics of Disability: A New Approach", *Disability, Handicap and Society*, 4(3), 1989, pp. 221-239.

13. M. Oliver, "Changing the Social Relations of Research Production?", *Disability, Handicap and Society*, 7(2), 1992, pp. 101-114.

14. M. Weber, "Some Categories of Interpretative Sociology", *Sociological Quarterly*, 22, 1981, pp. 151-180.

15. J. O'Brien and B. Mount, "Telling New Stories: The Search for Capacity among People with Severe Handicaps", in L. Myers, C. Peck and L. Brown (eds.), *Critical Issues in the Lives*, 1991 (see n. 10), pp. 89-92.

16. B. Glasser and A. Strauss, *The Discovery of Grounded Theory: Strategies for Qualitative Research*, Chicago: Aldine Press, 1969.

17. See G. Matthews, *Voices from the Shadows: Women with Disabilities Speak Out*, Toronto: Women's Education Press,

1983; and R. Bogdan and S. Taylor, *Inside/Out: The Social Meaning of Mental Retardation*, Toronto: University of Toronto Press, 1982.

18. D. Atkinson and F. Williams, *Know Me as I Am: An Anthology of Prose, Poetry and Art by People with Learning Difficulties*, London: Hodder and Stoughton, 1989.

19. John O'Brien, "A Guide to Lifestyle Planning: Using the Activities Catalogue to Integrate Services and Natural Support Systems", in B. Wilcox and G. Thomas Bellamy (eds.), *A Comprehensive Guide to the Activities Catalogue: An Alternative Curriculum for Youth and Adults with Severe Disabilities*, Baltimore, Md.: Paul H. Brookes Publishing Co., 1987.

20. Canada, Secretary of State, *The National Strategy for the Integration of Persons with Disabilities*, Ottawa: Government of Canada, 1991; Statistics Canada, *Health and Activity Limitations Survey*, Ottawa, 1986.

    Disability affects the lives of 13 per cent of Canadians. The impact, however, is wider than this, as a disability for one person will often affect the whole family, marginalizing the family with a pattern of social supports and service usage. A profile of people with disabilities in Canada gives the following facts:

    • People with disabilities are among the poorest members of society.

    • Only 40 per cent of adults with disabilities are in the paid labour force compared to 70 per cent of the general population.

    • There are long waiting lists for appropriate housing in every community.

- Only half of the people with disabilities who need specialized transportation services have access to them. Existing transportation system users face routine and repeated difficulties in travelling to work, school or elsewhere in the community.

- Barriers to education contribute to low literacy rates.

21. M. Sidell, "How Do We Know What We Think We Know?", in A. Brechin and J. Walmsley (eds.), *Making Connections*, London: Hodder and Stoughton, 1989.

22. W. Newman, *Social Research Methods: Qualitative and Quantitative Approaches*, Toronto: Allyn and Bacon, 1991.

23. See S. Kirby and K. McKenna, *Methods from the Margins*, 1989 (n. 3) for a discussion of the research methodology from the margins.

24. See Canada, Royal Commission on Equality in Employment, *Equality in Employment: A Royal Commission Report*, Ottawa: Supply and Services Canada, 1984; and L'Institut Roeher Institute, *On Target? Canada's Employment-Related Programs for Persons with Disabilities*, North York, Ont.: Author, 1992.

25. E. Boylan, *Women and Disability*, Women and Work Development Series, London: Zed Books Ltd., 1991; and R. Munford, "The Politics of Caregiving", paper presented at the Ninth World Congress of the International Association for the Scientific Study of Mental Deficiency, Brisbane, Australia, 1992.

26. See C. Baxter, K. Poonia, L. Ward and A. Nadirshaw, *Double Discrimination*, London: Kings Fund Centre, 1990; and R. Rieser and M. Mason, *Disability Equality in the Classroom: A Human Rights Issue*, London: London Education Authority, 1991.

27. Baxter, Poonia, Ward and Nadirshaw, *Double Discrimination*, 1990 (see n. 26).

28. I. Cocking and S. Athwal, "A Special Case for Special Treatment", *Social Work Today*, 1990, pp. 12-13.

29. See D. Demas, "Triple Jeopardy: Native Women with Disabilities", *COMPASS*, Special Edition, 1990, pp. 32-34; and M. Fine and A. Asch (eds.), *Women with Disabilities: Essays in Psychology, Culture and Politics*, Philadelphia: Temple University Press, 1988.

30. Government of Canada, *Women and Disability Forum*, Ottawa: 1988.

31. D. Driedger and H. Enns, *Statement on Equalization of Opportunities*, Stockholm: Disabled Peoples International, 1987, pp. 2-3. It further states: "to achieve the goals of full participation and equality, rehabilitation measures are not enough ... the needs of each and every individual are of equal importance, these needs must be made the basis for the planning of societies."

32. B. Blatt, *The Conquest of Mental Retardation*, Austin, Tex.: PRO-ED, 1987.

33. D. Polkinghorne, *Narrative Knowing and the Human Sciences*, Albany, N.Y.: State University of New York Press, 1988.

34. Research in social policy and intellectual impairment conducted at L'Institut Roeher Institute is representative of a critical studies paradigm. Research such as *On Target?*, *Poor Places, Income Insecurity, Nothing Personal, Vulnerable* and *How It Happens* led to a new conceptual framework on social well-being. They use both qualitative and quantitative analysis to reveal new insights to disability and social policy. The community living movement in Canada, and worldwide through advocacy groups

connected to the International League of Societies for Persons with Mental Handicaps, are engaged in a fight for equality through social action. Their struggle for social change has generated a new view of disability as an issue of human rights and citizenship. L'Institut Roeher Institute, *On Target?*, 1992 (see n. 24); L'Institut Roeher Institute, *Poor Places: Disability-Related Residential and Support Services*, North York, Ont.: Author, 1990; L'Institut Roeher Institute, *Income Insecurity: The Disability Income System in Canada*, North York, Ont.: Author, 1988; L'Institut Roeher Institute, *Nothing Personal: The Need for Personal Supports in Canada*, North York, Ont.: Author, 1993; L'Institut Roeher Institute, *Vulnerable: Sexual Abuse and People with an Intellectual Handicap*, North York, Ont.: Author, 1988; L'Institut Roeher Institute, *How It Happens: A Look at Inclusive Educational Practice in Canada for Children and Youth with Disabilities*, North York, Ont.: Author, 1992.

35. T. Kuhn, *The Structure of Scientific Revolution*, 2nd ed., Chicago: University of Chicago Press, 1970.

36. J. Nisbet, M. Clark and S. Covert, "Living It Up! An Analysis of Research on Community Living", in L. Meyer, C. Peck and L. Brown (eds.), *Critical Issues in the Lives*, 1991, (see n. 10), pp. 115-144.

37. A. Wight Felske, *Research by/for/with Women with Disabilities*, North York, Ont.: L'Institut Roeher Institute, 1991.

38. G. Zarb, "On the Road to Damascus: First Steps towards Changing the Relations of Disability Research Production", *Disability, Handicap and Society*, 7(2), 1992, pp. 125-138.

39. In the critical social science paradigm that supports the community living movement, the researcher is often a member of the group under study or has spent considerable time with the people in the study.

40. M. Oliver, "Guidelines for Funding Application to Undertake Disability Research", *Disability, Handicap and Society*, 7(3), 1992, pp. 279-280.

41. Outcome measures in the new paradigm embrace quantitative data sources such as the HALS (Health and Activity Limitation Survey) data base of the Canadian government as a way of addressing social reality. Qualitative information such as the participant's gender, ethnocultural and family roles are included as descriptive variables and outcome measures. The stigma of the role "disabled" is not seen as negating these memberships. It is precisely these roles that are severed by institutionalization and must be rebuilt, maintained and strengthened in community living.

42. A notable example is l'Institut Roeher Institute's plain language project in which straightforward versions of research studies have been published for a readership of people labelled intellectually disabled. Research in the critical studies paradigm will be available to people with disabilities and their organizations as well as the academia of mainstream disciplines such as law, political science, education, psychology and sociology. See, for example, L'Institut Roeher Institute, *The Right to Have a Job: A Straightforward Guide to Canada's Employment-Related Programs for Persons with Disabilities*, North York, Ont.: Author, 1994.

Chapter 9

The Social Semiotics of Disability

by Gary Woodill

W hat we refer to as disability in Western societies has been viewed differently in various historical periods. Before the Enlightenment and the rise of science, the view of disability can be characterized as "mythical" in that the presence of a disability was seen as a message from an other-worldly reality. For example, the ancient Greeks viewed the presence of visible differences as a disturbing message from the gods, one that required immediate appeasement. Infants who were born with unusual marks or limb configurations were sent back to the gods as offerings. Through the procedure of "exposure", the infant would be left to die on a mountain or beside a river.[1] Similarly, the ancient Hebrews viewed disability as a sign of imperfection that was incompatible with the sacred. They refused entry to the temple to persons with such physical differences as crooked noses, sores, missing limbs and crushed testicles. Christianity has a long tradition of ambivalence towards persons with disabilities, viewing them on the one hand as needing healing and assistance while on the other hand associating the presence of a disability with punishment for sin.[2]

The modern period of history in Western societies is characterized by the rise of science, the belief in progress and discovery of truth, and a view that reality can be known through rigorous empirical methods and technical instrumentation. Although medicine as a profession developed in the pre-modern period, its pre-eminent position in our society can be traced to its alliances with the scientific method and the strategic positioning of physicians as part of "the family".[3] As Michel Foucault[4] and others have demonstrated, professions in the human sciences have developed their positions of dominance over others through a knowledge/power spiral. This process includes the development of a professional discourse about a particular human group that is the object of that particular profession's practices. Starting with such scientific "discoveries" as germ theory, genetics, IQ and methods of rehabilitation, persons with disabilities have become the objects of both the discourse and practices of the professions of medicine, rehabilitation, psychiatry, psychology, education and social work. This has happened in such a way that, until recently, both the members of these professions and most persons with disabilities themselves have viewed the relationship between the professional, as "helper", and the person with a disability, as a "patient, client or student" in need of help, as a logical, positive and even natural state of affairs.

In recent years there has been a growing disenchantment with the modern world and its mostly positive images of science, professions and the relationships between professionals and their "patients" or "clients". This stance may be termed as "post-modern", although that term has been used to describe changes in everything from architecture to zoology. What is clear is that there has been, for many people, a shift in how they see and understand the social world. That change may be described as a shift from a "realistic" world view to a "constructivist" one[5] in which all reality is "mediated" by human perception and interpretation. In this new view, the world we generally take for granted is not "discovered" through science, but is "invented" through culture.

This new view has profound implications for the understanding of disability and persons with disabilities. From this stance one does not speak about "having a disability", in the sense that one actually possesses a particular condition, but rather of "the emergence of physical differences"[6] or the "invention of handicaps",[7] indicating the view that these "conditions" are social creations of a given culture. Because the meaning of disability can be seen as social creation, rather than designating a fixed and "natural" condition, the way is open for a change in the current meaning of disability through an analysis and reinvention of the way that disability is portrayed in this culture.

The very idea of a world of meaning that is socially constructed rather than discovered is the foundation for the development of the study of the semiotics of disability. The idea of the social construction of disabilities can be linked to the ground breaking work of Erving Goffman, who introduced such concepts as the "moral career of the mental patient", "total institutions" and "spoiled identity".[8] Another early work on the social construction of disability is Robert Scott's 1969 book, *The Making of Blind Men*.[9] In this book, Scott documents how persons who cannot see very well enter into an agency "for the blind" and come out with the identity of "blind person". That is, the process of socially constructing a person as having a "deviant personality" is one that involves professional diagnosis, labelling and treatment.[10]

In 1983 William Roth demonstrated how a theory of social construction changes the focus on disability from a medical problem to a political issue.[11] More recently, Philip Ferguson has shown how a constructivist perspective can be useful in analyzing the situation of persons with severe intellectual impairments,[12] while Robert Bogdan and Steven Taylor note that even the idea of a severely disabled person possessing "humanness" must be socially constructed.[13]

Yet these efforts to understand how disability is constructed lack depth because they do not show how Western society's view of disability is deeply rooted in the ways we communicate with and about our bodies and the ways language and myths have historically conditioned our views of what it means to be disabled. Professional power and privilege, for example, are not isolated phenomena but are linked to general cultural mythologies about science, sickness and the "normal". In order to better understand the roots of inequality, marginalization and disadvantage faced by persons with a disability, we must research the meaning and origins of the words and images about disability that form part of the cultural codes we all take for granted and in which we are all immersed. A semiotics of disability provides a framework for carrying out such research. It can provide an understanding of the role of communication in the construction and maintenance of dominant concepts of disability.

Semiotics

Semiotics is the study of the meaning of signs and has its roots in the work of the Swiss linguist Ferdinand de Saussure and the American philosopher C.S. Peirce. Signs are any aspect of our world that communicates a message. Spoken and written language is the most important system of signs for human beings, but many signs are non-verbal in that there are many ways of communicating besides the use of a formal language.[14] A set of signs that are codified constitute a text. Text does not need to be written language, although that is certainly one of its forms. Dress codes, gestures, art, stereotypical movements, accents, deliberate use of colours and so on are all codified signs that are open to our interpretation.[15] A semiotic analysis can focus on various aspects of signs, signification and text. In laying out directions for a semiotics of disability I will draw on three aspects of semiotic analysis: metaphor; the communication situation; and the standpoints or viewpoints of voices that are encoded into the text or excluded from it.

As a set of codified signs, texts are interpreted metaphorically in ways that are meaningful to the reader. As George Lakoff and Mark Johnson have argued in *Metaphors We Live By*, much of the meaning in our language is based on a set of physical metaphors.[16] The set of metaphors available to us are those learned through our cultural history and transmitted to us through schooling, parenting and the various media, or those metaphors we create on our own.[17]

When faced with a set of signs that evoke a particular

prototypical image, we tend to place that image into a category that we know and that seems to best fit with the person or image of the person we encounter, a process that is often called labelling. Metaphors may also be a form of dealing with a topic that is uncomfortable and, therefore, the metaphors for disability may also become *euphemisms*.[18]

Some visible signs that signify the differentness of disability are generally taken to be unambiguous (although they too have a history): wheelchairs, white canes and hearing aids are physical devices that mark a person as having a disability in our culture. Other signs are also visible but more ambiguous, such as dark glasses, "bizarre" behaviour and differences in speech. These ambiguous signs are open to wider interpretation and often need the combination of several cues in order to convey a clear message. Still other signs are invisible without mediating instrumentation and require the "confessional technology"[19] of psychological or medical testing for a difference to be noted and discussed. The signs of difference are read metaphorically as text in different ways by different people, depending on the position they hold in society and the position or stance they have in regard to the particular person with a disability they encounter. Therefore, any situation involving a person or persons with a disability can have both many different readings of the same text and "multiple voices"[20] representing the viewpoints of those who are able to speak about that situation.

A social semiotics approach to research can also look at some or all of the elements that make up the communication situation. The linguist Roman Jakobson[21] divided the communication process into the following six constituent factors:

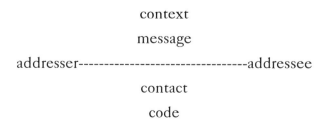

```
                    context
                    message
addresser--------------------------------addressee
                    contact
                    code
```

Much of the research to date on the social semiotics of disability has been the analysis of the content of the actual messages being conveyed, rather than such features as context or the relationships between addresser and addressee. For example, in their book *Social Semiotics*, Robert Hodge and Gunther Kress look at how messages of power and solidarity are conveyed between two people.[22] The use of first and last names, specific pronouns and terms of familiarity and formality are all involved in exchanges which convey a message that one party in the dialogue has much more power than the other. Observing interactions between persons with disabilities and professionals would likely provide a rich source of data on this type of interaction.

In reading social situations or texts for signs, one must be aware that there are many possible ways of making sense of a given scene or a reading of a text. As Mikhail Bakhtin, a Russian literary theorist (who had a disability), has indicated, for the novel, social situations can have many voices and many readers.[23] Voice, from a Bakhtinian perspective, represents the communication of the stance or viewpoint of the speaker in relation to the others in the situation in question. Therefore, I may speak (appropriately or inappropriately) as a professor, a critic, a spouse, a survivor or a victim, or in many other voices, depending on which "subject position" I occupy in relation to others involved in the same interaction.

In another paper,[24] my colleagues and I have identified at least five voices in social situations involving persons with disabilities: the popular voice; the intimate voice; the professional voice; the marginalized voice;and the analytical voice. The voice of a person with a disability is often absent, diminished or marginalized in situations where a person with a disability is in the company of non-disabled persons. As David Goode[25] has shown in his work with adolescents who had both visual and hearing impairments and who were without language, there are ways to hear the idiosyncratic voice of the non-verbal person, even when there is no written or spoken text for that person's voice. There is a greater chance that the voice of persons with less severe disabilities will be heard. However, there are still many reasons why this voice may also be marginalized.

First, the amount of text production and non-textual gestures by a person with a specific communication impairment may be limited. In electronic communications jargon, the *bandwidth* of communication may be very narrow, allowing only faint messages to be sent. This does not mean that communication is impossible, just that others might have to make an extra effort or find alternative means to listen.

Second, a person with a disability may have a different *footing* for communication. That is, in a conversation or presentation, a person's "alignment, or set, or stance, or posture, or projected self is somehow at issue".[26] Differences in the footing of communication can be manifested in many ways. There may be difficulties with *code-switching*, in that a person is unable to change posture or to modulate his or her speaking voice in order to indicate that the *frame* of the communication has changed. Because of a lack of mobility, a person may not be able to move away from a conversation and may therefore become an inadvertent bystander or eavesdropper. Persons with visual impairments or those with a lack of neck movement may not be able to indicate that they are listening through the use of eye contact. People who use wheelchairs may be at a disadvantage in communicating strength through actions such as standing or lifting. Research on the social semiotics would examine all these non-verbal components in the construction of the meaning of disability in our society.

Third, the voice of a person with a disability may be marginalized by the reactions of others. The reasons for miscommunication between people with and without disabilities have been recently explored by Lerita Coleman and Bella DePaulo.[27] If an encounter between a person with a disability and others, especially those who are not disabled, results in the other person reading the "disabled body" by interpreting signs in a stereotypical way (whether positive or negative stereotypes), then the result will likely be that the voice of the person with a disability will not be understood. What will likely be heard, instead, will be the *voice of the dominant other* — the person who often speaks *for* a person with a disability — or embarrassed silence.

If persons with disabilities are heard *in spite* of the efforts of non-disabled persons to dominate, then we could refer to this as the *voice of resistance*.[28] An example of this voice is a phenomenon developing as a counter to the language of professionals and the dominant non-disabled society. There is an emerging disability culture in which persons with disabilities appropriate language and transform it or invent new words, metaphors, myths and images that reflect their own experiences of the world. The beginnings of disability culture have been in the deaf community, which has talked about deaf culture for many years — a culture with its own language, history and traditions.[29] Other disability groups, such as members of People First or the Independent Living Movement, are now developing their own sense of pride and community which comes from having a positive, self-defined group identity. Part of the struggle for the development of a disability culture has been over the use of language and images.

Present research and theorizing on the social semiotics of disability has drawn on these elements of a semiotic analysis to pursue three distinct paths. One has been the analysis of the images of disability in popular culture and the media. Another has been the examination of the representation of disability in professional discourse, including how these images are reflected in the self-representations of persons with disabilities. A third area for research on the semiotics of disability, which is just emerging, is the study of the development of disability culture. The concepts used in these three approaches to the social semiotics of disability and their respective bodies of literature will be presented in the rest of this chapter.

The Image of Disability in Popular Culture

For a person who is not familiar with persons with severe disabilities, an initial encounter can be filled with shock and even horror.[30] This reaction has been attributed both to the relative lack of familiarity of non-disabled persons with persons with disabilities and to the presence of certain mythologies about people with disabilities which persist and are perpetuated in popular culture.

Perhaps the oldest and most durable image is that of the person with a disability as a monster or freak.[31] This image has been diffused throughout the culture in fairy tales, films, literature, circus side shows and even medical terminology. A recent computer search of the *Medline* database revealed over 30 medical articles published from 1985 to 1990 that used the term "monster" to refer to an abnormal fetus.[32] Table 1 indicates some of the various metaphors used for persons with disabilities in popular culture.

Table 1. Variations of the Popular Cultural Voice on Disability

Type of Metaphor	Example of Metaphor	Historically Related To
Humanitarian	Disability as misfortune	Giving to charity, telethons
Medical	Disability as sickness	Hospitals, medical care, cure, healing
Outsider	Disabled person as "other"	Monsters, strangers
Religious	Disability as divine plan	Charity, fortune/ misfortune
Retribution	Disability as punishment	Sin
Social control	Disability as threat	Monsters, horror shows
Zoological	Disabled person as pet, disability as entertainment	Freak show, circus, wrestling, dwarf tossing/bowling

As Irving Zola has argued, the types of disability metaphors used, and their methods of use, change with both the context and the type of media in which the metaphor is presented.[33] Briefly, here are some of the main sources of images of persons with disabilities in popular culture in Western societies.

Everyday language

Metaphors of disability, which ordinary persons use in everyday life to speak about their understanding and perceptions of disability (reading the text of the disabled body), can be used to understand and speak about other phenomena. Metaphors of disability are also used to make negative comments about non-disabled persons who are seen as lacking in some ability or as having characteristics outside societal standards (technically, a "dysphemism").[34] For example, employing the classification system of mental impairments in use until the 1960s, we can find people calling others "idiots", "imbeciles" or "morons" to denote a perception of stupidity in the other person. "Are you blind?" can be asked of a child who cannot find something around the house, "Are you deaf?" to a child who does not respond immediately to adult commands. As a counter to such negative images, Irving Zola suggests some positive uses of disability as a metaphor, such as survival and endurance.[35] To date there has been little other research on the use of disability metaphors in everyday speech.

Cartoons

One source of popular images of persons with disabilities is in cartoons, either those found in newspapers or collected in books. Brief studies in this area have been carried out in the United States, Canada and France.[36] This early work has shown that cartoons are often a good way to get at people's attitudes towards persons with disabilities, as one tends to react on an emotional level (laughing, being disgusted and so on) immediately and think about the reasons for the reaction later. This research also shows cross-cultural differences in how persons with disabilities are portrayed and what is acceptable in terms of images. For example, it is easier to find explicit sexual acts and stances involving persons with disabilities in French cartoons compared to those found in North America. In North America, images of disability, especially blindness, are often used as negative visual metaphors in political cartoons on editorial pages.

Literature and art

Perhaps the most pervasive source of images of persons with disabilities in popular culture is adult and children's literature. Keith Byrd has surveyed a list of over 16,000 literary characters to identify those that portrayed persons with disabilities.[37] Disabled characters are often brought into stories to add emotional elements such as horror, fear or sympathy. In France, René-Claude Lachal[38] has developed a large body of work on the portrayal of disability in Italian children's literature and proverbs, while Iain Davidson, Gary Woodill and Elizabeth Bredberg have analyzed the image of disabilities in 19th-century children's literature.[39]

A new book by David Hevey, *The Creatures Time Forgot*, shows the differences in the type of photographic images produced by charity advertising, mainstream photographers such as Diane Arbus and photography shot by persons with disabilities.[40] There is also a growing literature on the image of disability in paintings and sculpture. A recent inventory of works of art depicting disability in national museums around the world has been carried out by a team from Toronto and Paris.[41]

Newspapers and magazines

Newspapers and magazines are a good source for analyzing images of persons with disabilities. Extensive work on the image of persons with disabilities in newspapers and advertising has been carried out by René-Claude Lachal and Philippe Saint-Martin in France.[42] The production of stigma through media advertising for accident and injury prevention has been studied by Caroline Wang.[43]

Film and theatre

Every year there are dozens of films released that show one or more persons with disabilities in minor or major parts. Keith Byrd has recently reviewed the portrayal of persons with disabilities in American films from 1986 to 1988 and concluded that "disability can be used to manipulate the story line for entertainment purposes".[44] A French volume of articles edited by Olga Behar in 1984[45] shows the different roles that persons with disabilities have played in films, from the circus performers of Tod Browning's 1932 film *Freaks* to the angry Vietnam vet with paraplegia played by Jon Voight in 1978 in *Coming Home.*

Television images of persons with disabilities have been described by a number of authors.[46] In 1981 Joy Donaldson, using a random sample of television clips analyzed by independent observers, found that 3.2 per cent of the major characters, but only 0.4 per cent of the minor characters on television, were portrayed as having a disability. The majority of disabled characters viewed in this study were portrayed in a negative manner. Gerbner, Morgan and Signorielli, in an 11-year study, found that only about 2 per cent of television characters had a disability. Current estimates are that about 12 to 15 per cent of the North American population identify themselves as disabled.

Finally, the various theatrical portrayals of Joseph Merrick, "The Elephant Man", have been critically analyzed for the messages that each image has projected for a mostly non-disabled audience. To quote the book cover:

> In *Articulating the Elephant Man*, Peter W. Graham and Fritz H. Oehlschlaeger examine how the phenomenon called 'the elephant man' has been constructed and reconstructed — how Joseph Merrick has been transformed from a suffering individual into an exhibit, a shape-shifting curiosity whose different guises variously suit the needs of particular audiences, genres and interpreters.[47]

The Representation of Disability in Professional Discourse

The reading of signs in medicine has a long history, going back to pre-Hippocratic times, where indexical signs were important to ancient doctors. This practice of reading indexical signs has been linked to the reading of animal traces (such as feces and footprints) in hunting cultures.[48] Galen (131-201 AD), the Roman physician who developed early surgical techniques using pigs, was the first medical doctor to use the term "semiotics" to describe the reading of bodily signs we now call symptoms.[49] In the medical model, the body is "read" for "symptoms" under the power of the "medical gaze".[50] Diagnosis and treatment generally follow. Essentially, this is a one-way process for much of the time, with the body being treated as an object of practice.

The medical voice is only one variation of the professional voice in work with persons with disabilities, although it should be noted that many human service professions have adopted the medical voice in the development of a professional discourse of assessment, diagnosis and treatment. Other variations of the professional voice are found in Table 2. The idea of a professional voice refers to a particular stance or world view. There are professionals who do not speak in the professional voice about disability and there are parents and persons with disabilities who have incorporated the professional voice into their speaking about disability.

Table 2. Variations of the Professional Voice on Disability

Type of Metaphor	Example of Metaphor	Historically Related To
Deviance	Disability as violation of norms, social pathology	Pendulums, statistics
Educational	Disability as a deficit	Compulsory education
Humanitarian	Disability as misfortune	Feeding those in need
Medical	Disability as sign of sickness	Tracking animals
Positivistic	Disability as object of study	Physics
Social Service	Disability as a breakdown of functioning, imperfection	Repair shop, assembly line
Technological	Disability as a technical problem	Engineering

The medical metaphor has a long history and has been imitated and extended by other professional groups who want to have the prestige and power of the medical profession. "Diagnosis", "prescription", "treatment" and many other medical words are used today in education, social work and psychology. This medical metaphor, whether it is used in medicine or in allied professions, generally has negative consequences for the person who is labelled. As Irving Zola points out, "Being seen as the object of medical treatment evokes the image of many ascribed traits, such as weakness, helplessness, dependency, regressiveness, abnormality of appearance and depreciation of every mode of physical and mental functioning".[51]

A new metaphor is emerging within the disability community, which is to see people with disabilities as members of a minority group. The consequences of this shift are immense as the assumptions of the medical model are radically challenged by this new conception. Seeing a person with a disability as sick leads to one set of reactions towards that person, whereas the image of "member of a minority group" leads to another set of reactions. Defenders of the medical metaphor might argue that it is in place for humanitarian reasons but this argument says nothing about the fact that the medical metaphor empowers professionals rather than people with disabilities themselves. The sick role in our society has been described as follows:[52]

1. The patient is exempted from normal role obligations.

2. The patient is not held responsible for his or her state.

3. The state of being sick is considered conditionally legitimate if —

4. The patient cooperates with the source of help and actively works to achieve recovery.

5. The sick role will be temporary.

But the assumption of a sick role for a person with a disability, however humane the intentions, has profound and negative consequences.[53] First, the role is not temporary, which ultimately places the "medical tolerance" given by members of society into question. Second, not only is the person with a disability exempted from normal role obligations and expectations, he or she is often prevented from fulfilling normal roles even if that person is capable and willing to do so. Instead, the person is seen as always needing help and social support. Third, the sick role requires cooperation of the person with a disability in the professional management of, and intervention in, his or her "case". If the person refuses to obey the given prescriptions, he or she is seen as rebellious, defensive, ungrateful and resistant to treatment. Fourth, the sick role and the medical model locate the problems faced by a person with a disability solely in biology. This emphasis on the biological rather than the social environment as the cause of disability often means that disability is taken in research studies as an independent variable and, therefore, as an uncritically accepted given that produces various consequences. Fifth, when a person with a disability faces problems, it is often assumed that the person's impairment caused the problems. Sixth, since the sick role means that the person is not responsible for his or her state, a person with a disability is often seen as a perpetual victim.

Although circumstances causing disabilities can legitimately be seen as unfortunate or even tragic, research indicates that most persons with disabilities do not perpetually consider themselves as victims, especially those born with an impairment, or if a sufficient period of time has passed after an accident or onset of a disease that resulted in an impairment. A related assumption — that disability is central to a person's self-concept, self-definition, social comparisons and reference groups — is also an unfounded consequence of the sick role. This is more likely a projection of the non-disabled who are preoccupied with the prospect of their own future disabilities (and even death) when they confront a person with a disability.

The emerging minority group metaphor shifts the analysis from sickness to discrimination. The assumptions of this metaphor for a person with a disability also have profound consequences. Being a member of a minority group means:

1. The person is not automatically exempted from normal role expectations, but may be prevented from assuming a normal role by the actions and attitudes of persons not in the minority group.

2. The person is held responsible for his or her actions, but his or her situation may be limited by lack of opportunities and barriers.

3. The person has much in common with members of other minority groups and therefore —

4. The person is able to learn from the history and tactics of the civil rights movement about how to increase his or her freedom and reduce discrimination.

5. Solidarity with the members of the minority group and members of allied minority groups is a source of strength and help, and it may be necessary to limit the involvement of members of the majority group (non-disabled) in the decision-making process of the minority group's actions.

This is a far different prospect for a person with a disability than playing the sick role. Yet the power of the medical metaphor is such that this change will not come easily.

Language and Disability Culture

One of the interesting things about the work cited above is that much of it has been carried out by researchers who identify themselves as disabled. This is one indicator of a change in control over the language and images used to depict disability. The semiotics of disability are shifting and the images found in professional literature are increasingly being produced by persons with disabilities or by non-disabled people who have been sensitized by the vocabulary and actions of the disability rights movement. In addition, artists, writers, poets, dancers and photographers who are disabled are producing new images of the experience of disability both for the disability community and the public at large. In this new disability culture, words that were formerly seen as oppressive have been used by persons with disabilities to speak about their views of the world. A good example of this is the song "Spasticus Autisticus", written by Ian Dury in 1981 for the International Year of the Disabled. Dury had polio as a child and has a tendency to fall down. He has turned this into a positive attribute by incorporating it into his performances with his band, The Blockheads.

217

As Patricia Chadwick noted at the 1993 conference for the Society for Disability Studies:

> An empowerment strategy for disenfranchised groups is to change the frame of reference and through this begin a dialogue that challenges the dominant ideology ... This does not mean that every characteristic or experience of a particular group has to be defined as positive. What it means is that the members of the group should define for themselves and for the larger society what is positive and negative about their experience.[54]

This is most interesting when persons with disabilities reject well-meaning positive terms that actually cover up their experience of the world. The following poem illustrates these points.

I Am Not One of The ...

I am not one of the physically
challenged ...
I'm a sock in the eye with a gnarled fist
I'm a French kiss with cleft tongue
I'm orthopedic shoes sewn on the last of
your fears

I'm not one of the differently
abled ...
I'm an epitaph for a million
imperfect babies left untreated
I'm an icon carved from bones in
a mass grave at Tiergarten,
Germany
I'm withered legs hidden in a
blanket

I'm not one of the able disabled ...
I'm a black panther with green eyes and
scars like a picket fence
I'm pink lace panties teasing a stub of
milk white thigh
I'm the Evil Eye

I'm the first cell divided
I'm mud that talks
I'm Eve I'm Kali
I'm The Mountain that Never Moves
I've been forever I'll be here forever
I'm the Gimp
I'm the Cripple
I'm the Crazy Lady
I'm the Woman with Juice

Cheryl Marie Wade[55]

The semiotics of disability has taught us not to take for granted the language we use to describe disability and has uncovered the role of language in supporting professional power over persons with a disability. It has also pointed the way to the use of new words and metaphors as a tool for liberation.

An agenda for future research on the social semiotics of disability should include:

1. More ethnographic studies of various social situations in which persons with disabilities interact with each other and with non-disabled people, to see how signs are read by all participants.

2. Historical research on the development of terms and concepts to reveal their hidden ideologies and origins.

3. An analysis of the role of the concept of the "normal" in defining persons with disabilities. We also need to understand how science is used to legitimize the production of norms and the normal.

4. A study of how and when young children develop a vocabulary and understanding of differences among people.

5. Conceptual analysis of the link between theories of disability and vocabulary. In particular, a social semiotics of disability should not be developed in isolation from a critical theory of disability that recognizes power and oppression. Such a theory, now being developed, would connect with theories of sexism and racism.

The social semiotics of disability is a powerful tool in the analysis of the situation and social construction of persons with disabilities. It shows us how signs of difference that are learned and used from an early age by people both with and without disabilities can create our conscious and unconscious images of what it means to be disabled, and how these representations can perpetuate oppression and helplessness. By uncovering and debunking, by appropriating and redeploying the signs denoting disability, we can move towards emancipation of all.

Notes

1. Henri-Jacques Stiker, *Corps infirmes et sociétés*, Paris: Aubier-Montaigne, 1982.

2. Dominique Le Disert, "Entre la peur et la pitié: Quelques aspects socio-historiques de l'infirmité", *International Journal of Rehabilitation Research*, 10(3), 1987, pp. 253-265.

3. Jacques Donzelot, *The Policing of Families*, New York: Pantheon, 1979.

4. Michel Foucault, *The Archaeology of Knowledge*, New York: Harper and Row, 1972; Michel Foucault, *Power/Knowledge*, New York: Pantheon, 1980.

5. Lawrence Hazelrigg, *Claims of Knowledge: On the Labour of Making Found Worlds*, Tallahasee, Fla.: Florida State University Press, 1989.

6. Harlan Hahn, "Disability and the Reproduction of Bodily Images: The Dynamics of Human Appearances", in J. Wolch and M. Dear (eds.), *The Power of Geography*, Boston: Unwin Hyman, 1989, pp. 370-388.

7. Serge Ebersold, *L'Invention du handicap: La normalisation de l'infirme*, Vanves, France: CTNERHI, 1992.

8. Erving Goffman, *Asylums: Essays on the Social Situation of Mental Patients and Other Inmates*, New York: Anchor Books, 1961; Erving Goffman, *Stigma: Notes on the Management of Spoiled Identity*, Englewood Cliffs, N.J.: Prentice-Hall, 1963.

9. Robert Scott, *The Making of Blind Men*, New York: Russell Sage Foundation, 1969.

10. Robert Scott, "The Social Construction of the Conception of Stigma by Professional Experts", in J. Douglas (ed.), *Deviance and Respectability*, New York: Basic Books, 1970.

11. William Roth, "Handicap as a Social Construct", *Society*, 20(3), 1983, pp. 56-61.

12. Philip Ferguson, "The Social Construction of Mental Retardation", *Social Policy*, 18(1), 1987, pp. 51-56.

13. Robert Bogdan and Steven Taylor, "Relationships with Severely Disabled People: The Social Construction of Humanness", *Social Problems*, 36(2), 1989, pp. 135-148.

14. Terence Hawkes, *Structuralism and Semiotics*, Berkeley, Calif.: University of California Press, 1977.

15. Richard Brown, *Society as Text: Essays on Rhetoric, Reason and Reality*, Chicago: University of Chicago Press, 1987.

16. George Lakoff and Mark Johnson, *Metaphors We Live By*, Chicago: University of Chicago Press, 1980.

17. Gary Woodill and Iain Davidson, "The Language of Special Education Professionals: A Conceptual Framework", *Canadian Journal of Special Education*, 5(2), 1989, pp. 115-122.

18. Keith Allan and Kate Burridge, *Euphemism and Dysphemism: Language as a Shield and a Weapon*, Oxford: Oxford University Press, 1991.

19. Michel Foucault, *Discipline and Punish: The Birth of the Prison*, New York: Vintage, 1979.

20. Mikhail Bakhtin, *The Dialogical Imagination*, Austin, Tex.: University of Texas Press, 1981.

21. Cited in Hawkes, *Structuralism and Semiotics*, 1977, p. 83 (see n. 14).

22. Robert Hodge and Gunther Kress, *Social Semiotics*, Ithaca, N.Y.: Cornell University Press, 1988.

23. Bakhtin, *The Dialogical Imagination*, 1981 (see n. 20).

24. Gary Woodill, Jean-François Ravaud, Isabelle Ville and Elizabeth Bredberg, "The Disabled Body as Text: A Reading of Handicaps as Cultural Metaphors", paper presented at the International Conference on Language and Social Intervention, University of Rouen, Rouen, France, April 1992.

25. David Goode, "Socially Produced Identities, Intimacy and the Problem of Competence among the Retarded", in Len Barton and Sally Tomlinson (eds.), *Special Education and Social Interests*, London: Croom Helm, 1984, pp. 228-248.

26. Erving Goffman, *Forms of Talk*, Philadelphia: University of Pennsylvania Press, 1981.

27. Lerita Coleman and Bella DePaulo, "Uncovering the Human Spirit: Moving beyond Disability and 'Missed' Communication", in Nikolas Coupland, Howard Giles and John Wiemann (eds.), *Miscommunication and Problematic Talk*, Newbury Park, Calif.: Sage, 1991.

28. James Scott, *Domination and the Arts of Resistance: Hidden Transcripts*, New Haven: Yale University Press, 1990.

29. Carol Padden and Tom Humphries, *Deaf in America: Voices from a Culture*, Cambridge, Mass.: Harvard University Press, 1988.

30. Goode, *"Socially Produced Identities"*, 1984 (see n. 25).

31. Leslie Fiedler, *Freaks: Myths and Images of the Secret Self*, New York: Simon and Schuster, 1978; S. Thurer, "Disability and Monstrosity: A Look at Literary Distortions of Handicapping Conditions", *Rehabilitation Literature*, 41, 1980, pp. 12-15; H. Livneh, "Disability and Monstrosity: Further Comments", *Rehabilitation Literature*, 41, 1980, pp. 280-283; Randal Levenson, *In Search of the Monkey Girl*, New York: Aperture, 1982; Robert Bogdan, "Exhibiting

Mentally Retarded People for Amusement and Profit, 1850-1940", *American Journal of Mental Deficiency*, 91(2), 1986, pp. 120-126; Robert Bogdan, *Freak Show: Presenting Human Oddities for Amusement and Profit*, Chicago: University of Chicago Press, 1988; Daniel Mannix, *Freaks: We Who Are Not as Others*, Eugene, Oreg.: Re/Search Publications, 1990; Frederick Drimmer, *Very Special People*, New York: Citadel Press, 1991.

32. Gary Woodill, "Medical Monsters: A Brief History", paper presented at the conference Current Research on the History of Disabilities, l'Institut Roeher Institute, North York, Ont., November 1990.

33. Irving Zola, "Depictions of Disability - Metaphor, Message and Medium in the Media: A Research and Political Agenda", *Social Science Journal*, 22(4), 1985.

34. Allan and Burridge, *Euphemism and Dysphemism*, 1991 (see n. 18).

35. Zola, "Depictions of Disability, 1985 (see n. 33).

36. N. Weinberg and R. Santana, "Comic Books: Champions of the Disabled Stereotype", *Rehabilitation Literature*, 39(11-12), 1978, pp. 327-331; Iain Davidson and Gary Woodill, "Humour and Disability: Uses and Abuses", in *Actes, Congrès "Handicaps et Communication"*, CNAM, Paris, February, 1988; Jean-François Ravaud, "Le fauteuil roulant dans la bande dessinée, contribution à l'étude des représentations sociales du handicap", in *Actes des premiers Entretiens de la Fondation Garches*, Paris, 1988, pp. 168-170.

37. E. Keith Byrd, "A Review of Literary Characters and Disability", *International Journal of Rehabilitation Research*, 10(3), 1987, pp. 306-309.

38. René-Claude Lachal, "Infirmes et infirmités dans des

proverbes italiens", *Ethnologie française*, 2(1-2), 1972, pp. 67-96; René-Claude Lachal, "L'infirme dans la littérature italienne destinée à l'enfance et à la jeunesse: analyse typologique de 57 oeuvres", *Enfance*, No. 3-4-5, 1974, pp. 287-312; René-Claude Lachal, "L'animal infirme", *Italianistica*, 5(1), 1976, pp. 118-135; René-Claude Lachal, "L'infirme dans la littérature narrative italienne destinée à la jeunesse aux XIXe et XXe siècles", thesis for the Doctorat d'Etat, University of Bordeaux III, 1983; René-Claude Lachal, "Les stéréotypes de l'infirme en Italie d'après des proverbes et des livres pour la jeunesse", *Mediterranea*, No. 18, 1985, pp. 5-10; René-Claude Lachal, "Les représentations des personnes handicapées dans la littérature", *Cahiers ethnologiques de l'Université de Bordeaux II*, No. 7, 1986, pp. 177-183.

39. Iain Davidson, Gary Woodill and Elizabeth Bredberg, "The Image of Disability in 19th Century British Children's Literature", *Disability and Society*, 9(1), 1994.

40. David Hevey, *The Creatures Time Forgot: Photography and Disability Imagery*, London and New York: Routledge, 1992.

41. This unpublished survey lists over 1600 works of art depicting persons with disabilities. The work was carried out by Henri-Jacques Stiker in Paris, and Gary Woodill, Iain Davidson and Elizabeth Bredberg in Toronto. Contact the author for more information.

42. René-Claude Lachal, "Information du public et insertion sociale", *Pro Infirmis*, 36(4), 1977, pp. 158-168; René-Claude Lachal, "L'information sur les personnes handicapées à travers la presse régionale française (constantes et évolutions de 1977 à 1988)", *Cahiers ethnologiques de l'Université de Bordeaux II*, No. 13, 1991, pp. 39-75; Philippe Saint-Martin, "Images du handicapé proposées au grand public", *Réadaptation*, 262(7-8), 1979,

pp. 16-21; Philippe Saint-Martin and René-Claude Lachal, "Les personnes handicapées vues par la presse régionale française", *Cahiers ethnologiques de l'Université de Bordeaux II*, No. 4, 1983, pp. 2-44.

43. Caroline Wang, "Culture, Meaning and Disability: Injury Prevention Campaigns and the Production of Stigma", *Social Science and Medicine*, 35(9), 1992, pp. 1093-1102.

44. E. Keith Byrd, "A Comparison of Characters in Feature Films Who Are Disabled and Able Bodied", *International Journal of Rehabilitation Research*, 13, 1990, pp. 262-264.

45. Olga Behar (ed.), *CinémAction: L'écran handicapé*, Paris: Cerf, 1984.

46. E. Keith Byrd, P.D. Byrd and C.M. Allen, "Television Programming and Disability", *Journal of Applied Rehabilitation Counselling*, 8, 1977, pp. 28-32; Joy Donaldson, "Channel Variations and Effects on Attitudes toward Physically Disabled Individuals", *A.V. Communication Review*, 24, 1976, pp. 135-144; Joy Donaldson, "The Visibility and Image of Handicapped People on Television", *Exceptional Children*, 47(6), 1981, pp. 413-416; G. Gerbner, M. Morgan and N. Signorielli, "Programming Health Portrayals: What Viewers See, Say, and Do", in D. Pearl, L. Bouthilet and J. Lazar (eds.), *Television and Behaviour: Ten Years of Scientific Progress and Implications for the 80s*, Washington, D.C.: U.S. Government Printing Office, 1982, pp. 291-307; B.D. Leonard, "Impaired View: Television Portrayal of Handicapped People", doctoral dissertation, Boston University, 1978.

47. From book cover of Peter W. Graham and Fritz H. Oehlschlaeger, *Articulating the Elephant Man: Joseph Merrick and His Followers*, Baltimore, Md.: Johns Hopkins University Press, 1992.

48. Thomas Sebeok, "From a Semiotics of Nature to a Semiotics of Culture", lecture presented at University of Toronto, March, 1992.

49. For more on the semiotics of the medical symptom, see Eugen Baer, "The Medical Symptom", in John Deely, Brooke Williams and Felicia Kruse (eds.), *Frontiers of Semiotics*, Bloomington, Ind.: Indiana University Press, 1986, pp. 140-152.

50. Michel Foucault, *Birth of the Clinic: An Archaeology of Medical Perception*, New York: Vintage, 1975.

51. Irving Zola, "Self, Identity and the Naming Question: Reflections on the Language of Disability", *Social Science and Medicine*, 36(2), 1993, pp. 167-173.

52. J. Gliedman and William Roth, *The Unexpected Minority: Handicapped Children in America*, New York: Harcourt, Brace and Jovanovich, 1980.

53. Michelle Fine and Adrienne Asch, "Disability beyond Stigma: Social Interaction, Discrimination, and Activism", *Journal of Social Issues*, 44(1), 1988, pp. 3-21.

54. Patricia Chadwick, "Disability Culture", paper presented at the Society for Disability Studies Conference, Seattle, Wash., June 1993.

55. Cheryl Marie Wade, "I Am Not One of The ...", *Sinister Wisdom*, 1987. Used with the permission of the author.

Chapter 10

Setting One Agenda for Empowering Persons with a Disadvantage within the Research Process

by Paul Ramcharan and Gordon Grant

> Most social research has failed to acknowledge or even be aware of recent attempts by disabled people to reformulate and devise more appropriate definitions of disability ... The only way ahead is for disabled people and researchers to work together in constructing a more appropriate research enterprise, and failure of researchers to acknowledge this will inevitably mean that disabled people will construct their own research enterprise without them.[1]

The central thesis of this chapter is that disadvantaged groups[2] are commonly perceived to be unable to communicate in ways that are sanctionable and legitimized by a variety of people within society, and by the powerful structures and institutions created by the actions of such people. As such, these powerful individuals and groups have assumed, by default or through some system of authority, the right to speak and make choices on behalf of disadvantaged groups and individuals. These include medical, legal and governmental bodies. In assuming this right, they have tended to treat people and groups as commodities — to "commodify" them.

Mike Oliver points out that, at least formerly, prevailing definitions of disability have been largely tied up with a "personal tragedy" model.[3] Such definitions, he argues, construct disability as a problem and produce an interest in finding solutions. Many commentators have also argued that such solutions, at least in social policy terms, have been tied up with several devices for dealing with such people as a problem: the identification of socio-economic status, for example, in categorizing disabled people as "unemployable", as opposed to the "employed" and "unemployed";[4] the Great Imprisonment[5] in which placing people "round the bend" hid them from the rest of society; the emergence of a benevolent, and patronizing, social welfare state which seeks the alleviation of disability but not the celebration of people with disabilities and their worth.

We contend that the research process is one of the structures that perpetuates this "commodification" and that implicitly accepts the "personal tragedy model" of disability. A "tokenistic" research-process model prevails, in which the disadvantaged person is isolated from decisions about research commissioning, from setting the research agenda, from formulating appropriate research designs or from influencing the nature and content of research dissemination. By subjecting this model to criticism, an alternative and mutually exclusive "devolved research" model is developed. This model is characterized by the full devolution of funds to disadvantaged individuals who will set the research agenda, choose to contract which researchers they see fit or be empowered to undertake research themselves. The model is also characterized by the recognition of the status of researchers themselves as stakeholders in the research process.[6]

The authors recognize that within the continuum from "devolved" to "tokenistic" models of the research process lie a number of other possible "mentor or representational" models. These models may include one or more of the following characteristics: representation on funding, research advisory, personnel recruitment and dissemination bodies; and collaboration in the planning, operationalization and implementation of research. Given the limitations of space, these mentor models are referred to only in passing.

Rather, the emphasis is placed on producing a partisan account of the ways in which the "tokenistic" research process produces the commodification of the disadvantaged person. What is needed, it is argued, is a process of reverse commodification in which disadvantaged persons themselves are empowered to commodify the research process.

This reverse commodification differs from concepts such as "positive discrimination",[7] which relies on the idea of doing "to" or "for" the person, and social role valorisation[8] with its penchant for being prescriptive about the means and ends devalued persons should follow. Rather, it is the disadvantaged person who initiates and controls the process.

It will be demonstrated that the process of reverse commodification requires nothing less than a fundamental reappraisal of research epistemology, theory, methodology and dissemination practice. The research process that evolves out of the following critique is *not* meant as a replacement, but as a supplement, complement and addition to current research paradigms.

The authors also recognize a distinction between the new social movement or self-advocacy models of research and the research agenda being proposed in this paper. In the former, an "emancipatory interest"[9] is used as a mechanism through which social groups — members of which share some identity, for example, women, ethnic minority groups, disabled persons and so forth — formulate ways of pressuring changes to the dominant ideology that has generated their commodification and disablement.[10]

The value of this new paradigm or social movement research is accepted by the authors. However, the present argument rests on a slightly different, and we hope mutually elaborative, assumption. While such change in the structure of the dominant ideology continues, in the authors' view it will also be necessary to ensure that disadvantaged persons get the most out of, and be given the opportunity to reinforce, their individuality and their contributions to the system existing at any one point in time. In this model, the empowerment is of individuals in unison with their closest allies, such as family and friends. The empowerment is not necessarily of interest groups of which the person might also be a part. It is hoped that some of the ideas raised in this paper will place on the agenda for debate and action issues which the writers consider have some urgency.

Some Features of Traditional Research

Like a photographer, researchers may impose their own meanings on subjects and diminish their lives.[11]

Although a simplification, it may be asserted that the roots of social science research within the Enlightenment developed on the assumption that the research subject was a rational thinking being seeking to effect particular ends through chosen means. Such rational action meant that the position of research subjects within the social structure would in some way predispose them to act in particular ways. Hence, it was possible to seek certain similarities among such subjects on the basis of a number of variables relating to their position within that structure — for example, age, gender, race, socio-economic group and so forth. The function of such similarities for the researcher lies in their importance in formulating general hypotheses about any particular population showing a number of similarities, such as "the working class", demonstrating their predisposition towards a particular form of social action — for example, voting behaviour — and then testing the theory for its validity.

This hypothetic-deductive[12] or theory-testing model of research is considered below in order to demonstrate how the empowerment of the researcher and disempowerment of the research subject is achieved. This is done by considering the formulation of theoretical constructs and variables, operationalizing these variables, research analysis and then dissemination.

The Creation of Groups, Labels and "Otherness"

Researchers are commonly socialized into an accepted tradition placing value on results that can be generalized to large identifiable populations. Therefore, we still receive literature and expect to find literature in the libraries under the headings of "mental illness", "learning disability", "race and ethnicity" and so forth, with further subdivisions based on specialist interests.

There remains a tacit reliance by researchers on the work of a number of other professional groups who have, a priori, categorized people in a particular way. There is an inherent conservatism in this "unexplicated understanding collusive".[13] It is therefore ironic that, despite a high degree of acceptance by researchers of the labelling[14] and societal reaction models[15] within social science, researchers continue to be part of, and contribute to, the very system of labelling many of them seek to criticize.

In order to construct theoretical definitions and propositions, researchers rely heavily on an accepted literature review process and critique. Demonstrating a familiarity with this literature is one way in which researchers establish recognition and status among academic peers. However, in the large majority of cases, this review process and the theoretical constructs used are a product of logico-empiricist thinking rather than of knowledge from the subjects of the research themselves.

For example, it is the researcher, on the basis of the literature, who decides what categories constitute "depression", "schizophrenia" and so forth, or the elements that are constitutive of a "quality of life". To the writers' knowledge there has been no ontological philosophy (i.e., philosophy of being) which explicitly recognizes profound disability and disadvantage as an intrinsic aspect of the human condition, despite the existence of theories of the super-being.[16] Consequently, there has also been no research epistemology (i.e., philosophy of knowledge) which perceives the free agency of profound disability as a topic for its construction.

Rather, in much research writing, the subject moves in the social world as a "cultural dope"[17] of the researcher's own epistemology. Therefore, for example, the researcher might seek to discover the "efficacy" of service provision by seeking to elicit the subject's views on its accessibility, acceptability, availability, comprehensiveness and so forth. Although such concepts may be an essential part of the user's conception of service efficacy, their use as theoretical concepts decided in advance by the researcher, and imposed by fiat,[18] may place a filter on the meaning and phenomenological reality of such "efficacy" for the subject. In short, without first of all examining the meaningful social world of the subject, the researcher is implying that the rationality intrinsic to the researcher's own theoretical concepts has greater meaning and value than the rationality of the user.

Accountability to academic peers generates a number of other requirements that are tied up with what is considered to be accepted research practice. First, the researcher is driven to produce theoretical concepts that are reliable, repeatable and replicable. Second, both academia and funding agencies generally place a high value on converting "private problems into public issues",[19] and in seeking extraordinary solutions for groups as opposed to mundane solutions to the everyday problems of individuals. There is, therefore, a "generalization premium" in which the researcher establishes credibility and status through research that carries with it this generalizability and external validity.

In summary, researchers are generally seen to choose their areas of special interest, their substantive interests in these areas and their theoretical concepts without direct reference to the views of disadvantaged persons. Rather, accountability rests with an accepted academic tradition and with research funding agencies. By adopting these criteria for the conduct of the research, the researcher appeals to a particular system of rationality which may be at odds with that of the research subject. The need to maintain these systems of rationality at all costs is further compounded in the operationalization of the research as argued below.

"As If" and "Surrogacy"

Many theoretical concepts in consumer research are operationalized in the form of questions. For persons with profound disability and communication problems in particular, there has been an almost systematic and institutionalized exclusion of their views. This occurs in a number of ways that reflect the inability of researchers to find successful communications other than verbal.

For example, in a review of the literature on eliciting the views of people with a mental handicap,[20] a number of means through which researchers have variously sought solutions to this problem are described. Siegelman et al.[21] suggest asking positive and negative questions such as "Are you usually happy?" and "Are you usually sad?"[22] as a means of verifying the response and the respondent's propensity towards acquiescence. This "acquiescence" is treated as evidence of the unacceptability and invalidity[23] of a communication and not as a topic for research.

In other instances it is suggested that validity checks can be made by proxy through other sources such as parents, carers,[24] and service workers[25] or that the views of these third parties can stand as a "surrogate" for the views of the disadvantaged person. The implication is that if the subject's response does not fit the rational world created through the researcher's theoretical concepts, then the researcher should find a surrogate close to the person to answer on their behalf and so treat that data "as if" it were elicited from the subject. Although such surrogate and subject views may be in agreement, there remains room for conflicts of interest about which the researcher may well remain completely unaware.

In short, what it is permissible for the subject to say, and what is acceptable to the researcher, is confined to data that is commensurate with a certain notion of rationality. The methods used ensure the maintenance of this commensurability and the researcher thereby becomes restrained by methodological nuances, retracting from the alternative possibility of seeking to explicate the subject's own rationality as meaningful in their own terms.

The results and academic publications produced by such research are thereby converted into a form that is acceptable to the persons who count to the researcher, funding agency and academic peers. Having started with particular generalized theories and assumptions because it is accepted practice, it should not, therefore, be surprising that the researcher ends up with generalized results. What the researcher can legitimately say, however, can only possibly be a function of his or her own theorizing. She or he is constrained to describe and interpret the social world within the parameters set by the theoretical definitions used. Therefore, quality of life, despite possible differences in the views of users, is described in terms of aspects of their work, leisure, family, finances, living situation and so on,[26] whether or not these concepts as operationalized and analyzed carry the same importance, meaning and intent for the research subject.

It has been argued that researchers are accountable to their profession and to their funding agencies. Their success as researchers is tied, first, to a system that has been developed by academics for academics and, second, to the often politically loaded interests of funding agencies. That some accommodation occurs between the interests of funders and researchers is a reflection of their common concern and of a degree of collusion on the one hand and compromise on the other. They remain mutually interdependent, each sustaining the strength of the other.

Empowering the user within the research process must therefore begin by seeking to realign this interdependency through the development of a system in which the researcher becomes accountable to individuals with a disadvantage. This might be done through "mentor" models in which disadvantaged persons will have some representation on groups that plan, implement and disseminate research. However, representation of this sort implies some form of specified group identity and this can lead back to the thorny issue of labelling.

What follows instead is an agenda for action by researchers, proposed on the basis of the arguments made so far, which will avoid this issue of labelling. This will be done by retracing the research process from dissemination of research findings to the formulation of theoretical concepts. Each suggestion is nevertheless tentative and remains open to debate and testing. However, it is the nature of the agenda that concerns us here.

Empowering Disadvantaged Persons in the Research Process

> We are objectified ... We lose our individuality in the name of treatment ... We need research that finds out why we treat each other as we do. Let the product of research be part of something that benefits recipients, families, workers and so on.[27]

Disadvantaged persons involved as subjects of research are not generally concerned with academic articles or with the implications of research for public policy (i.e., in creating a public issue out of their own personal problems). They are more likely to be interested in what changes the research can bring about for them personally. To date, researchers in the field of social policy have, in general, sought to maintain their independence from changing the life circumstances of the research subject on the pretext that this will infringe the objectivity of the research. Instead, they suggest to the subject that there are no short-term gains for them, but hopefully long-term gains in terms of policy change. Researchers are, therefore, reliant upon the goodwill and consent of the subject to participate.

However, some solutions to disseminating research findings in ways that can be used by the research subjects are beginning to be discussed. For example, it has been suggested that short form and simplified versions of research results should be published and that material in braille or in the form of "talking books" should be made available to people with visual impairments. These can be useful techniques. However, simplifying the results can lead to accusations that the researcher is disparaging the intellect of the research subjects. Moreover, although the subjects may have a general interest in the ways the research may affect them, they are likely to be more interested in any changes that are specific to their present situation. Such changes are not especially evident in research results carrying generalized findings.

In unison with writers from the feminist movement then,[28] our first suggestion for an alternative research paradigm is that researchers relinquish and suspend their arguments relating to getting involved in the field and actively become involved in the person's life, perhaps as a citizen or paid advocate,[29] or in the promotion of self-advocacy.[30] Rather than disseminating through artificial mechanisms, the researcher should simply *tell* the subjects the findings and work with them to adjust the nature of their lives, *with, for and on their behalf.* This will be termed "milieu-sensitive dissemination".

This, however, is not enough on its own. The interests of the researcher will continue to lie with their funding agencies, as did the action research programs that sought to change the lives of the research subjects for the better in Britain's Community Development Projects.[31] Instead, mechanisms need to be found through which the funding for such research advocacy comes from disadvantaged persons themselves. This is likely to prove the most problematic aspect of the emergent research paradigm because few models of service provision are based on the full devolution of funding to the disadvantaged person. Until society's values change in this regard, there will always remain the problem that monies have to be secured from the larger and more powerful organizations that plan and implement services. This, once again, produces possible conflicts of interest between the research advocate and such organizations. It also leads back to accountability to these powerful groups rather than to the research subject.

The authors are aware of only one model that might meet the agenda being set for the research advocate, as she or he will be called. That is the service brokerage model developed in Canada. To summarize, service brokerage involves a broker, who is independent of service-providing agencies, discussing the needs and wants of the disadvantaged person with that person and other important people in their lives, such as family and friends. Brandon[32] has referred to such groups as Joshua Committees and they share a certain likeness to the circle of friends model developed by Perske and Perske.[33] Money allocated to the user and held by the broker is then used to buy the necessary services. The user and his or her committee can, therefore, suspend the use of a service if dissatisfied or if it has not achieved its aim. They shop around for the best options as would any other consumer of goods and services.

In such a model, the research advocates would themselves be bought in or "commodified". They would become a "partner in practice",[34] as well as carrying their own research interests. Their interest in continuing to secure funding would, therefore, be tied to the needs and wishes of the user. Their success would be judged by their use in their role as advocates. It is at this point that "reverse commodification" occurs, turning the researcher into a resource for their new employer and turning the disadvantaged person from research subject to "research participant".

This reverse commodification is an exceptionally important aspect of the emergent research paradigm, for it has a number of spin-offs. First, within our culture, time plays a major role. Research funding today is all too often time-limited. Efficiency and economy are the watchwords of such funding and yet time is often the one thing that is required to get to know persons whose communication abilities present problems for those who are used to communicating verbally. It is often necessary to spend long periods establishing rapport before even beginning to understand the social world individuals inhabit, much less the ways they express and pursue their own choices.

The role of research advocate, funded by the subjects themselves and based on the success or the use-value of the research advocate, may offer the opportunity for such time to be made available in a way that actively reflects the success of the researcher in their advocacy role. Neither would that role be one that is necessarily a product of a consumerist or welfarist mentality. The driving force would come from the disadvantaged persons themselves in terms of their life interests and preferences at any given moment — in other words from an unequivocally "humanist mentality".

Therefore, it would become unnecessary to employ the traditional tools of the questionnaire or to create variables that could be generalized. Instead, the researcher, like the anthropologist, will have to become immersed in the field in order to discover the subject's meaningful world and systems of rationality.

This pursuit is by no means totally at odds with the cherished edicts of the theory-testing and "tokenistic" research paradigm for a number of reasons. First, the dissemination of the research need not necessarily be confined to the research participant in terms of an instrumental advocacy input, but may also be translated by the researcher into a form that may be acceptable to the academic community. Second, the more research advocacy that is executed, the greater the possibility of generating theoretical definitions based on the rationalities of the subjects themselves. This may in itself lead to an ontology and epistemology based on the meaningful world of disadvantaged persons.

The use of such grounded theory[35] does not, therefore, preclude the researcher continuing their interests in the theory-testing model of research. Moreover, pursuing a research advocacy model does not constrain the researcher to seek funding from the research participant alone. The researcher may continue to pursue funding from a variety of sources given his or her own political choice and expediency.

Conclusion

Deinstitutionalisation, the shift towards consumerism, needs-led services and individual planning within contemporary social policy were initiated as far back as the 1950s. As the century draws to a close it is necessary to rethink the nature and emphasis of the research process to reflect these interests.

In this chapter an attempt has been made to prompt thinking about an agenda for such a paradigmatic shift[36] in the research process. We have argued the need to supplement theory-testing and deductive research with a research advocacy and inductive model. We have argued for a reordering of the research process and for the researcher, in the role of advocate, to give up claims to independence and objectivity. Instead, it becomes their research role to become immersed in, and to seek to understand, the meaningful world and the free-agency of their research subjects. This research advocacy goes beyond action research with its traditional funding and systems of accountability, and seeks to transfer research into the ownership of the disadvantaged person. It also goes beyond the culturally immersed paradigms pursued by such writers as Edgerton[37] and Langness and Levine[38] by providing an element of advocacy and change in the lives of the research participant.

Empowerment can only be accomplished if disadvantaged individuals are themselves facilitated to "commodify" the research process to their own ends, tying the interests of the researcher into the completion of practical advocacy, "milieu-sensitive dissemination" and perhaps other tasks on their behalf. It involves personal assistance in offering the disadvantaged person the opportunity and forum to demonstrate their value to society. It is also the private problems and solutions thereof that are most likely to interest disadvantaged people, and not necessarily the generation out of their problem, and those of other disadvantaged people, of a public issue with public solutions. While working within the research advocacy paradigm, researchers must, therefore, give up their interest in the generalization premium in their dealings with research participants.

We recognize that the ideas of "milieu-sensitive dissemination" and "reverse commodification" add jargon to the current debate. Their use has been purely heuristic and we recommend them being dropped if the agenda for action proposed in this article comes to fruition. However, in this article we have avoided the use of terminology for any specialization of disadvantage for fear of contributing to the labelling of such groups. It is perhaps only when society recognizes persons as citizens first, as persons who, for whatever reason, might need some assistance to achieve their full citizenship, and who have the right to redress if this does not occur, that such labelling will cease. In most countries this will require the political will to implement a Bill of Rights. In the absence of such a mechanism it remains incumbent upon the research establishment to seek to draw the disadvantaged into the mainstream of our culture by accepting their rationality and culture as being as important as that of the researcher. It is only through such empowerment in their everyday lives, and as research participants, that persons with a disadvantage can achieve full citizenship and acceptance within mainstream society.

Notes

1. M. Oliver, "Re-Defining Disability: A Challenge to Research", *Research Policy and Planning, Journal of Social Services Research Group*, 5(1), 1987, quoted from P. Beresford, "Researching Citizen Involvement: A Collaborating or Colonising Enterprise", in M. Barnes and G. Wistow (eds.), *Researching User Involvement*, Leeds: Nuffield Institute for Health Service Studies, University of Leeds, 1992, pp. 16-32.

2. Clearly the notion of disadvantage is itself highly problematic. We ask the reader to conceive of disadvantage in terms of a shortfall in both the statutory and everyday citizenship rights of individuals. It is only where the standards of meaningful citizenship are rendered knowable in some way that some measurement of disadvantage might be identified. It is only where such standards are backed up by redress that equal rights might be secured.

3. M. Oliver, *The Politics of Disablement*, Basingstoke: The Macmillan Press Ltd, 1990, pp. 1-11.

4. A. Scull, *Decarceration — Community Treatment and the Deviant: A Radical View*, Englewood Cliffs, N.J.: Prentice-Hall, 1977.

5. M. Foucault, *Madness and Civilisation: A History of Insanity in the Age of Reason*, New York, N.Y.: Plume Books, 1971.

6. M. Barnes, "Introducing New Stakeholders — User and Researcher Interests in Evaluative Research: A Discussion of the Methods Used to Evaluate the Birmingham Community Care Special Action Project", *Policy and Politics*, 21(1), 1993, pp.47-58.

7. L.G. Scarman, *The Scarman Report*, Harmondsworth: Penguin, 1982.

8. W. Wolfensberger, "Social Role Valorization: A Proposed New Term for the Principle of Normalization", *Mental Retardation*, 21(6), 1983, pp. 234-239.

9. J. Habermas, *Knowledge and Human Interests*, Boston: Beacon Press, 1972.

10. E. Cocks and J. Cockram, "The Participatory Research Paradigm and Intellectual Disability", paper presented at the 9th World Congress of the IASSMD, Gold Coast, Australia, August 1992.

11. Beresford, "Researching Citizen Involvement", 1992, p.16 (see n. 1).

12. K. Popper, *The Poverty of Historicism*, 2nd ed., New York, N.Y.: Harper and Row, 1964.

13. E. Bitner, "The Concept of Organisation", *Social Research*, 32, 1965, pp. 230-255.

14. H.S. Becker, *Outsiders*, New York, N.Y.: The Free Press, 1963.

15. E. Lemert, *Human Deviance and Social Control*, Englewood Cliffs, N.J.: Prentice Hall, 1967.

16. F.W. Nietzsche, "Thus Spake Zarathustra: A Book for Everyone and No-one", in R.J. Hollingdale, *Nietzche: The Man and His Philosophy*, Routledge and Kegan Paul, 1965, p. 196.

17. H. Garfinkel, "Studies in the Routine Grounds of Everyday Activities", in D. Sudnow (ed.), *Studies in Social Interaction*, New York, N.Y.: The Free Press, 1972, pp. 1-31.

18. A.V. Cicourel, *Method and Measurement in Sociology*, New York, N.Y.: The Free Press, 1964.

19. C. Wright Mills, *The Sociological Imagination*, Harmondsworth: Penguin, 1970.

20. H. Prosser, *Eliciting the Views of People with a Mental Handicap: A Literature Review*, Manchester: Hester Adrian Research Centre, University of Manchester, 1989.

21. C. Siegelman, E.C. Budd, C. Spaniel, and C. Schoenrock, "Asking Questions of Retarded Persons: A Comparison of Yes-No and Either-Or Formats", *Applied Research in Mental Retardation*, 2, 1981, pp. 347-357.

22. Prosser, *Eliciting the Views*, 1989, p. 9 (see n. 20).

23. Siegelman et al., "Asking Questions", 1981, p. 348 (see n. 21).

24. M. Cattermole, A. Jahoda and I. Markova, "Leaving Home: The Experience of People with a Mental Handicap", *Journal of Mental Deficiency Research*, 32, 1988, pp. 47-57.

25. D. Atkinson, "Research Interviews with People with a Mental Handicap", *Journal of Mental Handicap Resources*, 1, 1988, pp. 75-90.

26. A.F. Lehman, "The Well-Being of Chronic Mental Patients: Assessing Their Quality of Life", *Archives of General Psychiatry*, Vol. 40, 1983, pp. 369-373.

27. M. Lawson, "Survivors Speak Out", from Beresford, "Researching Citizen Involvement", 1992, p. 19 (see n. 1).

28. A. Oakley, "Interviewing Women: A Contradiction in Terms", in H. Roberts (ed.), *Doing Feminist Research*, London: Routledge and Kegan Paul, 1981.

29. K. Butler, S. Carr and S. Sullivan, *Citizen Advocacy: A Powerful Partnership*, London: National Citizen Advocacy, 1988.

30. P. Williams and B. Shoultz, *We Can Speak for Ourselves*, London: Souvenir Press, 1982.

31. R. Lees, *Research Strategies for Social Welfare*, London: Routledge and Kegan Paul, 1975.

32. D. Brandon, *Direct Power: A Handbook on Service Brokerage*, Preston, England: Tao Publications, 1991.

33. R. Perske and M. Perske, *Circles of Friends: People with Disabilities and Their Friends Enrich the Lives of One Another*, Nashville: Abingdon Press 1988.

34. For an interesting discussion of researchers as partners see P. Marsh and M. Fisher, *Good Intentions: Developing Partnerships in Social Services*, London: Joseph Rowntree Foundation in association with Community Care, 1992.

35. B. Glaser, *The Discovery of Grounded Theory: Strategies for Qualitative Research*, Chicago: Aldine Press, 1967.

36. T. Kuhn, *The Structure of Scientific Revolutions*, 2nd ed., Chicago: University of Chicago Press, 1970.

37. R.B. Edgerton (ed.), *Lives in Process: Mildly Retarded Adults in a Large City*, Washington: AAMD, 1984.

38. L.L. Langness and H.G. Levine (eds.), *Culture and Retardation*, Dordrecht, Holland: D. Reidel Publishing Co., 1986.

Chapter 11

Theoretical Framework for What Persons with Severe and Profound Multiple Disabilities Do in Context

by John J. Gleason

Introduction

Persons with severe and profound multiple disabilities present a particular challenge to the researcher interested in the ways in which individuals with particular differences become known and understood. The methods available to study these persons involve a variety of different methods for description and explanation. Each method entails a particular way of seeing, understanding, analyzing and explaining. Although the purpose and the focus of the methodology will vary, understanding and making sense of what is going on is the subject and the object of each form of inquiry.

The understanding of persons with intellectual disabilities evolved historically based on the application of scientific research to the study of each aspect of their lives. Our knowledge of persons with intellectual disabilities is primarily based on two sources of information: (1) medical interpretation — that is, the classification of the handicapping condition; and (2) psychological and educational statements about characteristics of the condition and resulting categories of deficit and ability. In both instances, interpretations rely on the clinical model's concepts and assumptions about the individual under study. Medical understanding interprets symptoms in terms of anatomical structures, physiological functioning and pathological processes in order to classify symptoms, prescribe treatment and determine prognosis.[1] Clinical thinking is also the basis of psychological and educational understanding that proceeds from a similar premise — that is, to determine developmental characteristics as states, stages and skills of the individual as the basis for intervention.

The study of persons with severe and profound intellectual disabilities has traditionally been conducted in clinical, quantitative and experimental modes.[2] In a review of 500 empirical studies of persons with severe and profound intellectual disabilities conducted between 1955 and 1974, Berkson and Landesman-Dwyer found that most description and assessment were based on formal testing of behaviour in four areas: the correspondence between medical syndromes and behaviour; the level of sensory and perceptual functioning; the measure of intelligence on standardized tests; and the rating of adaptive behaviours.[3] A fifth area was a search for environmental factors that evoked and maintained a behavioural response. Behaviour was understood in terms of prescribed labels and definitions of medical, psychological and educational categories and norms.

Other research methods commonly used for studying persons with intellectual disability include standardized psychometric instruments, task performance tests, questionnaires, interviews, adaptive behaviour measures and clinical judgements found to be appropriate with this level of intellectual and physical disability.[4] The appropriateness of these measures with persons with severe and profound intellectual disability was questioned by Sackett because they did not accurately predict the full range of actual behavioural adaptation to real life situations. Knowledge gained in this manner unwittingly interpreted the behaviour of persons with severe and profound intellectual disability in the researcher's own categorical terms. The dominance of the clinical orientation has led to a singularity of perspective with this population, even as new requirements for care and education are mandated.

This paper provides a framework for understanding persons with severe and profound multiple disabilities. In studying the everyday lives of persons with severe and profound multiple disabilities, the challenge posed is to look anew at how the rich medical, psychological, educational and therapeutic clinical information contributes to our understanding of these persons. Defining the contribution and relationship of the information to the understanding of everyday life events within a theoretical framework helps to place the disability in a different perspective. The ability of the person is then more readily perceived. Scientific inquiry into the lives of persons with severe and profound multiple disabilities involves unraveling patterns of complex human phenomena in the context of interaction. The basis of that inquiry is the discovery of the meaning in their behaviour.

The challenge is to understand human differences we do not share. Paul Deising offers a starting point — ourselves. He states:

> [T]he only instrument that is good enough for the study of human beings is man himself. Only the human observer is perceptive enough to recognize and appreciate the full range of human action, only the thinker is able to draw the proper implications from the complex data coming from human systems.[5]

Historically, persons with developmental disabilities have been understood primarily by comparison to non-disabled persons. Age and grade equivalents and developmental stages are the current basis for comparison in a long list of predecessors. The appropriateness of their behaviour is often assessed by social and cultural norms.

The comparison with others is artificial. The challenges faced by persons with developmental disabilities in figuring out the world around them are unfamiliar to us. We do not know their developmental path. Their experience is different.

The maturity of our understanding of human nature is tested by the degree to which we can investigate experience and tolerate the ambiguity expressed in the reality of the lives of persons with developmental disabilities. To see relationships among human systems and people is not the same as isolating variables and seeking correlations; rather, it is to explore the meaning of an event in a spatial and temporal context that respects the persons' patterns of interaction, communication and participation.

Although a connection to persons with developmental disabilities may be more difficult to establish, the concept of difference *is* familiar. We know that individuals have distinct differences. In human nature, we are connected and bound together in very fundamental ways. What are the common elements that connect persons with severe and profound multiple disabilities to us?

To understand persons different from ourselves is not just a challenge to see beyond their disabilities, to sense order in disorder, to understand without an urgency to compare. The behaviours of persons with developmental disabilities are not isolated entities, separate and distinct from other human qualities, characteristics and expressions. To understand demands comprehension of the whole of what they are doing in context, not just fragments of behaviours or aspects of individual actions.

Difference in human nature is part of the endless manifestation of variety in human form and content. Differences and variations are expressions of human dynamics. Human difference does not reveal itself in dichotomies of what the person can and cannot do, normal and abnormal, able and disabled. The challenge in giving meaning to people's behaviour is to see, understand and experience complex human phenomena outside of clinical dichotomies for explanation.

Understanding of persons with developmental disabilities evolved based on the methods available and the ways scientific research was applied to the study of their lives. When we understand Albert Einstein's comment, "The whole of science is nothing more than a refinement of everyday thinking," we all hold the potential for thinking scientifically about what we do. The eminent physicist offers some guidance: "Where the world ceases to be the scene of our personal hopes, and wishes, where we face it as free human beings admiring and asking and observing, there we enter the realm of Art and Science."

To refine my everyday thinking about persons with severe and profound multiple disabilities demands understanding the nature of their differences in a new way, in a scientific way. As an anthropologist, I had to approach the discovery of their day-to-day lives as a scientist refining my knowledge about the complex information inherent in their human systems. I had to free myself of personal hopes and wishes to change their lives and remain open to ask questions of what I observed them doing.

When I began to appreciate what they did beyond their multiple disabilities, I came to see patterns in their interactions. I could not describe their similarities by recognizing only their differences. I could not explain their ability by thinking in terms of their disability. The art of the language of description and explanation and the rigor and precision of scientific thinking revealed similarities in their experience that I could not share. I came to see the similarities and differences in persons with severe and profound multiple disabilities as shifts in the relationships among form, function and content.

Following a brief description of my research and an example, I will describe the patterns in the relationships I began to make sense of in their behaviour. Understanding of the shifts in form, function and content may illuminate the patterns in their human systems. Recognition of patterns allowed for the discovery of meaning and a fuller explanation of their ability.

Population

A comprehensive universal definition of the ability of persons with severe and profound multiple disabilities is difficult to achieve solely through the use of traditional clinical and psychometric measures. The archive records reveal no simple or consistent description of this population. A complicated array of physical handicaps constrains the individual's ability to function in the normal or expected fashion. The profound levels of intellectual disability, historically measured by an intelligence quotient lower than 20, impair the senses, disrupting the processing of information and affecting cognition. Many individuals are subject to seizures and central nervous system disturbances. The stable and uncompromising nature of their multiple involvements and disabilities generally necessitates assistance in the development of the skills of self-maintenance including movement, eating, dressing, bathing and communication.

Professionals and care-givers refer to these residents as the "lowest functioning on the grounds"; "they can't do anything"; "they're really bad off." These descriptions do not preclude their unique forms of communication, demonstration of awareness and understanding of others, communication of intent and purpose, and desire to belong and participate in everyday life.

Setting

The world experience of the residents is confined to two large living spaces: the activity area and the sleeping area. The room is partitioned into sections where residents are positioned on water beds, stretchers, sand-bag chairs and mats during free time for any general activity. The sleeping area is a maze of crib-style beds separated by metal cabinets with facilities for bathing and toileting. Intersecting both rooms is a glassed-in office from which staff observe the residents who live there. Across the hall from these living areas are classrooms, offices and therapy rooms for programmed activities. The event described here takes place on the floor and mats in the large activity area for the wards.

Methodology

My research began when I observed 64 persons labelled with severe and profound multiple disabilities, including intellectual impairment, living on an apartment ward over a five-year period.[6] I observed what individuals with severe and profound multiple disabilities did on their own before the introduction of legally mandated educational and therapeutic programs designed to teach skills, modify behaviours and present culturally appropriate tasks.

Being in the setting before the introduction of individualized educational programs allowed me the opportunity to compare and contrast what the residents were doing *before* the advent of the programs with what they were doing *after* the professional staff became involved in their lives. A natural experiment evolved.

The research role I assumed was that of an ethnographer. In contrast with other forms of qualitative research, I applied a social and cultural analysis to understand the everyday lives of persons with severe and profound multiple disabilities. As an applied anthropologist, I employed description and explanation to make sense of what I observed the residents do on the ward from day to day.

Formal analysis and explanation of the data were a comparison of my observations with the record of assessments from individualized educational programs. I contrasted interactions on their own with their participation in the structured, formal interactions with professionals in therapy and lessons designed to teach a skill.

By continuous elaboration of the patterns in the residents' behaviour, I was able to develop a description that revealed their messages in what they did. By freezing the account and analyzing the meaning underlying the residents' participation, I perceived intent and purpose in their actions. My explanation entailed the identification of the meaning made of behaviour, an abstraction of the underlying patterns that affected the course of their interaction.

Specifically, I was interested in the ways in which persons with severe and profound multiple disabilities participated with one another. I asked the very basic question: What do persons with severe and profound multiple disabilities do?

Illustration: Play Event between Danial and Thomas

I discovered examples of shared, learned patterns of interaction between and among the residents. The patterns of play in events became a starting place from which to describe the social and cultural boundaries of their experience. The play of Danial and Thomas came to symbolize what I observed the other residents doing. An excerpt of the event provides an illustration.

Danial swings a white-handled Fisher Price lawn mower.

Thomas crawls across the floor on his back, inch by inch, a distance of 20 feet. He positions himself parallel to Danial.

The attendant comes in, looks at the boys and says, "What are you fighting for?" She picks up Thomas and moves him to another mat 12 feet away. She gives Thomas a blue-handled Fisher Price lawn mower. With the toy, Thomas crawls back across the floor to lie parallel to, and behind, Danial.

Thomas hits Danial on the shoulder. Danial hides his toy underneath him. Thomas hits Danial on the shoulder again. Danial turns over to face Thomas with his toy in front of him. Thomas moves closer and grabs at Danial's toy. He misses. Danial grabs at Thomas's toy. He misses.

Thomas grabs at Danial's toy. He gets it. He pulls it over to him. Danial grabs at Thomas's toy. He gets it. He rolls over with the toy.[7]

Together, Danial and Thomas continued this sequence of play with the toy for two and one-half hours in spite of the constraints imposed by their multiple disabilities, the rules of the staff which required them to stay on the mats and repeated attempts by staff to separate the two because they were "fighting" and not playing.

Time and space are the defining properties that set the context of their play, not the setting, not their disability, not the rules of the ward, not our labels for what they are doing. This play sequence highlights the contradictions, paradoxes and gaps between what they are doing and what we know about what they are doing. The significance of this play example for persons with severe and profound multiple disabilities is that what staff understand about the residents in large measure determines the quality of their life.

The gulf widened when professional staff, who had assessed their ability and behaviours, developed individualized programs and designed a curriculum to teach them to play. Teachers and therapists directed lessons to develop socially and culturally acceptable patterns of play behaviours between these two. The play example described is ultimately richer than all the descriptions of skills in the professional reports of their ability following this event. For example, Thomas's educational program identifies skill objectives for the subsequent two years that are far more circumscribed than the skills I observed in the play event in March 1978. The following excerpts are from the annual statement of program objectives on his individual educational program.

Program Objectives (June 1978-June 1979)

Fine Motor: He will reach for an object while prone over a wedge daily for 30 minutes of a day. Response to activity of stimuli through change in facial expression, body movements and vocalizations.

Program Objectives (1979-1980)

Fine Motor: To lie prone on scooter board or supine in mat. Will place two-inch pegs into peg board four out of five trials in a one-to-one situation.

The elements of play described in objectives for programs such as socialization, recreation and fine motor ability fail to incorporate the intricate detail of what Danial and Thomas had mastered already.

Reports throughout 1979 document that Thomas needs physical assistance to pass an object and maintain his weight on his elbows and his head in a straight position for one and one-half minutes. In the play event, he maintains himself for over an hour without physical assistance. In the event described here he travels independently a distance of over 30 or more feet over the floor. Progress notes for June 1978 state that he can mobilize himself a distance of only five feet over a 20- or 30-minute lesson period.

Progress notes refer to the fact that Thomas plays games with staff, but there is no recorded observation of his play with other residents. As late as November 1978 (some nine months following the current event), a recreation specialist states that Thomas does not engage in any real interactions with others. Hence, staff continue to position him for prearranged activities, select the toys for play, determine the individuals with whom he is to interact, direct the play activity and evaluate his performance in the context of prescribed activities.[8]

The specialist in each instance conducts the evaluation in the context of prescribed performance at a prearranged activity. The evaluation criteria used by the teachers are the number of trials and percentage of correct responses in playing with the peer; these criteria do not clarify how to arrange the activity in order for Thomas to participate. The contrast between what the residents were doing and what we were trying to get them to do heightened my awareness of the contradictions in our understanding of their experience, the discontinuity in our curriculum and methods for understanding and interpreting their ability, and the challenges in appreciating the other ways of life they demonstrate.

Theoretical Framework

A theory of explanation of what these persons do — those with developmental disabilities in general and those with severe and profound multiple disabilities in particular — involves deciphering patterns expressed through their human systems. These are: (1) patterns of interference; (2) patterns of participation; and (3) patterns in ambiguity. Each pattern can be explained in terms of shifts in the relationships among form, function and content. The concepts will be explained first in terms of their application to persons with severe and profound multiple disabilities.

The differences are obvious. The first is difference in *form*. Multiple disabilities reveal themselves as differences in anatomical structures of the human body. For example, the excerpt used to illustrate points in this paper is a play event between two residents, Danial and Thomas. The physical characteristics of both are significant disturbances to the expected human form.

Danial is classified as having a profound level of intellectual impairment indicated by an intelligence quotient below 20. In 1969, Danial was admitted to the institution at the age of five; at the time of the study, he was 16 years old. Clinical manifestations of his physical condition include hydrocephaly, blindness, epilepsy, quadriplegia, Arnold-Chari malformation and psychomotor disabilities.

Thomas was admitted to the institution in 1962 when he was four years old. He was 22 years old at the time of the study. His level of intellectual impairment is recorded as severe. Thomas manifests clinical characteristics of organic brain damage and is considered blind, spastic and tetraplegic.

The second is difference of *function*. Differences in human form challenge our recognition of the ways the individual functions. Direct links are difficult to make. Disabilities affect the ability of the person to act in the natural, expected or required manner. In this interaction, Thomas's reaction to the therapist's presence is evaluated in isolation, divorced from the meaning of what he is doing when he repeatedly rolls away. The therapist figures out how his arms and legs move not by observing his movement but by how she is able to place them in order for him to roll. To discover his maneuverability, the therapist does not evaluate Thomas in the context of rolling for his own purposes. She evaluates his ability to roll by assessing functional attributes of his physical condition. In the context of trying to recreate the roll Thomas has earlier used to get away from the therapist, she places his hands and legs into position to roll in the manner she prescribes. For her, the problem in Thomas's inability to roll is lack of muscle tone rather than the nature of her interaction and involvement. Thomas rolls in play but does not cooperate with her for his own reasons. Nonetheless, his ability to roll is determined and prescribed by the therapist. The therapy will promote his ability to roll in the prescribed manner. Therefore, Thomas's performance in therapy does not correspond to his demonstrated ability outside of therapy.[9]

The third difference, then, may be that of *content*. Meaning in their action (whether Danial and Thomas or the population), or the content of their message, can easily go undetected and unappreciated for what it is to them. Interpreting behaviours of the residents rather than understanding them in terms of what the person is doing perpetuates a rift between what the residents do and what the teachers expect. Recording ability in terms of objectives with criteria for performance in the context of therapy reveals little of the ways in which Thomas goes about what he has to do. The focus becomes the handicap and the remediation of deficit areas rather than what the individual is doing. This orientation focuses on limitations of the individual rather than the ways in which Thomas has learned to adapt, interact and communicate within the constraints of his disability. The resident's performance is judged by the dichotomous criteria — "do" or "not do" — criteria not suited to the levels of their physical complexities or representative of resident patterns in the context of daily life. The content of the individualized educational plan does not match what the person does. The mismatch in evaluation is perpetuated in the program.

The patterns that must be deciphered are described below. First, *patterns of interference* are discovered in the ways variations in form disturb function. The effect of the disability on the person is recognized by the differences in the ways they look and act. Their ways of doing are different and challenge our perception and recognition of human form and function.

Pathology affects the balance, coherence and symmetry in their human systems and dramatizes the person's expressions, actions and movements. It alters the pathways available to the individual to convey content, interfering with the usual clues available for deciphering human expression and meaning. Expressions are not readily familiar. Because patterns of interference become associated with what the person *cannot do*, we run the risk of relegating content to the facts associated with the disturbance to form and function. In this way, what the person does is interpreted in terms of their disability. Generalizations about the profound and multiple level of the disability define staff expectations of their ability.

However, the disability and the associated qualities and characteristics are not the defining concept of the person nor a unifying feature of our humanity. Knowing the manifestations of the condition sets the stage for understanding another set of patterns.

Patterns of participation emerge when the relationship between form and function is recognizable and contributes to understanding. What the person does matches what we think he should be doing. We recognize expressions and behaviours as gestures that can convey meaning. Symmetry in form and function allows for the discovery of content beyond the disability. Specific behavioural repertoires of communication develop. We make sense of what the person is doing because their human systems function in a way that conveys meaning. Content becomes the meaning in their actions, expressions and movements. Content becomes what the person *can do*.

In an interaction, the direct relationship between form and function reveals order, which permits interpretation. In turn, analysis of the order may reveal the meaning implicit in their (whether Danial and Thomas or the population) explicit acts. The implicit meaning found in the shared, learned patterns between and among the residents defines their patterns of participation. Danial and Thomas's shared learned patterns of play, when viewed as reciprocal interaction, make sense to us as play.

Making sense of what is implicit in what they are doing is an avenue for discovering the capabilities and potential of the person. Therefore, patterns of participation represent a picture of the integrated and combined strengths of the person. They reveal the totality of their ability across the domains of human functioning available to them. For persons with severe and profound multiple disabilities, these patterns constitute a unifying feature in our shared humanity because they are a vehicle by which we can know them, understand the course of their development and participate with them.

There are clues for discerning patterns of participation. They are context, experience, purpose and meaning. Each is described here briefly.

The first is *context*. Primarily, what persons with severe and profound multiple disabilities learn is context. Context is used here to mean more than just the situation or circumstances within an environment. Context is the ongoing set of relationships in an interaction that make up an event. Learning context involves making sense of the set of explicit and implicit conditions and relations that influence the course of the interaction. Learning skills or abilities, behaviours or tasks is secondary. Danial and Thomas's skills are incorporated into their performance of play. Individual skills or behaviours taught in isolation may fragment the experience. Behaviours taught in mechanical fashion may not be incorporated into existing repertoires. Artificially derived tasks may be unrelated to their own performance.

They learn in the experience of doing. Danial and Thomas learned to play together. They are showing us what we need to know to provide experiences that will be meaningful to them. We have to arrange the context that allows them to play.

Patterns of participation are understood when the residents' actions match our expectations for the situation, when what they do seems to fit the context. Danial and Thomas's play is understood as play when we see the whole. The behaviours have a reference point within the circumstances of the situation. In context, patterns of interference can be differentiated because they interrupt the situation and the individual's participation. Such patterns do not fit.

A second clue is *experience*. The experience of persons with severe and profound multiple disabilities is defined by their ways of doing. Their experience develops from the ways they continue to initiate and maintain interaction among themselves and with staff.

Their experience is not defined solely in terms of pathology. Patterns of interference do not create experience, they disrupt it. The challenge to understand the complex processes involved lies in our ways of making sense of the nature of their experience.

In the rush to categorize their experience, it is often easier to compare what they are doing to what we do, judging what we recognize in their actions by the match to the situation. To accept the criteria for experience as what the person does requires understanding the intention and significance for the person in their own terms. Experience is not just doing, it involves knowledge.

To provide continuity in the development of their experience requires that we identify the native ability demonstrated in *their* ways of participating and doing things with others. I am not referring here to the practice of specific skills in lessons or behaviours in routines of daily life. The success of our involvement is directly related to how we build on the patterns of interaction that define the basis of the individual's relationship to, and association with, others.

The third clue is *purpose*. Shared learned patterns of behaviour are goal-directed. The purposeful ends towards which their actions are directed become a clue to the person's needs, wants and desires. How the individual participates in an interaction relates to the comparative strength of the patterns of interference and participation. What emerges is the unique and creative ways the person acts within the competing forces of these patterns demonstrating will. The resourcefulness in the play of Danial and Thomas lies in the way in which they mobilize their resources and abilities to play in the face of the misinterpretation by staff, the rules of the apartment and the constraints their disabilities impose.

To discover purpose requires that we respect their spatial and temporal context. When we interject ourselves prematurely into a situation through programs or interventions, we may override their purposes. Unwittingly, we can subvert what is most beneficial to know — that is, what they want.

This may change our intervention. But the purposes of Danial and Thomas are not a challenge to our control. Instead, they are a clue to the ways we can assist them to achieve their ends. To know their purposes allows us the opportunity to create the curriculum together. It can structure our involvement to support and aid their intent. Their purpose can open the opportunity to provide education and therapy in the context of what they are already doing — by expanding their experience in ways that are meaningful to them.

The fourth clue is *meaning.* Historically, we have passed over the discovery of meaning except as interesting anecdotal detail. However, order and repetition in shared, learned patterns provide the opportunity to define the meaning of events in a person's life. Attributes associated with their multiple disabilities do not define the person or assign meaning. To discover meaning in their terms at the implicit level is to interpret what they do with others based on their actions. The ability demonstrated in the combined patterns in the play of Danial and Thomas is greater than any recorded statement of their ability. The whole event is greater than any individual skill.

At first, the meaning of an event, a set of behaviours or accumulated experiences may seem remote. In attempting to derive meaning from an event we must accept the potential for alternative categorizations of their experience. Their experience and meaning challenge our own way of thinking, feeling and acting. To understand what is communicated by the individual requires that we interpret the meaning in their experiences *before* we seek to change, modify or alter existing behaviours by teaching mainstream ways of acting and behaving. The behaviours we seek to change may be their form of expression. Their form of communication may be lost with our intervention. If Danial and Thomas's actions were interpreted as play instead of fighting they would not have been separated and we would not have interfered with what they are doing. We need not make it harder for them to do what they can do. How we define what they are doing is the critical variable in our understanding of them.

The third set of patterns, *patterns in ambiguity*, are defined by the process of understanding the relationship between patterns of interference and participation. If we can think about patterns of interference and patterns of participation as two circles that intersect, then patterns in ambiguity represent the area of overlap between the two. Confronted with the challenge of understanding differences in persons with severe and profound multiple disabilities, it is easy to see all that the person is doing as ambiguous.

On the other hand, the ambiguity creates the opportunity for discovering links among form and function and content in what the person is doing. At the same time that the individual strives for expression and communication, pathological conditions constrain participation. The process of refining our thinking involves us in sifting and sorting through behaviours trying to make sense of them. To make sense, the observer learns to admire the form in their anatomical structures and human systems. I had to see function as how the person accomplished what he or she wanted to do. To further question the relationship between form and function is to discover content. The patterns in ambiguity represent the starting place for clarification and further discovery of the intent and purpose of the person's action. At first everything that Danial and Thomas did was ambiguous; when my categories for interpreting what they were doing were redefined as patterns rather than fragmented and isolated behaviours the meaning in their action began to emerge.

Conclusion

Difficulty in understanding what persons with severe and profound multiple disabilities are doing may be the result of overlooking the relationships among form, function and content and failing to use the appropriate clues and comprehend the patterns. The challenge is to make sense of what the individual does, teasing out patterns of interference and patterns of participation from the ambiguity.

When we regard teaching and learning as a mutual act of interpretation, we have a different starting place, a different approach to making sense based on the common ground in our humanity. The significant differences shift from the discovery of their pathology to understanding our ways of interpretation.

What is significant about the play of Danial and Thomas is that it shattered illusions that we have to teach them to play. Together, they learned one another's behavioural repertoires, they differentiated patterns and they developed shared meanings. In what they do, they show us what we need to do.

With persons with severe and profound multiple disabilities participating in our homes, schools, communities and workplaces, we all will be asked to refine our everyday thinking scientifically to discover the common qualities in our life together. When we discover these qualities we will be in a position to qualify and quantify what was previously unknown.

Notes

1. F. Erickson, "The Nature of Clinical Evidence", in Daniel Lerner (ed.), *Evidence and Interference*, Glencoe, Ill.: Free Press, 1958.

2. Lester Mann and David Sabatino, *The First Review of Special Education*, Philadelphia, Pa: Buttonwood Forums, 1973.

3. Gershon Berkson and Sharon Landesman-Dwyer, "Behavioral Research on Severe and Profound Mental Retardation", *American Journal of Mental Deficiency*, 81, 1977, pp. 428-454.

4. Gene Sackett, "Theory and Applications in Mental Retardation" and "Data Collection and Analysis Methods", Vols. 1 and 2 of *Observing Behavior*, Baltimore, Md.: University Park Press, 1978.

5. Paul Deising, *Patterns of Discovery in the Social Sciences*, New York, N.Y.: Aldine Atherton, 1971, p. 141.

6. John J. Gleason, *Special Education in Context*, Cambridge, England: Cambridge University Press, 1989.

7. Ibid., pp. 93-106.

8. John J. Gleason, "Meaning of Play: Interpreting Patterns in Behavior of Persons with Severe Developmental Disabilities", *Anthropology and Education Quarterly*, 21, 1990, pp. 59-77.

9. John J. Gleason, "Underlying Meaning in the Behavior of Persons with Severe and Profound Mental Retardation and Multiple Handicaps: Implications for Clinical Intervention," in A. Vermeer (ed.), *Motor Development, Adapted Physical Activity and Mental Retardation*, Basel: Karger, 1990.

Chapter 12

The Politics of Care-giving

by Robyn Munford

T he very nature of the care-giving relationship reflects and is part of the practices that contribute to the way disability is defined in our society. In order to challenge this and the existing ways of organizing *care* one must have an understanding of what *care* means for the participants. This chapter explores this and looks at the ways in which the care-giving relationship can be transformed and alliances with people with intellectual disabilities can be formed. It is based on the argument that, as non-disabled researchers and writers, we must situate ourselves in the research project and in the particular context one is writing in and about.[1]

In order to obtain a precise understanding of a phenomenon, one must be cognizant of the experiences that have constructed our subject positions. These positions and the experiences informing them are multiple — something that many non-disabled writers on disability have not often acknowledged. Morris[2] emphasizes that non-disabled people may not make explicit their subject positions and ground themselves as non-disabled individuals:

> holding certain cultural assumptions about disability; because the understanding and theorising have not been treated as taking place in the context of an unequal relationship between non-disabled people and disabled people; and because the *act of knowing* which in this case is predicated on the social meaning of disability, has not been examined as the crucial determiner of what is known.[3]

I have been involved in providing *care* and researching care-giving for a number of years. Given my experiences, my views will be grounded in a particular social, cultural and political context.

This has influenced how I have written this chapter and the themes I choose to address. The chapter is divided into three sections. The first provides a context by discussing important influences on the research and writing process. I argue that we must understand how our research could reinforce the powerlessness of those we are researching. Before we can discuss how we perceive and research care-giving, we must make explicit our views about the research process and articulate our commitment to reconstructing this process and developing equitable relationships with people with disabilities.

The second section builds upon the first in that it identifies some important concepts for exploring the key elements of the care-giving process. If the care-giving relationship is to be transformed, we must have a precise understanding of what takes place in this relationship.

The final section discusses the role social policy has in determining how disability is to be defined. It illustrates this discussion with some examples from New Zealand.

Research and Writing: The Context

The context of a research process as a piece of writing must be located in terms of the writer's own perspectives and experiences. As Kondo suggests, our accounts are "partial" and "located". Our experiences are "multiple".[4] There is a diversity and richness in people's lives and, rather than constrain this, the researcher and writer must discover ways to illuminate the complexity of experience. By situating oneself in the context of the research or writing, one makes explicit what "glasses" one has on and how this influences our view of the world. Embedded in this process is the theory we adopt. I agree with Kondo in that I do not wish to adopt theoretical models that push me to search for the "typical" individual.[5] I certainly do not want to invoke the collective noun, "the disabled", which can infer that people with disabilities are part of a "unified" group where all experiences are seen to be in common.

Although there is no denial that there are certainly common experiences that can help one identify mutual goals and visions, the search for the "unified self" can lead us to rigidly categorize the experiences of people with intellectual disabilities. This standpoint ignores diversity and can result in unacceptable perceptions about this group of people. For example, both Morris and Keith talk about the ways in which people with disabilities are represented as "the other, the non person".[6] In the situation of care-giving they "are rarely seen as having valuable lives in the way their able-bodied carer or partner does".[7]

As non-disabled researchers and writers, do we (given our own subject positions and experiences) portray people with disabilities as "helpless" and "passive" in the care-giving relationship? Our tendency towards binary divisions among individuals, groups, ideas and experiences may lead us to "essentialized" and, at times, exclusionary and elitist conceptions of the "self" which do not leave us any space for celebration, diversity and transformation.[8]

Assumptions about certain social phenomena can function to empower those we research or they can act to disempower them.[9] As a feminist writer, I base my work on feminist principles. One of the key aims of feminist research is to make visible women's experiences and to provide validation of women's experience. In the process of carrying out research, women and, in this instance, people with disabilities should not be further alienated. The very process of doing the research can be used to reveal and expose some of the relations of power individuals experience on a daily level.

Feminist research is also about challenging existing frameworks for explaining women's experience. In the process of seeking better ways of validating and writing about women's experiences it attempts to find mechanisms for changing women's reality. In working towards the empowerment of women, feminist researchers should base their research process on "reciprocity". It is here that the "researched" and "researcher" form a relationship where certain components are exchanged. The researcher must give something back in exchange for carrying out the research and entering the "researched" life.[10] Lather believes that "reciprocity" is an essential part of the empowerment of women.[11] Feminists must use the research process to discover emancipatory knowledge and empower the participants. Oliver also emphasizes the emancipatory potential of research:

> The issue then for the emancipatory research paradigm is not how to empower people but, once people have decided to empower themselves, precisely what research can then do to facilitate this process ... researchers have to learn how to put their knowledge and skills at the disposal of their research subjects, for them to use in whatever ways they choose.[12]

My work has attempted to take into account these key principles. However, in reading the care-giving literature I began to feel a sense of disquiet with what I was reading. As Morris and Keith[13] point out, many of the feminist research principles have not been emphasized when researching and documenting the lives of people with disabilities.

Much of the care-giving literature focuses on the experience of the care-giver.[14] This research is important for helping to make the care-giving experience visible. However, there is now a move to extend this writing to more fully document the experiences of people with disabilities. Rather than viewing care-giving as a burden and as stressful, and perceiving care-givers and those requiring personal assistance as "passive" participants, one needs to analyze these perceptions in order to discover why the care-giving process is viewed in this way. Care-giving should not only be analyzed in terms of the needs of care-givers but also from the perspective of the person receiving care. Care-giving, I argue, has traditionally been seen as a "professional/practice problem" to be solved from the perspective of the care-giver.

What about the reality of the person with a disability? Dossa emphasizes that we must not merely add in disability to our frameworks but also acknowledge the complexities of the lives of people with disabilities.[15] As Morris also argues:

Disabled people — men and women — have little opportunity to portray our own experiences within the general culture, or within radical political movements. Our experience is isolated, individualised, the definitions which society places on us centre on judgements of individual capacities and personalities. This lack of a voice, of the representation of our subjective reality, means that it is difficult for non-disabled feminists to incorporate our reality into their research and their theories, unless it is in terms of the way the non-disabled would see us.[16]

If we take up the challenge offered by writers such as Morris, our goal is not to "add on" women with disabilities but to rethink our ideas and practice. We must constantly ask ourselves, "how we can do research which empowers disabled people".[17]

In New Zealand, disabled researchers are insisting that non-disabled researchers adhere to certain fundamental principles of research. Wicks and Terrell identify these in their paper *Speaking a Silence*.[18] They emphasize the importance of acknowledging the diversity of individuals' experiences. In our country disabled people have often been defined as a homogenous group. This means that not only have the experiences of people with disabilities been misrepresented but also that cultural, gender and class differences have been ignored. Ballard points out that the experiences of Maori, the indigenous people of New Zealand, have often been excluded from the research process.[19] He argues, as does Barton,[20] that unless we have a socio-political perspective that takes into account the structural conditions of disability, the research process will be sanitized and homogenized and ignore unequal social relationships and conditions.

Wicks and Terrell argue that disabled people are rendered silent when non-disabled researchers determine the research agenda:

> Theirs have been the questions that have been asked, and the manner in which the research has been conducted. Nobody has stopped to ask if this research is what we wanted, or how we might participate. In this process, it has been assumed and defined who we are, how we are, and what we need, hope or think.[21]

Wicks and Terrell challenge non-disabled researchers to become allies of disabled people and to be active participants in a struggle for change. In carrying out this research one cannot ignore the operation of power and how certain discourses function to uphold the meanings given to disability.

The Experiences of Care-giving

In order to understand the care-giving process and the nature of disability, we must explore not only the ways in which power relations shape our very existence but also the meaning given to this existence.

Foucault's ideas about the nature of power relations and the production and operation of discourse can help in our understanding of how relationships such as that of care-giving are produced and maintained. Discourse refers to a set of statements that function to regulate the way we think and live our lives. Practices are regulated through ideas, language, institutional behaviour, rituals, social relations and practices. Foucault proposed a "genealogical" method of analysis in order to identify and understand the operation of discourse. It is in this way that competing discourses can be located and their role in maintaining oppressive structures can be exposed.[22] As Fairclough points out, discourses:

> constitute key entities (be they "mental illness", "citizenship", or "literary") in different ways, and position people in different ways as social subjects (e.g., as doctors or patients) ... [23]

We are constrained by the discourses we are subject to, but we can also be part of the production of discourses and contribute to their maintenance. To understand why certain discourses dominate, we need to examine power relations. Power relations function to legitimize certain discourses. An understanding of power relations not only helps one understand how certain practices are maintained, it can also help one understand how resistance to these relations can occur.

Many writers are now exploring how, within power relationships, people with disabilities are placed in subject positions and how their lives are given meaning. My own work in New Zealand with families who have a child with a disability has shown how they can be subjected to behaviours and activities that non-disabled people would not tolerate for themselves or for other non-disabled people.

One of the most common experiences reported by the women in my previous research and in my ongoing work with care-givers concerns the energy they must invest in coming to terms with the ways in which society devalues people with disabilities.[24] In a society where disability has been socially constructed as a problem based on a notion of individual pathology, people with intellectual disabilities, and those who personally assist them, are continually devalued. The care-givers feel the effects of this in very intense ways. Many cite the example of the medical profession and, more recently, helping professions such as psychologists and social workers who intervene in, and have the authority to determine, what will happen to individuals. They also have the authority to decide what resources will be granted.

Morris gives detailed accounts of how the subject positions of people with disabilities are shaped by social practices and social relations:

> Assumptions that our lives are not worth living are only possible when our subjective realities find no place in mainstream culture. Where disability is represented in the general culture it is primarily from the point of the view of the non-disabled and so their fears and hostility and their own cultural agendas dominate the way we are presented ... Non-disabled people feel that our differentness gives them the right to invade our privacy and make judgements about our lives.[25]

These actions have a profound effect on the care-giving process. They place pressure on the relationship and are reflected within it. Care-givers at times find themselves mirroring the behaviour of others in society because this has become so firmly entrenched as an acceptable way to treat people with intellectual disabilities. When the person cared for is viewed as the devalued "other", the care-givers may feel that they are also viewed in similar ways. In the media, in the professional literature and in research, people with disabilities may be portrayed as "feeble" and "passive". Care-givers can also internalize these perceptions. When viewed in this way it is difficult for the person with disability to contribute in an equal way to the relationship. It may be difficult for them to assert their rights. What they value as important may conflict with what the care-givers view as important goals. Care-givers are caught in a double bind where their activities are determined and shaped by the ways in which society prescribes the needs and goals of people with disabilities.

The points outlined provide just a few examples of how the lives of people with disabilities and their care-givers may be constructed. Although one cannot deny the physical or intellectual restrictions of disability, we must emphasize how, in an "able-bodied" society, these restrictions are given particular kinds of meaning. Social policy reflects society's perception of people with disabilities and functions to reinforce their position. In the next section I show how current social policies may in fact function to exclude people with disabilities from the "mainstream". One must ask if people with disabilities and their care-givers are part of important decision-making activities such as resource allocation.

Social Policy: Constructing the Lives of People with Disabilities

Power relations operating within the care-giving relationship may be reinforced or directed from a more global level such as at the policy level. Barton argues that social policy reflects our views about the nature of society and the kind of society we desire.[26] The construction of the meaning of disability can take place in the social policy arena where multiple discourses will lead to different interpretations of the nature of disability. Certain discourses will dominate. Bryson emphasizes the importance of understanding the ways in which social policy debates are framed and promoted.[27] The concepts are never neutral but are part of the political process and are a reflection of competing interests. The very nature of processes such as consultation are subject to certain discourses.

In New Zealand we are currently experiencing a reorganization of the provisions of the welfare state. Since the election of the 1984 Labour Government, social policy has taken a particular direction. Free market advocates have dominated all aspects of social policy. The New Right agenda emphasizes a reduced role for the State with market forces becoming the mechanism for increasing efficiency and accountability.

Shirley critiques the "theology" of New Right thinking. He argues that it ignores the social and cultural histories of individuals by focusing upon an individualistic view of human behaviour.[28] Bunkle and Lynch endorse this argument. They point to the free market view as one that emphasizes "individual desires over group or community-based ones".[29] There is an assumption that individuals are able to meet their social needs in the marketplace. According to Bunkle and Lynch this free market ideology ignores the social nature of individuals and denies the "naturalness of dependency".[30] The model disguises our needs for interdependency by commodifying social relationships.

It is important to discuss these social policies and their critique in light of the changes to social policy for people with intellectual disabilities. The current social, political and economic context in New Zealand contributes to the processes of rethinking how disability will be taken into account. The New Zealand experience may have relevance for understanding the nature of disability in other countries.

For many years people with intellectual disabilities and their care-givers have struggled to have their experiences acknowledged by policy makers. Given the current burgeoning of social policy initiatives for people with disabilities, one could assume that they had succeeded in this task. However, authors such as Oliver[31] and

Barton suggest we must be aware of romantic rhetoric. Barton states:

> For those of us who are committed to the pursuit and realisation of a truly democratic society in which issues of social justice and equity are central concerns, then in terms of the prevailing situation, it is crucial that we do not underestimate the difficulties involved. Romantic visions and idealistic rhetoric have too often resulted in human suffering, disappointment and disillusionments.[32]

The Health and Disability Services Bill in New Zealand aims to improve access to health and disability services. The government, in its introduction of the Bill, argued that it would encourage flexibility and innovation in the delivery of health and social services. It is important to discuss this Bill in light of the changes that people with intellectual disabilities and their care-givers have achieved and are likely to achieve. A critique of the Bill enables us to ascertain whether the lives of people with intellectual disabilities will be improved by increased opportunities. We need to recognize the contradictions in policies, some of which may further restrict the lives of people with intellectual disabilities but, conversely, could also provide possibilities for change.[33] We must ask how the material conditions of people with intellectual disabilities will be improved.

Disability rights groups in New Zealand have addressed a number of questions to those designing and implementing the new legislation. Those people providing personal assistance to people with intellectual disabilities add their voice to the concerns.

When we examine the stories of care-givers, we see the concerns of people with disabilities about how to deal with professionals who have the authority to determine how their lives will be constructed. People with disabilities have historically been subjected to procedures that have assessed, ranked and classified their activities. These procedures have not always resulted in the provision of "inclusive" services; they have often resulted in the provision of services that have excluded individuals from the "mainstream". Professionals such as those in the medical profession have had the authority to determine all kinds of service provision, even those services that have no immediate relevance to medical needs. In a medical model there is an emphasis on deficiencies and inabilities.[34]

Oliver critiques the activities of professionals who have a medical frame of reference and who define disability from an individual pathological view.[35] This view defines disability as emerging solely from personal limitations. It does not focus upon the disabling nature of society. Oliver emphasizes that definitions of disability must be related to the ways in which society chooses to organize itself.[36] Will legislation in New Zealand and other countries have unrealistic goals for people with disabilities — goals focusing on rehabilitation aimed at encouraging the person with a disability to become a "productive" member of society (in economic terms)? Parent organizations are concerned that caregiving work will not be adequately funded as it does not relate to any notion of production and is not measured in economic terms. If care-giving cannot be rated as an economic activity contributing to the well-being of society, will the current social policies take into account the needs of families?

Writers such as Oliver alert us to the characteristics of the "disability industry".[37] Drawing on some of the ideas of Illich, he talks about how professionals may manufacture needs that have little relationship to the real needs of their clients. He argues that professionals have built up a service industry that meets the professional need for career advancement rather than meeting the needs of their clients. Although the legislation in New Zealand talks about incorporating people with disabilities into decision-making processes and supports consultation with communities about disability support needs, it is still not clear who will have the final say on assessment procedures. Does the knowledge incorporated in these assessment procedures include the ideas that have been developed by people with disabilities and their families?

There have, in the history of services for people with disabilities, always been concerns about whether needs are assessed in ways that maintain the dignity of the individual and that do not further restrict life opportunities. Disability rights groups in New Zealand are calling for guarantees that they will be part of the decision-making processes about assessment of needs and related activities such as service development. Will professionals have the authority to define what "disability" actually means? Will these professionals form alliances with people with disabilities?

Chappell alerts us to the problems that arise when professionals take over a service industry wherein they begin from their own perspective and knowledge base rather than that of the person with a disability.[38] Time is spent on solving service provision problems that may become removed from the original focus of the service — that of meeting the needs of people with disabilities.

Disability rights groups are concerned that the diverse aspects of the lives of people with disabilities may still not be acknowledged. They argue that, politically and economically, people with disabilities are still viewed as "other". In this situation people may be still sidelined into "special" services that do not encourage "inclusion". These groups wish to emphasize the interdependent nature of society. They point out that a society in pursuit of the independent, self-sufficient, competitive economic being does not acknowledge the necessity for interdependence among individuals. This view functions to ignore the connectedness between human beings. We must ask whose definition of independence current policies adopt.

One must also critique how the care-giving relationship will be supported in a market economy. Kendrick makes some important points about what happens to social services in such an economy. Her comments are particularly relevant for understanding the care-giving relationship. She argues that there are a number of factors we must consider when:

> care is treated like any other commodity that is sold for profit ... Care can be minimised-restricted just to those services which preserve life. It can be maximised to embrace the notion of Quality of Life.[39]

Kendrick identifies unique aspects of the care-giving relationship. These include the independence-dependence debate, issues of control and the nature of the care-giving relationship. Caring for someone as a social service has a different process and goal from that of a commercial service. Caring is different than "purchasing a joint of meat from the butcher."[40] Kendrick urges us to carefully examine current policies that see *care* as a commercial commodity, to be packaged and sold like any item in the marketplace.[41]

Social policy and the nature of disability are complex. In order to understand them we must examine the ideological and material conditions and challenge the dominant discourses that continue to devalue people with intellectual disabilities. In a society where people with disabilities are still not included in the "mainstream" it is important to critically analyze social policy initiatives. As Barton suggests, disability as a social and political category not only entails regulation but also embodies within it possibilities for choice and empowerment.[42]

Bringing About Change

In New Zealand the needs of people with disabilities are on the social policy agenda. However, we must be involved in ongoing political action in order to ensure that the issues of people with disabilities are to remain on the political agenda and their voices are heard. We must challenge the historical views of personal tragedy where people with disabilities are to be pitied and where they are subjected to discriminatory policies and practices.[43]

In this chapter I have shown how our knowledge about the care-giving process will be enhanced if we understand the power relations that pervade it. These relations do not take place in a vacuum but are part of a wider global context which functions to reinforce and direct power relations within the care-giving relationship. Power operates to construct and regulate individuals. As Kondo suggests, others seek power over us and assign us to categories regardless of, or at times because of, our personal characteristics.[44] This then determines how we will be treated and what is expected of us. People with disabilities may be placed in subject positions in ways that function to hide their multiple subject positions in order to uphold society's notion of "the disabled".

However, where there are power relations there is also room for resistance. As writers and researchers, we should be asking why the subjective experience of people with disabilities is "missing from the general culture".[45] We should take up Morris's challenge and turn the "spotlight on the oppressors".[46] The prejudice emerging from power relationships must be exposed. As we work alongside people with disabilities we can challenge the discourses and the meanings attached to the subject positions of people with disabilities. We can challenge the discourses in our society that uphold the exclusion of certain groups.

An important part of this process of change is related to our understanding of the discourse of social policy. How are we to ensure that policy makers understand the daily lived experiences of care-givers and the people they personally assist? What is society's commitment to supporting care-givers? The answer to this question is intricately related to the ways in which society values the lives of people with disabilities. As Kendrick emphasizes, we must clearly document the outcomes of new policies.[47] Are safeguards in place to ensure that the needs of "consumers" are met? Will current changes to the delivery of services ensure that services are more effective?

In an environment where there is a reluctance to support the welfare state, will economic rationalization herald a return to restrictive environments for people with disabilities?[48] As researchers and writers we must precisely document the effects of these current social policies. This means that planning for the future must incorporate an understanding of what is happening to care-givers and people with disabilities in the care-giving relationship. This is why it is important to have theoretical frameworks that help us understand the daily lived experiences of individuals. We must use this information to educate the policy makers. As Brown and Smith state:

> We want the reality of caring to be made public and political, to encourage the women who do this work to speak out without feeling guilty or disloyal. We urge professionals who work in the field of community care to unite to create political pressure for real changes in the material circumstances of their lives.[49]

Brown and Smith advocate a shift of focus from the individual to the context within which she or he is cared for. Support given to people with disabilities and their carers:

> should be collective and flexible, wherever possible within their control and accessible without the indignity of means tests and professional assessments.[50]

Brown and Smith, writing about the English situation, suggest that, despite current public policy which encourages individual contracts, carers and those they assist should be encouraged to support one another and come together to challenge these policies. Parent organizations have a key role in supporting and bringing families together. They also encourage families to reveal the impact of current policies. They ask pertinent questions about whether services have improved for their daughters or sons or whether there has been a return to earlier times when people with disabilities were totally excluded from the "mainstream".

Highlighting care-giving as a public issue is essential. Encouraging others to take more responsibility is part of this process. Edgar emphasizes the community's responsibility in caring. He argues that it is "absurd" and "myopic" to view care as a private family matter and believes that there must be a better balance between public service provision and family care.[51]

As a feminist working alongside people with intellectual disabilities, I can use feminist strategies for bringing about change. This includes linking personal troubles to political issues, building alliances with other groups, redefining struggles in our own terms and reflecting on change in order to move on and continue the struggle. The struggle for change happens at several levels: in the daily lives of people with intellectual disabilities; in challenging the discourses on disability; and in critiquing the social policies that construct the lives of people with intellectual disabilities.

We have made progress in our journey of change for people with intellectual disabilities. If we are to continue this struggle, we must continue our commitment to filling the silence with the words and knowledge of people with intellectual disabilities. I leave the last word to my friend Alan:

> Robyn, what's all these things called conferences? Will these people make sure I get a job? Will my worker be able to help me get my new stereo? Will I be able to still come on holiday with you? Will they stop calling me handicapped?

The dignity and life opportunities Alan refers to are what being human is all about. These should inform our struggles.

Acknowledgement

The author wishes to acknowledge the role of people with intellectual disabilities and care-givers in the generation of ideas for this chapter.

Notes

1. Lois Keith, "Who Cares Wins? Caring and Disability", *Disability, Handicap and Society*, 7(2), 1992, pp. 167-175; Dorine Kondo, *Crafting Selves: Power, Gender and Discourses of Identity in a Japanese Workplace*, Chicago: University of Chicago Press, 1990; Patti Lather, "Research as Praxis", *Evaluation Studies Review*, Sage, 1987; Jenny Morris, "Personal and Political: A Feminist Perspective on Researching Physical Disability", *Disability, Handicap and Society*, 7(2), 1992, pp. 157-166.

2. Morris, "Personal and Political", 1992 (see n. 1).

3. Ibid., p. 159.

4. Kondo, *Crafting Selves*, 1990 (see n. 1).

5. Ibid., p. 8.

6. Morris, "Personal and Political", 1992; and Keith, "Who Cares Wins?", 1992, p. 196 (see n. 1).

7. Keith, "Who Care Wins?", 1992, p. 196 (see n. 1).

8. Jean Scott, *Gender and the Politics of History*, New York: Colombia University Press, 1988.

9. Liz Stanley, *Feminist Praxis: Research, Theory and Epistemology in Feminist Sociology*, London: Routledge Kegan Paul, 1990.

10. Anne Oakley, "Interviewing Women: A Contradiction in Terms", in H. Roberts (ed.), *Doing Feminist Research*, London: Routledge and Kegan Paul, 1981, pp. 30-61.

11. Patti Lather, "Issues of Validity in Openly Ideological Research: Between a Rock and a Soft Place", *Interchange*, 17(4), Winter 1986.

12. Michael Oliver, "Changing the Social Relations of Research Production?", *Disability, Handicap and Society*, 7(2), 1992, p. 111.

13. Morris, "Personal and Political", 1992; and Keith, "Who Cares Wins?", 1992 (see n. 1).

14. Janet Finch and Dulce Groves, *Labour of Love: Women, Work and Caring*, London: Routledge Kegan Paul, 1983; Gillian Dalley, *Ideologies of Caring*, London: MacMillan Education Ltd., 1988.

15. Parin Dossa, "Women and Disability: The Myth of the Autonomous Individual", *Journal of Practical Approaches to Developmental Handicap*, 14(2), 1990.

16. Jenny Morris, *Pride against Prejudice: Transforming Attitudes to Disability*, London: Women's Press, 1991, p. 8.

17. Morris, "Personal and Political", 1992, p. 164 (see . 1).

18. Wendi Wicks and Vicki Terrell, "Disability Research: Speaking a Silence", *Association of Social Science Researchers Newsletter*, Wellington, New Zealand, 1993.

19. Keith Ballard, "A Socio-Political Perspective on Disability: A Comment from the New Zealand Context", *Disability and the Necessity for a Socio-Political Perspective*, Monograph 51, The International Exchange of Experts and Information in Rehabilitation, 1992.

20. Len Barton, *Disability and the Necessity for a Socio-Political Perspective*, Monograph 51, The International Exchange of Experts and Information in Rehabilitation, 1992.

21. Wicks and Terrell, "Speaking a Silence", 1992, p. 4 (see n. 18).

22. Michel Foucault, *Power/Knowledge: Selected Interviews and Other Writings, 1972-1977*, C. Gordon (ed.), Brighton, England: Harvester Press, 1980.

23. Norman Fairclough, *Discourse and Social Change*, London: Polity Press, 1992, p. 3.

24. Robyn Munford, "The Hidden Costs of Caring: Women Who Care for People with Intellectual Disabilities", unpublished PhD thesis, Massey University, New Zealand, 1989.

25. Morris, "Personal and Political", 1992, p. 29 (see n. 1).

26. Barton, *Disability and the Necessity for a Socio-Political Perspective*, 1992 (see n. 20).

27. Lois Bryson, "Contemporary Policy Directions and the Welfare State: Who Benefits?", paper presented at the Health Promotion Forum, Auckland, New Zealand, 1992.

28. Ian Shirley, "Social Services in a Market Economy", *Social Work Review*, 4(4), 1992.

29. Phillida Bunkle and Jo Lynch, "What's Wrong with the New Right?", in C. Briar, R. Munford and M. Nash (eds), *Superwoman Where Are You? Social Policy and Women's Experiences*, Palmerston North, New Zealand: Dunmore Press, 1992, p. 33.

30. Ibid.

31. Oliver, "Changing the Social Relations", 1992 (see n. 12).

32. Barton, *Disability and the Necessity for a Socio-Political Perspective*, 1992, p. 2 (see n. 20).

33. Ibid.

34. Ibid.

35. Michael Oliver, *The Politics of Disablement*, Basingstoke: Macmillan, 1990.

36. Ibid.

37. Oliver, "Changing the Social Relations", 1992 (see n. 12).

38. Anne Chappell, "Towards a Sociological Critique of the Normalisation Principle", *Disability, Handicap and Society*, 7(1), 1992.

39. June Kendrick, "Accountability, Quality Assurance and the Business of Care", *Social Work Review*, 4(4), 1992, p. 10.

40. Ibid.

41. Ibid.

42. Barton, *Disability and the Necessity for a Socio-Political Perspective*, 1992, (see n. 20).

43. Kendrick, "Accountability", 1992 (see n. 39).

44. Kondo, *Crafting Selves*, 1990 (see n. 1).

45. Morris, "Personal and Political", 1992, p. 165 (see n. 1).

46. Ibid.

47. Kendrick, "Accountability", 1992 (see n. 39).

48. Janet Finch, "The Politics of Community Care in Britain", in C. Ungerson (ed.), *Gender and Caring*, London: Harvester, 1990.

49. Hilary Brown and Helen Smith (eds.), *Normalisation: A Reader for the Nineties*, London: Tavistock, 1992, p. 168.

50. Ibid.

51. Don Edgar, *Sharing the Caring: Re-thinking Current Policies*, policy document of the Office of Women's Interests, Western Australia, 1992.

Contributors

Michael Bach, M.E.S., is a senior researcher on public policy and disability at l'Institut Roeher Institute, Canada, and is Assistant Professor (part-time) in the Faculty of Environmental Studies at York University. His current research includes critical analysis of competency-related law and policy in Canada and evaluation of deinstitutionalization and community development initiatives in Canada.

Jerome E. Bickenbach, Ph.D., LL.B., is Professor of Philosophy and Law at Queen's University, Kingston, Canada, and is the author of *Physical Disability and Social Policy* (University of Toronto Press, 1993). His research interests focus on social policy concerning intellectual and physical disability.

Margaret Flynn, Ph.D., is an Assistant Director of the National Development Team, an agency which provides advice and consultancy to those who plan, commission and provide services to people with learning difficulties in the U.K. Her most recent publication is *Taking a Break: Liverpool's Respite Services for Adult Citizens with Learning Difficulties*, which she co-authored with self-advocates.

Gordon Grant, Ph.D., is co-director of the Centre for Social Policy Research and Development at the University of Wales, Bangor. He holds joint responsibility for research in two streams of work relating to elderly people and persons with a learning disability.

John J. Gleason, Ed.D., is an Associate Professor in the Department of Special Education, Rhode Island College. With 30 years of experience in the field of special education, his research has focused on the competing forces at play within the human systems of persons with developmental disabilities which influence their ability to act and communicate. His published works include *Special Education in Context*, which challenges the predominant frameworks within which we presently examine the lives of persons with severe and profound disabilities.

Robyn Munford, Ph.D., lectures in the Department of Social Policy and Social Work, Massey University, Palmerston North, New Zealand. Her teaching and research interests focus upon disability studies, feminist research, social policy analysis, social work practice and community development. She is active in advocacy organizations for people with disabilities.

John P. Radford, Ph.D., is Associate Professor and former Chair of the Department of Geography at York University in Toronto, Canada, and the editor for the Americas of the *Journal of Historical Geography*. His main research is in the social and spatial structure of cities in the 19th century. He has also written widely on constructions of intellectual disability during the asylum era.

Paul Ramcharan, Ph.D., is a research officer at the Centre for Social Policy Research and Development at the University of Wales, Bangor. He is involved in evaluation of different aspects of the All-Wales Strategy for Persons with a Mental Handicap.

Marcia H. Rioux, Ph.D., is Executive Director of l'Institut Roeher Institute, Canada's national institute for the study of public policy affecting persons with disabilities. She also teaches Social Policy in the Faculty of Environmental Studies at York University. She has directed a large number of research studies on Canadian public policy and disability. Her forthcoming book is *The Equality-Disability Nexis*.

Fred E. Stockholder, Ph.D., is presently a professor of English on the faculty of the University of British Columbia. He has been an English professor at the University of Ghana and has published articles on British modern literature.

Linda Ward, Ph.D., is Senior Research Fellow at the Norah Frye Research Centre, University of Bristol, England, and Programme Advisor (Disability) to the Joseph Rowntree Foundation. She has researched and written widely in the field of learning difficulties and has a particular interest in equal opportunities issues. Her publications include *Double Discrimination: Issues and Services for People with Learning Difficulties from Black and Ethnic Minority Communities* and *Values and Visions: Changing Ideas and Services for People with Learning Difficulties* (in press).

Aileen Wight Felske, Ph.D. (Cert. Psyc.), is a lecturer in the Rehabilitation Studies Program at Mount Royal College in Calgary, Canada. Her research interests include gender and disability, equality of opportunity and social policy. She has published numerous books and articles including *Reseach by/for/with Women with Disabilities*; *The Law and Your Rights: A Plain Language Guide*; and *Dialogue on Disability: A Canadian Perspective.*

Gary Woodill, Ed.D., is a professor of Early Childhood Education, Ryerson Polytechnic University in Toronto, Canada. He is author of many books, articles and papers on disability. He has served on the board of directors for the Centre for Independent Living in Toronto for six years.

Irving Kenneth Zola, Ph.D., is a professor of sociology at Brandeis University in Massachusetts. He is the editor and publisher of *Disability Studies Quarterly* and a founder and board member of both the Society for Disability Studies and the Boston Self-Help Centre. His latest work ranges from a paper on disability statistics to short stories dealing with disability to analysis of national health care reform. He was a member of the Clinton Health Care Transition Team. His published works include *Missing Pieces: A Chronicle of Living with a Disability* and *Ordinary Lives: A Collection of Short Stories.*

Selected Publications of L'Institut Roeher Institute

- **Social Well-Being,** 1993

- **The Canadian Disability Resource Program: Offsetting Costs of Disability and Assuring Access to Disability-Related Supports,** 1994

- **Direct Dollars: A Study of Individualized Funding in Canada,** 1993

- **Just Technology?** From Principles to Practice in Bio-ethical Issues, 1994

- **On Target?** Canada's Employment-Related Programs for Persons with Disabilities, 1992

- **Income Insecurity:** The Disability Income System in Canada, 1988

- **Poor Places:** Disability-Related Residential and Support Services, 1990

- **Nothing Personal:** The Need for Personal Supports in Canada, 1993

- **Comprehensive Disability Income Security Reform,** 1992

- **Changing Canadian Schools:** Perspectives on Disability and Inclusion, 1991

- **Literacy and Labels:** A Look at Literacy Policy and People with a Mental Handicap, 1990

- **Vulnerable:** Sexual Abuse and People with an Intellectual Handicap, 1988

- **The Power to Choose:** An Examination of Service Brokerage and Individualized Funding as Implemented by the Community Living Society, 1991

- **Right Off the Bat:** A Study of Inclusive Child Care in Canada, 1993

For more information please contact:

L'Institut Roeher Institute Kinsmen Building, York University, 4700 Keele Street, North York, Ontario M3J 1P3 Telephone: (416) 661-9611 Fax: (416) 661-5701 TDD: (416) 661-2023

entourage: **L'Institut Roeher Institute's quarterly bilingual magazine**

entourage is on the leading edge of constructive ideas and theories in the field of mental handicap and disability. Its timely articles identify the latest directions for changes and new ways of understanding inclusive communities and economies. For information on subscriptions, contact l'Institut Roeher Institute.